MAN AND WOMAN

MAN AND WOMAN:
A Study of Love and the Novel
1740-1940

A. O. J. COCKSHUT

Such, then are First Principles; sovereign, irresponsible, and secret — what an awful form of government the human mind is under from its very constitution!

> Newman, *Present Position of Catholics* (1851)
> Lecture VII, Section 3

'In our days' continued Vera — mentioning 'our days' as people of limited intelligence are fond of doing, imagining they have discovered and appraised the peculiarities of 'our days' and that human characteristics change with the times.

> Tolstoy, *War and Peace*, (1868-9) Book VI, chap. xxi
> (Trans. by L. & A. Maude O.U.P. 1933)

COLLINS
St James's Place, London
1977

William Collins Sons & Co Ltd
London · Glasgow · Sydney · Auckland
Toronto · Johannesburg

First published 1977
© A. O. J. Cockshut, 1977

ISBN 0 00 216503 1

Set in Monotype Garamond
Made and Printed in Great Britain by
William Collins Sons & Co Ltd Glasgow

Contents

For Eda with love

Preface

It will be obvious to all who note the length of this book in conjunction with its sub-title that the author does not dream of aiming at completeness. A dozen volumes like this one could easily be devoted to the subject without prolixity.

My choice of examples is, inevitably, arbitrary; but I hope it is defensible.

I have tried:

1 To achieve a fair balance between well-known and little-known books.

2 To give special weight to some unusual cases, without suggesting that they are more representative than they really are.

3 To avoid repeating anything in my previous books (which has involved the omission of some material well-suited to the theme).

4 To stress the diversity often concealed under blanket terms like *Victorian*.

The quotations which precede each chapter are offered for their general suggestiveness; there is no attempt to restrict this to the meaning intended by the authors in the original context. Anyone who finds any particular quotation puzzling is advised to ignore it or pass on. The quotations in the body of the chapters, naturally, are a different matter. There the question of the meaning in the context in which they appeared is vital.

I have been more concerned to record what novelists actually thought and felt than to evaluate it. How far my personal beliefs and attitudes are apparent in what follows, I don't know. But it seems sensible to state my position simply here. I have been a convinced Catholic for over thirty years and a happily-married man for nearly twenty-five.

A.O.J.C.

CHAPTER I

Love and the Novel

Miss Mackenzie was written with a desire to prove that a novel may be produced without any love; but even in this attempt it breaks down before the conclusion.

> Trollope, *Autobiography* (1883) chap. X

Bessie blushed, as becomes the Englishwoman of mature years when she is gracefully supposed to be ignorant of all it most behoves her to know.

> George Gissing, *The Nether World* (1889) chap. XXXVIII

'Oh, it's so different. Girls – women – are good. There's nothing unpleasant to be known about them.'

> Eustace in *The Crown of Life* by George Gissing (1899) chap. XXIII

The difficulty and the strangeness of the subject of this book can be illustrated by a comparison of the phrase 'love poetry' with the phrase at the head of the chapter. Every reader will feel at once that the two phrases suggest entirely different things. Why? The answer seems to depend on a contrast of public and private. Love, as traditionally conceived by poets, is private, intimate, intense, even ecstatic. Most love poems are lyrics, dealing with intense moments. Even when there is talk of love as a permanent state, this state may often be conceived as an eternizing of the moment, as if the mutabilities of time were, in this unique case, simply inapplicable. Complaints about the ravages of time (as in Shakespeare's sonnets) are simply the obverse of this denial of time. Love poetry seldom traces the time process in detail. Nor does it often deal with love's relation to religion, to duty, to society or to work, money, recreation and friendship.

It is characteristic of the novel, the longest and most minute of imaginative forms, to deal with time and society. The novel shows the consequences of things; and if it deals with anything intense and personal, then it shows the effect of personal experience and action on other people who did not share the experience; and it shows the effect over many years on the ageing personality of the one (or the pair) who had the original experience. For the novelist, as for common sense, love, which is the most private and intense thing is at the same time public, institutional, responsible. One could read a great many love poems in many languages without learning, if one did not know already, that sexual intercourse is procreative, and thus potentially contains consequences which persist as long as the world lasts. Society, which everywhere and at all times has attempted to regulate the play of sexual instincts, by law or by custom or by both, can never forget this. Nor can the novelist.

A minor work of Lawrence, *The Trespasser* (1912), can help to illustrate the difference between love poetry and love in the novel. The first half of the book contains a lyrical account of five days spent on holiday in the Isle of Wight by a married man and a girl. The narrative concentrates entirely on their sensations. Then they part, and the man goes back to his wife and children, who receive him coldly, so that he is forced to realize the blighting effect of a brief episode on his family and on himself. The girl goes to Cornwall with some women friends, and then hears that the man has hanged himself. The book ends by showing the effect of time in softening the shock felt by the mistress and the wife. Whatever accusations, fair and unfair, have been made against Lawrence, no one has ever said that he was oblivious of passion. But he is a novelist, and therefore he writes of love in terms of time and society. If the book had ended with the end of the holiday episode, it would not have been a novel, but only an inflated prose-poem.

This double character of love, private and public at the same time, makes general thinking about it peculiarly difficult. It is easy enough to think of love in personal terms, romantic, sensual, faithful, inconstant, predatory or sacrificial. It is easy to think of moral duties, marriage laws and courting customs. But it is extremely difficult to think and write accurately about the strange, shifting no-man's-land between the two. It is hard to capture the actual (as opposed to theoretical) standards of a society or a generation, hard to isolate and describe the sentiments that are really active in people's hearts and to distinguish them from conventions, pretences, self-deceptions.

The history of general statements about the tone and standards of any given time and place is a history of unsupported and often wild panegyrics and diatribes. And there is a strong tendency to contrast the present state of affairs with an imaginary ideal future or with an ideal (and perhaps equally imaginary) past. Thus in a letter to Johnson's *Rambler* of 19 February 1751, the anonymous writer (apparently the novelist Samuel Richardson) wrote:

Oh, Mr Rambler! forgive the talkativeness of an old man! When I courted and married my Laetitia, then a blooming beauty, every thing passed just so! But how is the case now? The ladies, maidens, wives, and widows, are engrossed by places of open resort and general entertainment . . .

and he goes on to speak of 'the general dissoluteness of manners'. Yet it is doubtful whether there exists evidence that would convince a historian that the mid eighteenth century was more dissolute than the world of fifty years earlier.

Again, Mrs Lynn Linton, writing in the very middle of Victoria's reign,[1] is convinced that she is living in a time of extreme sexual licence and degradation, strongly contrasting with earlier times, not specified, but presumably in or near the reign of George IV, in which she was born.

She writes:

If we must have only one kind of thing let us have it genuine; and the queens of St John's Wood in their unblushing honesty, rather than their *imitators and make-believers* in Bayswater and Belgravia.*

And she exhorts her readers to

wait patiently until the national madness has passed, and our women come back again to the old English ideal, once the most beautiful, the most modest, the most essentially womanly in the world.

Alternatively, and just as subjectively, a new and noble present may be contrasted with a barbarous past. Havelock Ellis writes:

The vulgar crowd has lost much of its brutal selfishness, its sordid ugliness; a new graciousness has become interfused with life, a faint perception that living is an art. I cannot see a girl walking along the street with her free air, her unswathed limbs, her gay and scanty raiment, without being conscious of a

---

* My italics. St John's Wood was an area of fashionable courtesans and kept mistresses; Bayswater and Belgravia the home of the 'best' society.

thrill of joy in the presence of a symbol of life that in my youth was unknown.[2]

The inner meaning of fashion in dress is an obscure and controversial subject; but the clothes themselves, one would think, were less prone to misrepresentation, being in the realm of visible facts. But I can only say that I was very young when Havelock Ellis was old, and I do not remember it so.

Two points, at any rate, seem clear. First, that there is a strong and perennial tendency to believe in unique and extraordinary sexual revolutions. (Virginia Woolf, perhaps a little with tongue in cheek, professed to identify the precise month and year when one occurred.) Second, both men and women habitually chose the conduct of women as the true index of morals and manners.

I called the area between the public and the private aspects of the matter a no-man's-land; and it possesses, in particular, one characteristic of a no-man's-land in trench warfare. It is always there but it is always liable to change its position. What can acceptably be said in public about what was felt or said or done in private varies from age to age and almost from year to year. There is always a question about reticence and there is always a question about honesty. The mid nineteenth century, when reticence was at its strongest, offers us perhaps the most revealing examples of a perennial dilemma.

More than his contemporaries, Thackeray felt the agreed standards of literary decorum in his age as inhibiting; and a close study of his work would furnish many examples of evasiveness as he sulkily kept to the letter and violated the spirit of rules he would not openly flout. At times he makes us picture two separate audiences for his work. Novels were supposed to be most eagerly read by young unmarried girls; and often, too, they were read aloud by fathers or mothers to large families including young children. Yet this father, who read aloud, might be a knowing man of the world with memories of Paphian escapades, and just as fond as Thackeray himself was of bawdy talk at the club. There is one moment in chapter XLIII of *Vanity Fair* which may stand as an emblem of a whole society's mixed and contradictory ideas. (And that is not to pre-judge the question whether the ideas of other times and other societies were not equally contradictory or more so.)

The passage runs:

    people remember Lady O'Dowd performing a jig at Government House, where she danced down two Aides-de-Camp, a Major of Madras Cavalry, and two gentlemen of the Civil Service; and, persuaded by Major Dobbin, C.B., second in command of the ——th, to retire to the supper-room, *lassata nondum satiata recessit.*

'She retired, weary but still ready for more.' What could be more natural and innocent in a healthy, hearty, virtuous officer's wife with an enthusiasm for dancing? And so, no doubt, the young ladies felt it when papa translated, correctly, and roughly as above. But if papa was the sort of man Thackeray was aiming at, if he had a classical education, had a fair memory and some literary sensibility, and a little taste for elegant naughtiness, then he may have had difficulty in preserving his paternal gravity as he answered his daughters' question about the meaning of the Latin. For he would recall that this was Juvenal on Messalina; and that the occasion was a wager between women about how many gallants each could receive in succession before admitting to exhaustion.

The striking thing about this little touch of naughtiness is its complete irrelevance to the issues of *Vanity Fair*. There is no slur at all on Lady O'Dowd's character. The *double entendre* is there for its own sake, not for the story's sake. It has all the marks of a rebellion which is not meant seriously. Thackeray no more means to overthrow accepted standards than the young men in Wodehouse are planning revolution when they steal a pig or a policeman's helmet. It is very good fun to score off the police, but it would be dreadful to have to do without the police.

Bagehot, a more straightforwardly honest man than Thackeray, expressed the accepted mid-Victorian view of the broader eighteenth-century style of novel-writing in his essay on Sterne:

It is quite true that the customary conventions of writing are much altered during the last century, and much which would formerly have been deemed blameless would now be censured and disliked. The audience has changed; and decency is of course in part dependent on who is within hearing. A divorce case may be talked over across a club-table with a plainness of speech and development of expression which would be indecent in a mixed party and scandalous before young ladies. Now a large part of old novels may very fairly be called club-books; they speak out plainly and simply the

notorious facts of the world as men speak of them to men.³*
Thackeray was unusual, then, not in considering two quite
different styles and two standards of decency appropriate for
men alone and for mixed company; he was unusual in pluming
himself a little on the risky cleverness of talking to both audiences
at once in the very same words with different meanings for
each.

Thackeray himself, in different mood, occasionally speaks more
cautiously than the previous example of his method would lead
us to expect. In the preface to *Pendennis* he complained that since
Fielding died, it had been forbidden to describe a MAN. 'We
must drape him and give him a conventional simper.' And in
chapter LXIV of *Vanity Fair*, he inveighs against the 'moral
world' that has 'no particular objection to vice, but an insuperable
objection to hearing vice called by its proper name.'

It would be wrong to take such statements too seriously. The
reading public cannot have found them very upsetting; they
certainly did not prevent Thackeray from winning both critical
esteem and wide popularity. So far as we can guess at feelings
that were not often stated, we may suppose that the reading
public instinctively recognized and respected the petulant
docility with which he bore himself under irksome restrictions.

But there was another question which Thackeray perhaps did
not ask. If it was impossible to speak of some topics plainly and
honestly was it wise to speak of them at all? A reviewer of Hardy's
The Return of the Native in *The Athenaeum* of 23 November 1878
had this interesting comment:

> Eustacia Vye belongs essentially to the class of which Madame
> Bovary is the type; and it is impossible not to regret, since this
> is a type which English opinion will not allow a novelist to
> depict in its completeness, that Mr Hardy should have wasted
> his powers in giving what after all is an imperfect and to some
> extent misleading view of it.⁴

We are dealing here with the question of reticence, not of
morals. It is impossible to find any correlation between personal
concepts of moral virtue and degrees of fictional latitude.

---

* Bagehot's view about young ladies was general, but not quite universal. Beatrice
Webb records (*My Apprenticeship*, 1926, p. 11) that when she was thirteen (about
1871) her father said 'If you were a boy I should hesitate to recommend *Tom Jones*,
but a nice-minded girl can read anything.' She says that he was the only man she
ever met who genuinely believed that women were superior to men.

Thackeray, who, as we have seen, was one of the most easily exasperated literary men on the point, was firm and sincere in his adherence to the high ideal of marriage. By contrast, we find a comparatively lax moralist, G. H. Lewes, writing in prim tones. In reference to the passage in Goethe's *Wahlverwandtschaften* in which two married people lie together while each is dreaming of another beloved person, he writes:

There is, it is true, one scene, which although true to nature, is nevertheless felt to be objectionable on moral and aesthetical grounds. The artist is not justified in printing every truth; and if we in this nineteenth century often carry our exclusion of subjects to the point of prudery, that error is a virtue compared with the demoralizing licence exhibited in French literature.[5]

That phrase 'moral and aesthetic' provides a classic instance of the vulnerability of unchallenged assumptions. When Lewes's *Goethe* was published in 1855, few readers will have paused on this linking of the two ideas. Their conformity, almost their identity, will have appeared as a self-evident truth. At this time, Swinburne had recently left Eton for Eton's good, and was about to go up to Balliol, while Oscar Wilde was not born till the following year. The time was coming when one part of the literary world would place moral and aesthetic values in violent opposition, so that even those who least agreed with these iconoclasts would never again be able to take for granted that conflict between them was an impossibility.

We have been dealing so far only with what people felt it was right to say in public. All the authors quoted assumed that men talked differently in the club; all assumed that there were many things one knew which one did not say, even in the club, and still less in public. But, of course, what is said or not said, will gradually and insensibly influence what is thought. The influence of mid-nineteenth-century reticence upon actual beliefs about life is a fascinating and obscure subject. But we get a glimpse of it occasionally, and sometimes in a startling form. Take the following passage from a review in *Fraser's Magazine* of September 1848:

... Are there not women ... capable of nobler things than are here set down for them? Are they all schemers and *intrigantes*, worldly-wise, shuffling, perfidious, empty-headed?[6]

Most of us would take many guesses before we hit on the name of the book here described. It is *Vanity Fair*; now *Vanity Fair* did not actually offend agreed standards of decency. It merely, as we have seen, stretched them to the limit. And it certainly is not a book which denies the possibility of real, straightforward goodness. The reviewer appears to be perfectly sincere; so we must suppose that literary convention strongly influenced his sense of social reality. He had come to see people as they usually were in books. That is to say, man's capacity for wickedness, and even, in large part, his weakness, though written plain at this time as at all others on the face of life, had become obscured by the coloured spectacles of books. It is unlikely that this reviewer was very unusual in this. Respectable literature tends to make for a belief in a respectable world; and what begins by not being said out of good taste may end by not even being thought.*

It is noticeable that the reviewer is most affronted by Thackeray's portraits of women. The double sexual standard was unfair, of course, as several novelists from Mrs Gaskell to Hardy did not fail to point out. But it is important to realize that it was not based solely on biological and social facts. It received support also from a genuine conviction that women were, naturally and habitually, morally superior to men; and so, much more culpable when they fell. The Victorians no more thought it unfair to blame a woman more than a man for unchastity than a commander-in-chief would think it unfair to punish an officer more severely than a private for running away from the enemy.

This concept of feminine virtue was interwoven with another idea, quite different in its fundamental nature, but inextricably interwoven with it in fact, the idea of feminine *refinement*.

Elizabeth Barrett gives us an amusing sidelight on this in a letter of 17 January 1846 to her future husband, Browning. (She is quoting her father.):

Don't read Gibbon's history – it's not a proper book. Don't read *Tom Jones* – and none of the books on *this* side, mind! So I was very obedient and never touched the books on *that* side, and only read instead Tom Paine's *Age of Reason* and Voltaire's *Philosophical Dictionary* and Hume's *Essays*, and *Werther* and Rousseau and Mary Wollstonecraft.[7]

---

* There were, of course, many novels in the 1830s and 40s dealing with murder, robbery and the life of the criminal classes. But these will not have had the same startling effect. They were about the 'other' people, not about 'us'. In the same way, people who would be horrified to hear of cannibalism in Mayfair may read of its occurrence in the South Seas with untroubled placidity.

This is very revealing in three different ways. We notice
that Gibbon's subversive views on religion were ignored, while
the coarseness of some of the things he describes (usually in
chaste and reticent language) was an important issue. Then, it
never occurred to Mr Barrett that any book could be improper
for a man. Finally, it never occurred to him that his daughter, an
extremely clever girl on the way to becoming a woman of learning, could really be affected by an intellectual influence.

And the idea that women ought to be very refined frequently
extended to the claim that they actually were. Thus a reviewer of
Hardy's early novel *Desperate Remedies*, uncertain whether it had
been written by a man or a woman, decided that it was too coarse
to have been written by a woman. A passage in the first draft of
George Eliot's *Scenes of Clerical Life* about a few ladies being
'less sure of their equilibrium' (through drink) was omitted from
printed texts. [8] Mrs Ewing records in *Six to Sixteen* a case of the
historical books of the Old Testament being rejected as unsuitable
reading for girls. An extreme case, described satirically and perhaps with some exaggeration by Charlotte Brontë, shows us that
it could be considered more culpable for a well-brought-up girl
to *speak* of a man's profligacy than for the man himself to have
deserved the criticism.*

This last example points to an odd feature of the stock concept
of feminine refinement. It was held to be compatible with
marriage to a rake; as if the girl's innocence of any information
about his life could somehow sterilize that life. Thus in *Daniel
Deronda* (1876), Gwendolen Harleth's clerical uncle, who knows
that the man she is to marry has a mistress and several children,
assumes (wrongly) that Gwendolen, since she has accepted him,
cannot know about it.

Gwendolen Harleth's case is especially interesting because it
shows what few other novels show – the actual effect in life of
society's agreed standards of reticence. Gwendolen is a spoiled and
wilful girl, whose father is dead, and whose mother and younger
siblings are much in awe of her. She is impatient of control, and

---

* An example from a much earlier period is perhaps unusual enough to be worth
quoting:
    'To me a common rake is as odious as a common prostitute to a man of the nicest
feeling.' The speaker is Miss Milner, and her female friend replies: 'Strange that you,
who possess so many follies incident to your sex, should, in the disposal of your
heart have sentiments so contrary to women in general.' Mrs Inchbald: *A Simple
Story* (1791) Vol. II, p. 68.

fond of appearing unconventional and even startling. Mrs Glasher, the mistress of the man she is thinking of marrying, finds her out and tells her: 'Mr Grandcourt ought not to marry any one but me. I left my husband and child for him nine years ago . . . My husband is dead now.'[9] Gwendolen's 'uncontrolled' reading, we are told, had not prepared her for this encounter with reality.

When Grandcourt proposes, he asks, 'Is there any man who stands between us?'

Inwardly the answer framed itself, 'No; but there is a woman.' Yet how could she utter this? Even if she had not promised that woman to be silent, it would have been impossible for her to enter on the subject with Grandcourt.[10]

This is a moment eloquent in implied comment on the conventions of its age. It suggests that reticence, which is so undeniably necessary to civilized life, since without it the whole idea of what is fitting to an occasion is lost, can turn into a destructive tyrant. Gwendolen, no bread-and-butter miss, but a bold girl, and very much her own mistress, finds it impossible to speak of the very thing that it is most necessary to speak of, the thing she must elucidate in order to know her duty and to safeguard her hope of happiness. And this inability to speak is not due to ignorance or to parental control, but to an ethos so pervasive that it never needs to be stated, as inescapable as a substance dissolved in the drinking-water by an invisible authority. And, George Eliot encourages her readers to reflect, how strange this reticence is when one examines it; how odd that it should be impossible to speak of sex, when the issue is marriage.

To reinforce the point, we have a powerful portrait of the evening of the wedding day, when Gwendolen receives back from Mrs Glasher the diamonds Grandcourt had given her with a letter of fierce reproach, telling her, accurately enough, that she 'will have her punishment.' The reader is being asked to remember what it was tempting in those days to forget, that what is suppressed, what is unspoken, is still there.

George Eliot was contributing here, with the higher power and suggestiveness which art can achieve, to a long-standing debate, in which men of sincerity and high talent were on opposite sides. The case for reticence was perhaps best put by Bagehot in that same article on Sterne quoted above. He writes:

What is disenchanting or even disgusting in reality does not become enchanting or endurable in delineation. You are more angry at it in literature than in life; there is much which is barbarous and animal in reality that we could wish away; we endure it because we cannot help it, because we did not make it and cannot alter it, because it is an inseparable part of this inexplicable world. But why we should put this coarse alloy, this dross of life, into the *optional* world of literature, which we can make as we please, it is impossible to say.

And he goes on to speak severely of *Tristram Shandy* for offending in this respect.

On the other side, Coventry Patmore says:

The 'art' of the present generation is in great part more immoral than any that has preceded it in England. Modern English readers tolerate any amount of corruption, provided only the terms in which it is suggested be not 'coarse'; ... the delicate indecency of so much modern art is partly due to deficiency of virility.[11]

Bagehot and Patmore were born within a year or two of each other. This was no 'war of generations'; but an honest and respectable difference of opinion between contemporaries.

Gradually, insensibly, manners change. We know we are in a new world, aptly symbolized by the presence on the throne of the old queen's disreputable son, when we come to Howard Sturgis's *Belchamber* (1904). The following is a dialogue between Sainty, a very correct and honourable young nobleman of effeminate bearing and the girl who is trying to marry him for his wealth and position. Sainty's younger brother has recently married his mistress, a courtesan known as Cynthia de Vere:

'Of course one knew all those girls by sight,' she remarked, with engaging candour, 'but I'm not sure just *which* was Cynthia de Vere; it *was* the tall one with the beautiful legs and the rather big mouth, wasn't it ...?

'I didn't know young ladies knew anything about such things,' Sainty said rather severely.

'They do now,' said Cissy, 'whatever they used to; but I suspect they always knew more than they let on. There was a friend of mine who married Teddie Hersham last season; I was one of the bridesmaids; she was awfully proud of taking him away from Tottie Seymour; she used to boast of it to all her friends.'[12]

Gwendolen Harleth might have nodded ruefully at that 'always knew more than they let on'.

Belchamber throughout is a break with the tradition that
'Women are pure, but not men. Women are unselfish, but not
men.'[13] Here the pure innocent is a man, and the predatory sen-
sualists may be women. This remained, in the twentieth century,
as in the nineteenth, an exceptional view.

Earlier there had been a long desultory debate about the moral
effects of loss of chastity on a woman. Trollope, ever the calmest
and coolest among the Victorian novelists, was able to present a
realistic and credible, though rather sketchy, account of two
meetings between a reckless society rake, Burgo Fitzgerald, and
a London prostitute, impressed with his exceptional physical
beauty.[14] The two meetings are separated by a long time and many
chapters. Trollope is particularly unusual in showing the girl as
hungry on the first occasion, and comparatively prosperous on
the second. She says:

'You gave me supper one night when I was starving. I ain't
hungry now. Will you give me a kiss?' 'I'll give you a shilling
and that's better,' said Burgo. 'But give me a kiss too,' said
the girl. He gave her first the kiss, and then the shilling, and
after that he left her and passed on. 'I'm damned if I wouldn't
change with her!' he said to himself.

Given Burgo's character and history, this desperate wish rings
absolutely true, as does the whole of this and the previous
episode. And, since there was no question of Burgo wishing to
make use of the girl's services, Trollope was able to present the
human aspect of a topic generally clouded with literary pretence
in a manner that was at once genuine and well in accord with
agreed standards of decency. He equals here, in honesty if not in
subtlety, George Eliot's treatment of Mrs Glasher.

I reserve the fullest and most interesting example of the
'fallen woman' theme for separate treatment;* here I select
examples, one from each end of the queen's reign. In *Oliver Twist*
(1837–9) we have a poignant interview between the 'good'
woman, Rose Maylie and the 'bad' woman, Nancy.

'Do not turn a deaf ear to the entreaties of one of your own
sex; the first, I do believe, who ever appealed to you in the voice
of pity and compassion. Do hear my words, and let me save you
yet, for better things.'

---

* See discussion of *Ruth* in chapter V on Mrs Gaskell.

'Lady,' cried the girl, sinking on her knees, 'dear, sweet, angel lady, you *are* the first that ever blessed me with such words as these, and if I had heard them years ago, they might have turned me from a life of sin and sorrow; but it is too late, it is too late.'

'It is never too late for penitence and atonement.'[15]

When Nancy is murdered by Sykes,[16] she is just able, in her dying agony, to hold up the white handkerchief that Rose had given her, which thus becomes an emblem of repentance, and of the effective influence of the good woman on the bad, saved from despair at the last moment, and expiating her guilt in her innocent blood.

One should not be hasty in judging this passage. Dickens's great genius was only at the start of its long development, and the unreal, rhetorical quality of the dialogue is fairly general throughout the book (except in some of the comic passages) even though the subject may be quite different. But when all allowances are made, it remains true, I think, that we have here an episode which is not so much an expression of Dickens's immaturity as an artist as of a shared, public delusion. It was comforting to suppose that the bad woman reverenced the good, and that the good exercised a profound moral influence. But suppose the fallen woman resented, disliked, even despised the pure one? What then? Suppose the pure woman despised and spurned the fallen one? Suppose even, as Tolstoy rather startlingly suggests in the case of Dolly Oblonsky, the pure woman envies the fallen one? It is not for me to determine how much truth there is in Pope's aphorism:

Every woman is at heart a rake.

But whatever grain of truth it contains was excluded from consideration at this time and for many years after.

In *Trilby* (1894) George du Maurier, with no less sentimental unreality, exactly reverses Dickens's procedure. He has the 'good' woman fall at the feet of the 'bad'. Moreover the 'good' woman is the mother of the boy who has been in danger of marrying Trilby:

Mrs Bagot, who was as impulsive, emotional, and unregulated as her son, rushed forward, crying, 'Oh, my poor girl, my poor girl!' and caught her in her arms, and kissed and caressed her, and burst into a flood of tears, and forced her back into her chair hugging her as if she were a long-lost child.

'I love you now as much as I always admired you – pray believe it' . . .

and a little later:

'Forgive a poor jealous mother. As if *any* man could help loving you – or any woman either. Forgive me.'[17]

Here it is the virtuous woman who needs to purge her pharisaism; the fallen woman has taken Rose Maylie's place as the beneficent moral influence. Like many opposites, the passages really have much in common. Both are staged to avoid awkward questions and the real embarrassing harshness and incomprehension to be expected in the long-delayed meeting of people with different experience and conflicting desires and interests. Each passage conveys an illusion of real feeling which is achieved only by ignoring the feelings the character portrayed would really have.

It would be easy, but tedious, to give many more examples. A full consideration of them might have the effect of increasing our admiration for those, like George Eliot, who avoided sentimentality when the temptations to it were so pressing.

We find, then, that the 'fallen' woman is a constant preoccupation of the nineteenth-century novelists; and their reticence about her is really much less extreme than it has often been said to be.*

And we find, to our surprise, that the real absentee from the novel is often marriage. Naturally, there are innumerable accounts of marriage as it appears from outside; and the most memorable of them are often, like the treatment of the Bennets in *Pride and Prejudice*, full of sarcasm and mutual incomprehension. But the experience of being married, so important in the world, is generally overlooked,† or relegated to a hasty summary in a final chapter. Why is this?

The venerable plot derived from ancient stage comedies, and exemplified by *Tom Jones*, gives one pattern where the experience of marriage is left to the imagination. It is omitted because it is the long-delayed goal of all the action; and so gradually takes on an unearthly, absolute quality for the yearning participants and for

---

* I pass over, regretfully, a case remarkable for the honesty, dignity and compassion of the author's treatment, only because I have written about it before. This is Effie Deans in Scott's *Heart of Midlothian*.
† There are exceptions. Notable are Trollope's account of the Pallisers and *Wives and Daughters* by Mrs Gaskell.

the sympathetic reader. The humdrum nature of everyday domestic life, even at its happiest, the feeling of 'Monday morning', would be fatal to the book's structure in such cases, for it would damage the sense of a thirst finally satisfied and a painful quest achieved.

On the other hand, an attempt to describe a permanent state of ecstatic bliss would be sure to fail. In cases like these, the long-delayed wedding becomes a secular equivalent of a happy death with a hope of heaven; and it becomes impious to enquire minutely into the nature of that happiness.

On the explicitly sexual side, the wedding at the end of the volume provides a neat method of avoiding the consummation. And we find that the shyness about speaking of this, is, for most novelists, far greater than any that would afflict them in describing an illicit relationship. In this, the novelists seem to be following closely the practice of earlier poets and dramatists. The paradoxical conclusion is that in the interests of morality and decency, sexual intercourse is usually excluded from literature when it is legitimate, moral, pure and loving. Various degrees of nearness of approach to it become permissible when it is cynical, casual, lustful and adulterous. Here, as in other respects, Lawrence was the founder of a new tradition in *The Rainbow*.

Very often, the last chapter of a long novel is meant to be read differently from the rest. The air of fictional reality begins to be dropped. The author is personally addressing the reader rather in the way a leading actor does at a curtain call after the play is over. The close family likeness between one description of wedding bells and another need not then have the effect of boring repetition. The last chapters of (say) *Tom Jones*, *David Copperfield*, *Dr Thorne* and many, many others have an air of pleasant traditional formalities. The author is ceasing to create for himself and retreating into a realm of quasi-liturgical repetition. The reader's transition from suspension of disbelief in the story to his own ordinary world is thus gradual and easy. He does not need to blink mentally, as when leaving the cinema. Perhaps this has its advantages.

We have seen that women were thought more culpable than men because they were supposed to be naturally better; but it was also a general assumption that women loved more strongly, more fiercely and above all, more faithfully. It might seem to follow from this that their temptations might be more severe, and lapses, therefore, more excusable. Occasionally (as, for instance, in *Trilby*) we do find this judgement made. But, in general, the idea of women's stronger love is balanced by its greater purity.

The whole question of passion and will bristles with difficulties, which many novelists simply ignore. One who did not ignore them was Samuel Richardson. When Pamela, in the sequel, is safely married to Mr B., and he has reformed, she has a most instructive conversation with his sister about his bachelor life:

he has assured me, that in all the liberties he has taken, he never attempted a married lady, but always abhorred the thought of so great an evil.

'Tis pity, said her ladyship [B.'s sister] that a man who could conquer his passions *so far*, could not subdue them entirely. This shews it was in his own power to do so; and increases his crime: and what a wretch is he, who scrupling, under pretence of conscience or honour, to attempt ladies *within* the pale, boggles not to ruin a poor creature *without*; although he knows he thereby, most probably, for ever deprives her of that protection, by preventing her marriage, which, even among such rakes as himself, is deemed, he owns inviolable and so casts the poor creature headlong into the jaws of perdition.[18]

Richardson, as he was to show more brilliantly, in *Clarissa*, was abundantly aware of the mental elements in lust. He knew that a professed rake soon ceased to find interest in the mere routine satisfaction of the promptings of the body. He would then turn to satisfying an idea of himself, as conqueror. He transforms his lust from a weakness of the flesh into an instrument of diabolical strength. Mr B.'s early career is a bit shadowy; but we are left to assume that its motive was similar to that of Lovelace. In both it was a willed lust, that set itself obstacles as a sop to pride and as a remedy for boredom.

What Mr B.'s sister is saying here is that lust as a weakness of the flesh is far more easily pardonable than lust as an instrument of a conquest which feeds an insatiable, diabolic will to power. Now, lust as a weakness is wayward and unpredictable; it will be attracted by a face, a figure, a voice, a mere idea. Since many of the most attractive women are married, it will often be directed to one of them. A man who deliberately excludes married women from his calculations is a man who has conquered the weakness of

lust; and instead has by strength of will transformed his lust into
a willed channel. By moving half-way towards conventional
morality, Mr B. has forfeited the excuse of overwhelming carnal
temptation.

Richardson drops the issue very quickly, as if a little nervous
of the boldness of the paradox that the greater sin is less culpable
than the smaller. We feel here as so often in his work a tension
between a deep moral insight and a wish to be conventionally
correct. But the paradox advanced is a truth in terms of the wisest
traditions, according to which pride is a far more deadly sin than
lust.

This willed passion, this lust as an instrument of power, is
Richardson's great subject. And we find another, softer, version of
the same thing in the eighteenth century, in Sterne and Henry
Mackenzie, and other sentimentalists. Here the desire is also
controlled, but not in the interests of conquest, but rather of the
character's own conception of himself as a man of delicate sensibility. He prides himself on the power to feel more exquisitely
than others. To do this it is not necessary to succeed. A hopeless
love can be a certificate of a more exquisite sensibility than a
seduction (or a marriage). Lust may even be diluted out of exist-
ence; but, if so, the purpose of the remaining sentiment is still
the same. Love is still being used competitively, in the service of
a man's idea of his superiority to others. The Don Juan gratifies
his pride by conquest of many; the sophisticated Don Juan (like
Lovelace) especially by attempting the most difficult case, the
most strong and virtuous woman; the sentimentalist by assuring
himself that he feels more deeply, more beautifully than anyone
else can.

This aspect of the matter is less prominent in the nineteenth
century than the eighteenth. Two patterns, which ignore the
place of the will to power in sexual psychology, are commoner
in the nineteenth century. According to one, usually to be found,
for instance, in Scott, A's love for B is simply part of the donnée.
No questions are to be asked about reasons and motives. According to the other, love, in either sex, is a power, almost like the
madness of Aphrodite, which leaves the sufferer no choice about
the identity of the beloved, though it still leaves desire subject
to moral control. Even if, as often happens in Trollope, a
character is undecided between two possible loves, the relative
strength of each is supposed to be almost beyond the power of

conscious decision to alter. Compared with Lovelace the men of the nineteenth-century novel are, for the most part, modest and humble. But we do find a soft, feminine version of sexual pride and power in the person of the coquette. Rosamund Lydgate 'welcomed the signs that her husband loved her and was under control. But this was something quite distinct from loving him.'[19] And her flirtation with Will Ladislaw makes her dream of a royal position where a husband was only the leading member of a cohort of adorers. The whole point here is that the less she returns the feelings of her adorers, the more numerous and the more devoted they will be. George Eliot reminds us forcibly here that love cannot be a separate area of the soul where the everyday character has little effect. Some novelists wrote as if love was a magic potion that acted in the same way whoever drank it. And we find a totally different kind of willed passion in the same book when Dorothea Brooke lectures herself into loving Casaubon, because he appears to minister to her idea of herself as a learned lady, a helpmeet of genius and intellect, and a Lady Bountiful for his tenants.

At the other end of the scale the overpowering, unwilled, nature of love is shown in characters whose will and personality suffer total collapse at its onset. Such are Dickens's Mr Toots, or the son of the millionaire, Tringle, in Trollope's *Ayala's Angel*. Both these are treated in terms of broad comedy. Very good comedy it is, in both cases; yet one is led to ask whether something is being hidden or evaded here. The disintegrating, destructive power of passion, as in the *Hippolytos* of Euripides, or *Othello*, or Proust's Charlus, is surely a real part of the subject, and one, as the above examples show, capable of being used for the grandest literary effects. Its almost total absence* from the English novel is, perhaps, an aspect of its generally domestic character. There is no lack of novels with tragic plots and sad endings, as can be seen in my chapter devoted to *The Pessimists*. But nearly all the characters there retain their dignity in their sufferings; and so, the authors have not quite envisaged the worst.

And one might be tempted to suppose, taking a bird's-eye view of the course of the English novel over two centuries, that there was also a much more serious and fundamental lack. Do the

---

* A notable exception is to be found in Trollope's *He Knew He Was Right* (1869). See my *Anthony Trollope* (Part II, chap. 3, *The Drama of Loneliness*).

English novelists ever pause to enquire into the fundamental bases of morality? In so far as it is not merely conventional, morality rests on religion or, for those who do not accept religion, on whatever general view of the world they adopt in its place. No reason that will hold water for a moment can be given why sexual morality should claim exemption from this general condition of all morality. Of how many English novelists can one claim that they emancipate themselves from convention, from convenience, from mere personal impressions and predilections, and present a coherent view of the world, with sexual morality in its due, logical place? Richardson, certainly, Jane Austen (with perhaps an uneasy caveat about her attitude to money) and D. H. Lawrence, and how many others?

In chapter XXII of Manzoni's great novel *I Promessi Sposi*, there is an account of the early years of Cardinal Federigo Borromeo, Archbishop of Milan. It describes how, brought up in surroundings of wealth and privilege, he had listened, since childhood, 'to those maxims about the vanity of pleasure, about the injustice of pride, about true dignity and true riches, which are handed down from one generation to the next (whether heeded or not by men's hearts) as the most elementary teaching of religion.'

He listened, I say, to those lessons and maxims, he took them seriously, tested them, and found them true; he saw that, in that case, other opposing lessons and maxims which had also been handed down from generation to generation *with the same certainty, and sometimes by the same lips,* could not be true.*

Anyone emerging from a prolonged course of reading in the English novel will recognize a perfectly accurate analysis of something that he has found constantly present, but hardly ever discussed. The other maxims that could not be true, if the radically Christian ones were, were, of course, maxims about family pride and dignity, about the glory of wealth, about the duty of marrying 'well' in the eyes of the world, about health and worldly content being the highest goods. And that terrible phrase 'sometimes by the same lips' points exactly to the dilemma

---

* My italics. The original reads: Bado, dico, a quelle parole, a quelle massime, le prese sul serio, le gusto, le trovo vere; vide che non potevan dunque esser vere altre parole e altre massime opposte, che pure si trasmettono di generazione in generazione, con la stessa sicurezza, e talora dalle stesse labbra.

of so many heroines, whose mentors had never seriously asked themselves which of their precepts were religious and really moral, and which were dictated by worldly prudence. Such confusions in the minds of characters, as Manzoni reminds us, are true to life. But the weakness of the English fictional tradition is to be found in the fact that, often, the authors are as confused as their characters. Did Fielding ever ask himself why it was inconceivable that the heroine of *Tom Jones* should be unchaste like the hero? If he ever did, he left no sign for us that he had done so. He simply did not know that he had mingled some of the basest maxims of the world ('Boys will be boys – but girls is damaged goods') with high-sounding moral and even religious professions. Really, Dickens is no better; though the conventions of his age prevent him giving himself away quite so obviously.

A fair example to take, perhaps, is the dilemma of Griselda Grantly. Griselda is the daughter of a serious, working arch-deacon who sees no inconsistency between being this and being a wealthy, ambitious man, eager for the worldly success of his children. His daughter, absorbing, like the Bertram girls in *Mansfield Park*, what was implied rather than what was stated in her education, has married the heir to a marquisate and a great property. She is flirting with Plantagenet Palliser, the heir to a dukedom, and an even greater property. Reports reach her mother that she is about to leave home as Palliser's mistress.

She receives a letter from her mother, which says in part:

I will not say a word as to the injury in a worldly point of view which would come to you from any rupture with your husband. I believe that you can see what would be the effect of so terrible a step quite as plainly as I can show it to you. You would break the heart of your father, and send your mother to her grave – but it is not even on that that I may most insist. It is this – that you would offend your God by the worst sin that a woman can commit, and cast yourself into a depth of infamy in which repentance before God is almost impossible . . .[20]

If Griselda had been other than she was, and had seriously desired to extract the real moral message from this, how difficult it would have been for her. The religious feeling in the letter is perfectly sincere, but how exquisitely muddled. Who said it was the worst sin *for a woman*? Only worldly prudence. Who made this one exception to the universal Christian principle that all sins may be repented and forgiven? And then, what about the marriage with Lord Dumbello? The man is almost an idiot, while all the Grantlys are clever. How hollow it sounds to invoke a high sacramental view of marriage as a subsidiary and an after-thought, when the only object of the marriage was devotion to the great god of 'getting on'. And yet, muddled as it is, of course the letter does contain a Christian idea of indissoluble marriage, and having married the man, for whatever motive, it becomes Griselda's duty to stick to him.

But Griselda is not one to enquire into deep meanings. Having shown the issues with such unobtrusive and brilliant skill, Trollope characteristically liquidates the scene with a magnificent piece of satirical comedy. Griselda has no intention of going off with Mr Palliser; she knows it would not pay. There is poignancy in Trollope's comment on Mrs Grantly's feelings when she receives her daughter's cool and safe reply:

She has thrown all her heart into that which she had written, but in the words which her child had written not a vestige of heart was to be found. In that reconciling of God and Mammon which Mrs Grantly had carried on so successfully in the education of her daughter, the organ had not been required, and had become withered . . .

I do not know whether Trollope read *I Promessi Sposi*; but if he did he might have seen a parallel. Muddled and inconsistent views, mingling religion and worldliness, go on being accepted from generation to generation. Then comes one who is wholly consistent and clear-sighted. Cardinal Federigo casts off all the worldly maxims in his zeal for the gospel; and Griselda cast off every impulse that could interfere with worldly success. By show-ing us Mrs Grantly's grief at this, mingling with relief at avoidance of the feared catastrophe, Trollope shows that in his unemphatic way he is aware of the dilemma of which Manzoni speaks so eloquently.

In *The Small House*, the comic upshot is that Griselda shows her mother's letter to her husband, sets his mind at rest, resolves to snub Mr Palliser at their next encounter and receives from her husband a 'wonderful green necklace, very rare and curious'. Griselda, as she counts the sparkles, 'triumphed inwardly, telling herself that she had played her cards well'. A fine and convincing ending to the episode, thoroughly consistent with all the characters involved. But it leaves a nagging difficulty. If religion and base worldly prudence here counsel the same thing – fidelity to the husband – how is the infinitely powerful contrast between them, which really exists and which Cardinal Federigo understood, and Mrs Grantly and the archdeacon did not, to be made manifest?

Newman complained that it was hard to wind an Englishman up to a dogmatic level. And we have throughout most of the period of two centuries with which this book deals a curious paradox. Marriage was held to be sacred, and an offence against its sanctity very serious. But few asked in what way it was sacred or why. Just as Newman was amused to hear that an Anglican bishop, on reading his tract on the Apostolic Succession, could not tell whether he held the doctrine or not – that is to say, was quite happy as a bishop without ever asking himself what a bishop was – so with marriage. Everyone was sure that marriage was wonderful, precious, sacred; few asked whether the basis of this precious sacredness was sacramental or legal or merely empirical. Times change and customs change. Those who imagine that they will rub along very well without fundamental principles because custom is so powerful, and old England is so traditionally minded, wake up one day and find old England has changed. Then they find that the comfortable absence of fundamental principles has suddenly become an aching void.

> Water and fire shall rot
> The marred foundations we forgot

The Victorian public rested comfortably on conventional views of marriage. Their twentieth-century successors woke up and found that conventions had dissolved. The thirty-year controversy over *Lady Chatterley's Lover*, culminating in the obscenity trial of October 1960, revealed the extraordinary confusions of thought which were left as the thick sediment of this Victorian complacency.

The confusion between decorum and morals on the 'respectable' side of the argument seemed at times so strong that some people appeared to be saying: 'The moral law is that you may do anything provided you do not employ to describe it words which every boy of twelve knows but which should not appear in print.' The confusion on the 'progressive' side (which was on the whole more inexcusable since it contained more people who claimed to be intelligent students of literature) was so extreme that the difference between marriage and adultery was being concealed under a smoke-screen of words derived from the more muddled passages in the literary criticism of Matthew Arnold.

All this followed naturally from the failure of the Victorian novelists to guide their public to ask themselves what marriage was and why they valued it, and what elements were essential, and which fortuitous. Thackeray occasionally hinted at the question; Trollope for a moment put it plainly, in Mrs Grantly's letter and Griselda's reply. But both were more interested in their own masterly psychology and their own comic brilliance than in these skeletons in the national cupboard their probing hands had rattled for a moment.

On one point in particular the reticences of the nineteenth century served the future ill; and something of importance in the eighteenth-century novel was lost. Some of Richardson's most powerful and morally serious passages describe events in a brothel. And brothels, of course, in the nineteenth century, as in the eighteenth, were not institutions in rebellion against the conventions of society, but entirely in accordance with them. They were the embodiment of the commercial ethic, the *reductio ad absurdum* of Manchester economics, the pitiless consequence of the 'respectable' double standard of morality for male and female. They were also, above all, living proof that the teachings of religion and the dictates of conventional respectability were utterly different, and that hypocritical endeavours to harmonize them could not survive a clear view of the facts.

Richardson showed this. The Victorian novelists did not, though perhaps some of them knew it too. No novelist was willing to say to the public: '*This* is the corollary of your respectable marriage market and your "purity" which only applies to one sex (or rather the respectable part of it); and this is the measure of the gulf between what most of you think you believe about Christian marriage and what most of you really believe about Mammon's marriage.' The price of decency can be too high.

CHAPTER II

Richardson and Fielding

He [Johnson] said that he was praising to Richardson his account of a house of bad fame. Richardson said it was all done from fancy for he never had been in one in his life.
Boswell in Extremis Edited by C. Weis & F. A. Pottle. Entry for 21 September 1777

'I think it ought not to be set down as certain, that a man must be acceptable to every woman he may happen to like himself.'
Fanny Price in *Mansfield Park* by Jane Austen (1814) chap. XXXV

... 'to go to a masquerade at Ranelagh, for which my lord had furnished her with tickets.'
At these words, Amelia turned pale as death ...
Henry Fielding, *Amelia* (1751) Book VII, chap. VI

Unlike other parts of my subject, the running controversy of Richardson and Fielding has been much discussed. I wish, therefore, to avoid much detail and to draw attention to a few simple points. The key scenes in the early part of the controversy occur in chapters V and VIII of *Joseph Andrews*. Here, more subtly and much more amusingly than in *Shamela*, Fielding sought to discredit Richardson's heady mixture of principle, prudence and cupidity in *Pamela*. The essence of his complaint against Richardson is that he allowed Pamela to regard her resistance to Mr B.'s sexual importunity as a bargaining counter in a campaign for a socially and financially advantageous marriage. She seems to treat Mr B.'s violence, deception and treachery as mere tactical features in her struggle. She allows for them as a far-seeing tactician allows for the weather and the nature of the terrain. It does not seem to occur to her that men, and even squires of broad acres, vary; that not all are brutes, and that a man's character is at least as relevant as his social position in assessing a girl's chances of happiness in marriage.

Here is the crucial passage of Fielding's answer: (Lady Booby is lying provocatively in bed, as the servant Joseph rejects her advances.)

'Your virtue,' said the lady, recovering after a silence of two minutes, 'I shall never survive it. Your virtue! intolerable confidence! Have you the assurance to pretend, that when a lady demeans herself to throw aside the rules of decency, in order to honour you with the highest favour in her power, your virtue should resist her inclination? that when she had conquered her own virtue, she should find an obstruction in yours? ... Did ever mortal hear of a man's virtue! Did ever the greatest, or the gravest, men pretend to any of this kind!'[1]

A very neat and effective comic scene, certainly. But what as a critique of Richardson, is it really saying? At first it seems that Joseph stands alone, contrasted both with Lady Booby, and with Richardson's Mr B. and Pamela. He takes virtue to be a word with real moral substance. They, all three, assume it is merely a cant word for a weapon in the sex-war. Certainly Lady Booby, Mr B. and Pamela would express themselves differently, but at heart they all mean the same thing. Since women have babies and men don't, since the world condemns female unchastity and winks at male unchastity, since every man, whatever his own history, wishes his bride to be a virgin, virtue, that is chastity, becomes an exclusively feminine concern. It is no more than a function of worldly prudence. A girl who is careless of her chastity is as ill-advised as a man who is reckless with his money – more so, since recovery is more difficult or, in most cases, impossible.

Taken like this, the scene suggests that Lady Booby is only saying openly what Pamela means, but hypocritically won't say. And each woman appears to have very similar expectations of the male. Pamela is harassed, but not in the least surprised, and hardly at all shocked by Mr B.'s lustful behaviour. Lady Booby is staggered and incensed by Joseph's restraint.

But it is not quite so simple. Neither Richardson nor Fielding, at this stage in the debate, appears to have thoroughly considered the double standard of sexual morality upon which both are commenting. One might suppose, here, that Fielding was entirely rejecting it and Richardson was uncritically accepting it. But this is deceptive. To analyse the double standard, one needs to try to separate worldly wisdom from moral truth; eventually, in *Clarissa*, Richardson would do this with unequalled artistic power, but the time was not yet.

Fielding, though his intentions are not completely clear, seems to be encouraging us to ask, since Joseph's refusal of Lady Booby is uproariously comic, why not admit that Pamela's evasion of Mr B. is uproariously comic too? Lustful woman and chaste man – lustful man and chaste girl, there is no fundamental difference. But, we soon see, this will not quite do. We have to consider facts as well as principles. And two very important facts of the Pamela situation have been reversed. There is an advantage which nearly all men have over all women in physical strength. This is given by nature. There is an advantage which a member of the squirearchy has over a servant. This is given by the particular social conditions of the time. And there is an advantage of men over women in the degree of moral licence society agrees to allow them. This is not unalterable, or inscribed in the nature of things. But it is much more lasting than any particular class arrangements of a given historical society; and it is related, however unfairly, to certain unalterable facts of nature; for instance, that men cannot become pregnant, and that an adulterous wife can foist her child upon her husband as his, while an adulterous husband may conceal his fault, but can never persuade his wife or the world that she bore the child that another woman bore.

If then, we adopt this fourfold division, morality, natural facts, class discriminations and social assumptions about sexual roles, we find that all the last three are on Mr B.'s side. He has an advantage in strength, in class, in the double standard. Added to all this, he has the advantage of seclusion, and of willing and corrupt female associates. All this means that Pamela's situation cannot be comic, even though one or two scenes may be in danger of lurching temporarily into comedy through improbability of event or inadequate psychology.

In the contest between Joseph and Lady Booby, the odds are much fairer. Lady Booby has the advantage of class that Mr B. had; and, unlike Pamela, she has no particular reason to fear pregnancy, her husband being only a short time dead. Joseph has the unalterable advantage possessed by the feeblest male, that he can't be raped by a woman. The scene is comic, not only because it comments wittily on *Pamela* but because much less is at stake. Joseph has nothing to lose but a not very desirable position. Lady Booby has nothing to lose by his refusal but her own self-esteem. In *Pamela*, however faulty the morality may be, the issues are truly momentous. The heroine can lose everything.

Fielding appears to be saying obliquely here, what he said unequivocally in *Shamela*, that Richardson's Pamela is a creature of pure calculation. Richardson laid himself open to this charge, of course, by showing her triumphant in her eventual matrimonial conquest of a man whom the whole previous story showed to be worthless. Yet it is not quite true; there is something else which Fielding may have missed. Fielding is above all a moralist; Richardson is a psychologist first and a moralist second. Distasteful as the ethical implications of *Pamela* are, it has elements of a humbler truth. Pamela's resistance is not, as Fielding rightly saw, wholly virtuous, but neither is it wholly calculation. It is deeply rooted in her femininity. She has an unconscious desire to be bullied, to be made to yield, to make herself valuable by delay. There is an element of sensuous enjoyment in her perfectly genuine terror.

Fielding was generally oblivious of subtleties, or else, when he was aware of them, he was impatient of them. It was natural to him to suppose that every person and every act was either sincere or insincere. He was honestly bewildered, perhaps, by a genuinely mixed case like that of Pamela. When was Blifil ever sincere, or when was Tom Jones ever insincere?

Sincerity is the great canon of judgement in Fielding's sexual morality. Theory is always suspect. Even the admirable Parson Adams becomes foolish with too much theory when he lectures Joseph as bridegroom-to-be on the wickedness even of marital love if it causes a man to set his heart too much on one person.[2] He is immediately deflated by his own wife:

> Marry come up! Fine doctrine, indeed! A wife hath a right to insist on her husband's loving her as much as ever he can; and he is a sinful villain who doth not . . . Besides, I am certain you do not preach as you practise; for you have been a loving and a cherishing husband to me . . .

Principles, Fielding seems to say, are only clumsy formulations of feelings. If the feelings are right, we can dispense with them.

In *Tom Jones*, Fielding was able to deploy his moral opinions more fully, and when he does so we find that they are full of paradoxes. This is not surprising, for the effort to treat complex moral questions as matters of mere common sense is bound to lead to difficulties. Let us take first the episode of Tom and Molly Seagrim. The scene in which Tom, going to visit Molly, finds the

philosopher Square in her bedroom, deserves particular attention.
It is much more than a farcical effect of situation. It is a scene
cunningly devised to gloss over one of the chief difficulties in
Fielding's moral scheme. It is this. A healthy, uninhibited,
unreflective young man like Tom will be unlikely to resist Molly's
solicitations. But when he yields to them, he sets up obligations.
She may be fond of him; she may have a child. She may acquire
a right to expect him to marry her. The morality of generous
feeling, which Fielding preaches and Tom is supposed to be
following, will make it impossible for him to be insensible to her
claims. If the ensuing inner struggle were allowed to run its
course, Tom would be in danger of being ruined as a novel hero.
He might have to spurn the woman who was about to bear his
child; or he might have to marry an ignorant village slut. Square's
presence is urgently needed. And it is particularly lucky for Tom
that it is this man and no other. A high-minded Platonic philosopher can be convicted of hypocrisy as well as of lust. His pre-
varications are amusing, and help to distract attention from Tom's
moral dilemma. Fielding takes the opportunity to press home his
case against theory:

> Philosophers are composed of flesh and blood as well as
> other human creatures . . . though such great beings think
> much better and more wisely, they always act exactly like other
> men. They know very well how to subdue all appetites and
> passions, and to despise both pain and pleasure; and this
> knowledge affords much delightful contemplation, and is
> easily acquired; but the practice would be vexatious and
> troublesome . . .[3]

In Fielding's scheme one weak or insincere professor of a
theory is almost enough to refute it. It does not seem to occur to
him that insincere professors of his own 'good-chap' morality
might also be found.

So Tom gets off, without a stain on his character, and without
the tedious necessity of marrying Molly to save his credit as a
man of feeling. Indeed, he actually acquires some moral kudos:

> The infidelity of Molly, which Jones had now discovered,
> would, perhaps, have vindicated a much greater degree of
> resentment than he expressed on that occasion; and if he had
> abandoned her directly from that moment, very few, I believe,
> would have blamed him.[4]

Tom, who, just before discovering Square, had been asking

himself 'Can I be such a villain?', when he contemplated deserting Molly, now receives that special halo which is reserved for works of supererogation. And his original guilt as seducer is neatly transferred to an uncomplaining third party, who is introduced into the story solely for the purpose of bearing this burden, and then is speedily dismissed:

This Will Barnes was a country gallant, and had acquired as many trophies of this kind as any ensign or attorney's clerk in the kingdom. He had, indeed, reduced several women to a state of utter profligacy, had broke the heart of some, and had the honour of occasioning the death of one poor girl, who had either drowned herself . . .

'What a wicked man!' we are asked to think, 'and how different from our dear Tom!' But Fielding does not tell us how he knows that none of these terrible consequences will ever follow any of Tom's escapades. Nor does he explain why, if Tom thought he was Molly's first lover, he was not just as guilty as if he really was. This is odd, since Fielding always stresses intention as the key point of moral judgement.

But it is wrong to see Tom simply as the creature of impulse. His impulses are strong, but he is governed just as much by a primitive sense of honour. Certainly, it is not always easy to distinguish the two. We are told that his sense of honour forbade him to refuse a challenge in love, just as it forbade him to refuse a man's invitation to fight. In simple cases this will come to much the same as saying that his senses could not resist much female provocation. But the case of Lady Bellaston is more complicated.

Here, Tom feels no love and little desire. She is much older than he is, and her beauty is marred by bad breath. The dislike of refusing any love-challenge is combined here with gratitude. 'It is owing, perhaps, solely to her, that I have not, before this, wanted a bit of bread. How can I possibly desert such a woman?'[5] Tom escapes by a trick which he does not himself understand, but which is suggested to him by someone else. An offer of marriage will be treated as an insult by such a woman, so much richer and more fashionable than the boy she dotes on. Tom dutifully performs this trick, like a person delivering a message in a code he does not understand. And it is effective at once.

But what about sincerity? Fielding clearly saw the difficulty here. Sincerity had always been his one claim for his hero in all his scrapes and indiscretions. Here is Fielding's last line of defence;

and if he abandons it, his whole cause will be lost.

He has no intention of abandoning it; and he approaches this most awkward of all the tasks of his special pleading with great skill. First, Tom did not understand fully the deceit he practised. He was put up to it, so he can remain a simpleton while doing a clever thing. Then, when he does at last dimly understand what he is going to do:

> There was in this scheme too much of fallacy to satisfy one who utterly detested every species of falsehood or dishonesty . . . surely the reader will allow that every good principle, as well as love, pleaded strongly in favour of Sophia.[6]

Why the reader who has willingly made the latter admission should be deemed to have also conceded that deceit is the same as honesty, is not clear. But in case we should linger on this point, Fielding neatly follows it up with an exhibition of Lady Bellaston's vicious resentment which leads her to incite her friend to have Tom pressed for the navy. Lady Bellaston then does not deserve kindness. We only need to forget that kindness and sincerity are not the same to find all this convincing.

But why, we may wonder, does Fielding require to go to such lengths to deceive us? Actually, quite a lot is at stake. In one sense, Fielding plays very fair. The plot sets the hero many difficult problems; had the issues been fairly stated, Fielding would be entitled to claim that Tom and his morality of untutored impulse had been thoroughly vindicated. A boy who can emerge from encounters with Molly Seagrim, Mrs Waters and Lady Bellaston without a serious stain upon his character would certainly be credited with a degree of heroism.

Fielding knows that chastity is not natural to healthy, high-spirited and attractive young men. But he wants to say that such young men may nevertheless be the salt of the earth if only they have sincerity and generous instincts. His strategy, therefore, is to insulate sexual morality from all other kinds of morality. 'I will show you', he seems to be saying 'a man who is unchaste, (which I admit is a blemish) but so deserving in every other respect that you will be forced to admit that the blemish has not deeply affected his character. And, to play fair, I will bring him up against some very dangerous female opponents, ordinary, like Molly Seagrim, and unusual, like Lady Bellaston. His sense of honour, his integrity, his generosity will survive intact. Thus you will see that chastity is only a detail, and, most important, a *separable* detail, involving nothing beyond itself.'

This is very persuasive, but it fails with discerning readers. For discerning readers of any novel are those who work out the consequences for themselves, and then compare their own version with the one the author offers. If cause and effect had been permitted to work normally, Tom would have been guilty of heartless conduct in deserting Molly Seagrim, and of tricky deceit in deserting Lady Bellaston. And this in spite of the fact that he is by nature kinder and more truthful than most. This would tend to show that sexual morality is not a separate compartment of conduct; that the world is so arranged that every virtue and every vice affects every other, that momentary, unconsidered actions have long consequences, that any shared sexual act sets up a relationship with another person, which can be evaded but not cancelled. The intelligent, good-hearted man of the world, whether Fielding himself or his reader, does not want to be told this. He wants to hear that unchastity can never threaten his sense of honour as a truthful gentleman. Fielding is very comforting.

II Noble Women

Fielding's letter to Richardson of 15 October 1748 is very surprising, and it is not as well known as it might be. Having just read *Clarissa*, he wrote:

God forbid that the Man who reads this with dry eyes should be alone with my Daughter, when she hath no Assistance within call.

Fielding and Richardson are generally billed in literary history, truly enough, as opponents. But they can also be seen in a paradoxical way as collaborators. It may be partly because of the criticism embodied in *Joseph Andrews* that *Clarissa* is so infinitely superior to *Pamela*. And the appreciation of *Clarissa* may have contributed to *Amelia*. In any case, Fielding's letter is much to his credit. It took an unusual degree of detachment to see that *Clarissa* was something new, which the boisterous moral criticism of *Joseph Andrews* and *Shamela* could not touch; and it took a generous spirit to confess it so freely.

Clarissa is superior in many ways to *Pamela*, some of which are not relevant here. For our purposes, its great superiority is this:

it draws a clear distinction, at once subtle, firm and flexible between the morality of conscience and the morality of the respectable world. This is precisely where *Pamela* had failed.

From the first, Clarissa is in a paradoxical position. She is admired for her virtues and accomplishments; she is a special favourite. She has been chosen, contrary to all normal customs of primogeniture, for her grandfather's inheritance. At the same time, her conscience and her natural feelings as a woman are forcing her to act so that she is disgraced both in the eyes of those who admired and loved her and of those who envied and resented her. Her relations talk much of duty, but their duty is not her duty. 'For a girl to lay so much stress upon going to church', her brother writes,[7] 'and yet resolve to defy her parents . . . is an absurdity.' Unwittingly, James Harlowe here puts his finger on the key point. The respectable world finds itself confronted by traditional moral principles. Some of these are indifferent to them, some; like the injunction to love your neighbour as yourself, are too strange and exacting to be taken seriously by respectable minds. A few, like the duty of honouring parents, are just to their taste. St Paul, who said that the foolishness of God was wiser than men, also enjoined obedience to the powers that be. By choosing out a few subordinate moral principles, and neglecting all the others, by fastening on details and ignoring the logic of the system, members of the respectable world can often justify to their own satisfaction the most selfish motives and cruel actions.

But the trick can only be performed if a wide variation is allowed in the precepts selected for temporary approval. At one moment family obligations are paramount. But when it comes to Solmes's family obligations, quite a different canon is invoked. (Solmes in his eagerness to marry Clarissa has promised settlements that will deprive his blood relations of their legitimate expectations, and strongly excite the avarice of the Harlowe family.) Clarissa asks:

> Can *he* be an honest man who offers terms that will rob all his own relations of their just expectations? Can *his* mind be good – You, Clary Harlowe, for whose sake he offers so much, are the last person that should make this observation.[7a]

It is always Clarissa who is pleading for a wide and general orthodox moral view, with its roots in the Sermon on the Mount; it is always her family who restrict their moral vision to a

single moral department at a time, which may be obedience, or
chastity or prudence, but which never shows any sense of connection between the categories of morality.

Clarissa writes:

The principal thing objected to Mr Lovelace (and a very
inexcusable* one) is that he is immoral in his loves – is not the
other in his hatreds? Nay, as I may say, in his loves too . . .
if *the love of money* be *the root of all evil.*[8]

Clarissa is constantly being told by her friends that Solmes
has no vices. Characteristically and unanswerably, she widens
the issue, and removes the concept of vice from a respectable
worldly sense to a religious sense.

At first sight, Lovelace, the other horn of Clarissa's dilemma,
seems at the opposite pole from Solmes and the Harlowe relations. And so in some important ways he is. He is bold and
dashing, when they are sly and cautious. He is ruled by pride,
they by avarice. Yet we come more and more to see that it is the
similarities just as much as differences that are destructive for
Clarissa. Lovelace is not respectable, but he is, just as they are, conventional. He has received from the surrounding society certain
truisms about the roles of male and female. That the woman pays,
that a woman once conquered is conquered for ever, that any
woman will be thankful to marry her seducer, that men can retrieve
their sexual reputation at any time, but women never, that a promiscuous or inconstant man may be disliked and feared, but will not
be despised, while an unchaste woman will be rejected by society,
and especially by women, whether virtuous or wicked – all these
truisms he has found to be true by experience. The great blindness
of the worldly-wise is that they never realize that the occasional
person is really different. Generalizations about how people will
behave, sound enough in their way as practical guides, will fail
before the uniqueness of Thomas More or Dr Johnson. They will
fail with Clarissa too. This blindness is shared equally by the
Harlowe family and Lovelace at first; but Lovelace is less slow to
learn, less self-deceived, less hypocritical.

Even for him, though, learning is a long process. He is catastrophically wrong, yet he would have been right with any of
ninety-nine other women, when he writes of the sequel of his
proposed rape or seduction, 'Art thou not in my POWER?'

* Clarissa uses words precisely here. She means *inexcusable*, but not *unforgivable*.

and '*A wife at any time!* Marriage will be always in my power.'[9]

What does Lovelace really want? Obviously he wants many things, excitement, the admiration of his companions, a high idea of himself and his own irresistible appeal to women. But with Clarissa there is something else. He wants to make a final test of his way of life as a rake.

And now, if I have not found a virtue that cannot be corrupted, I will swear there is not one such in the whole sex. Is not then the whole sex concerned that this trial should be made? And who is it that knows this lady, that would not stake upon her head the honour of the whole?[10]

He is half-joking, of course, but truthful in a way when he says 'I am no sensual man'.[11] He knows that one woman is like another in body, and very much like in sexual response. If men were exclusively sensual in their sexual desires, they would have no difficulty in being faithful to one woman. The life of the imaginative rake is sensual only in its operation, not in its essence. He is searching for uniqueness of mind and soul. The long drawn-out irony of the book is this: he has enough perception to see that he has really discovered this uniqueness in Clarissa. But a mixture of habit, scepticism and fear of his friends' scorn of abandoned rakish principles, works upon him to prevent his admitting it. He must always make one more test. He must be sure; he must be even more sure, and (here lies the irrevocable miscalculation) he deludes himself that he has nothing to lose.

If, as he really hopes, all his efforts to subdue her fail, if the proofs of her uniqueness become so plain that he can deny them no more, *then* Clarissa, being after all of the weaker sex, will have to give in and marry him.

Lovelace fails to follow his own logic, and this is why I earlier called him conventional. The assumptions of the world about the sexual roles are too deeply engrained in him to enable him to see the necessary conclusion of his thought. If Clarissa is really unique among women, so that she cannot be bullied, deceived or cajoled – well then, perhaps she really *is* unique, and then it will be impossible to make amends. The idea that, even if he rapes her, marriage will still be in his power depends precisely upon that weak position of woman in the world. What he is looking for, and what he has actually found, is a woman who is independent of the world. What Lovelace is saying to himself is this: if she really is uniquely true to herself so as to be independent of the opinion of the world, then I shall be able to use the pressure of the world to save her and myself from the consequences of the trial. If I rape her in my effort to attain absolute certainty that she cannot possibly be seduced, she will have to marry me. But he does not see that if she were to bow to this necessity she would show that she was, like other women, dependent for her self-respect on public opinion. 'He who can resist an angry crowd has a footing outside time,' said Carlyle. Clarissa has that footing outside time.

If Lovelace's logic is faulty at this crucial point, Richardson's is inexorable. The novel is the longest of all forms of imaginative literature. And *Clarissa* is one of the longest novels in the language. The justification of length in a novel is that there, and nowhere else, we can follow an issue to the end. But we can only do this if it is focused clearly throughout, and if the logic is impeccable. Otherwise, if a mere impression of things is all that is wanted, a short story can do the work as well. By this test, every word of *Clarissa*'s length is justified, and *Tom Jones* might as well be a third or a quarter as long as it is.

Clarissa, like all the most memorable fictional characters, is unique; and the circumstances of her case are most unusual. She could not be treated as a model for young girls in the way of ordinary heroines. Her courage is so great as to be beyond even the imitation of ordinary people. Her one mistake, her elopement, receives a terrible retribution, usually reserved in novels, though not in life, for monstrous wickedness. She may be a saint, but she is not what parents want their daughters to be, a respectable and happy young woman.

With Fielding's Amelia, we are back in the ordinary world. She has her serious troubles, and she needs courage to bear them. But they are similar to the troubles of thousands of other women, rooted in the unsatisfactory character of her husband. They love each other, and he admires and stands in awe of her. But he is unfaithful, through impulse, imprudent and spendthrift.

The most striking thing about Amelia's situation is something that is wholly natural in life, but surprising in a novel. She is married when the story begins. Easily, deliberately, and most sensibly, Fielding challenges a familiar assumption of literature, that marriage is humdrum, that marital love, at its best, is gentle and affectionate, perhaps, but not passionate. This assumption is present alike in the customary ending of a novel (or a play) with wedding bells, and in the other kind of work which deals with the excitements of intrigue and adultery.

A visitor from Mars, after reading many novels, could be pardoned for supposing that love and sexual passion, and even sexual intercourse were facets of human life entirely separate from marriage. He might well think that marriage had to do only with stability, parenthood (apparently free from the preliminary of conception), property, on the one hand, and on the other with quarrelling, infidelity and passion seen only as an escape from the bond of marriage. Fielding, with his robust common sense, punctured all this. He centred attention on the sexual delights as well as on the comforts and conveniences of marriage. And in *Amelia*, he did so boldly, by eschewing an idyllically happy marriage, and showing one marred by the husband's weak character, and harassed with many external troubles. Great credit is due to a man who draws attention to the obvious when there is a conspiracy to neglect it. Put bluntly, the question Fielding asks his readers is this: If it is delightful to have a beautiful, loving, loyal and responsive woman in bed with you, why should it be any less delightful because she is wearing your ring? And he answers his own question by saying, 'Not less delightful but much more.' Unanswerably true, and yet almost the whole of Restoration comedy, and shoals of novels, French and English, had been written on the opposite assumption.

Amelia has often struck later readers as an early anticipation of the Victorian heroine, an impression heightened, no doubt, by Thackeray's repetition of her name for his very different character in *Vanity Fair*. But the differences are quite as notable as any similarities. She is, of course, like them, chaste, loyal and loving. But this leaves room for enormous variations of emphasis. She is, unlike her Victorian successors, very much a woman of the world. She is surrounded by distressing, sordid circumstances. They do not surprise her. She is vain of her beauty. When the reliable family friend, Dr Harrison, teases her by saying he could cure her of her admiration for his character by denying her beauty, she replies: 'Perhaps I might blame the goodness of your eyes.'[12] She has a keen sense of the ridiculous and a robust tolerance of female frailty. She reads Farquhar to cheer her spirits in anxiety about her husband's absence. She speaks jokingly and colloquially about serious things, as when she talks of being in a 'strange pickle'.[13] She is firm against the wealthy man who tries

to seduce her, but touched to a momentary inward response to the
'plain, honest, modest, involuntary, delicate, heroic passion' of a
poor man to an extent that might have displeased her husband
if he had known.[14] Mild and forgiving in general, she is capable
of being driven completely out of patience by her husband's
vagaries. On one occasion she goes so far as to reply to her child's
anxious enquiry about 'poor Papa':

> Mention him no more, your papa is – indeed he is a wicked
> man – he cares not for any of us.[15]

The irony of this last scene is that the wretched husband has
not deserted her in quest of pleasure, but in a desperate attempt to
prevent his earlier infidelity from becoming known to her. Booth's
fear of her is here entirely credible. There is something imperious
about her submissiveness, and something gritty in her mildness.
Here, though different in so many other ways, she resembles
Clarissa, and both are unlike their Victorian successors.

They are alike, too, in their unprotected stance as against life.
Their creators are too much in earnest to be chivalrous to them.
Clarissa spends a long time in a brothel, exposed to the meanest
insults from bawds and prostitutes. Fielding tells us with no
particular emphasis or surprise that when Amelia went to visit
her husband in his detention for debt, she was of course mistaken
for a whore by the bailiff's wife. They both live, in fact, as
Victorian heroines do not, in the public world, the man's world
with all its brutality, coarseness and misrepresentation.

All this means that, though they are both emphatically feminine,
the qualities in them which are held up to our admiration are
not, as in Victorian heroines they are, exclusively feminine. They
are human and heroic, before they are 'good women'. Above all,
they are both courageous.

It is not surprising then, that it is to the women writers of
the Victorian period, to Emily Brontë and George Eliot especially,
that we have to look for female characters who are not restricted
to a narrow interpretation of feminine roles. Clarissa and Amelia,
like Dorothea Brooke, share with men the whole range of moral
choices, a moral arena as wide as life.

CHAPTER III

Sterne

'But there's more than one person in the world. Remember that.'

> Beatrice in *The Trespasser* by D. H. Lawrence (1912)
> chap. XXV

Like Richardson and Fielding, Sterne has remained a figure of controversy. But there is a difference; while they bring the reader to re-examine his own principles, Sterne resists moral classification. His real view of the relation between the sexes, like his narrative technique, is easier to experience than to analyse. It is difficult to take him seriously, but somehow impossible not to. He has often been condemned – and by very intelligent and sympathetic readers – and yet the adverse verdicts have been delivered with hesitation or regret or simple puzzlement. Perhaps the only point on which nearly all the critics agree is that Sterne is *worrying*.

Scott, in his plain, sensible way, conveyed some distaste for his 'indecency and affectation' with an acceptance of the plea that it was mainly harmless. He said:

It is a sin against taste, if allowed to be harmless as to morals. A handful of mud is neither a firebrand nor a stone; but to fling it about argues coarseness of mind and want of common manners.[1]

Coleridge spoke of a 'certain oscillation in ... the mind between the remaining good and the encroaching evil of his nature' and concluded with a much more severe reproof: 'Sterne cannot be too severely censured for thus using the best dispositions of our nature as the panders and condiments for the basest.'[2]

Thackeray wrote with great severity of his philandering and accused him of cowardice and of 'a horrible baseness of blasphemy'[3] because he quoted the Lord's Prayer as a proof that he did not wish to be led into temptation.

Leslie Stephen wrote even more forcefully:

Sterne's sudden excursions into the nauseous are like the

brutal practical jokes of a dirty boy who should put filth into a scent bottle.[4]

The scent bottle is a very exact image here. He does not say that he desecrates something pure and natural, but something elegant and artificial. (And after all, dirt is not offensive in a field.) And Stephen conveys very well the sensation which many readers must have had of being tricked by Sterne, when he appeals to finer feelings. He pictures the 'sham Yorick . . . chuckling quietly at his successful imposition.'[5] He says too that Sterne is an almost solitary exception to the general rule that we enjoy humour only in so far as we love the humorist's character. The whole essay testifies to his sense that Sterne is deeply worrying.

Scott, who had edited Dryden, was not disturbed by coarseness, and Thackeray, though he lived in a more outwardly decorous age, rather liked it. All four, with varying degrees of penetration, are bothered by the unique combination of feelings aroused by the reading of Sterne. Scott, with his Augustan traditions, assumes that Sterne commits a breach of artistic decorum by mixing the modes of sentiment and earthiness. Coleridge sees a deeper moral danger if the animal passions are allowed to acquire a colouring of fine sentiments. Thackeray, the most severe and perhaps the least comprehending, assumes a basic insincerity in a man who can be so variable. All are pleading for a separation of the different parts of our nature, and of their literary equivalents. Man is angel and beast, satyr and sober citizen; but let us have different seasons, different clothes, different books for the fulfilment of all these roles. Let us stick to the point. Sterne never will.

Scott quotes an anecdote, in which Sterne excused himself to a lady who had been told that his books were improper by comparing himself to a three-year-old boy rolling on the carpet. 'He shows at times a good deal that is usually concealed, but it is all in perfect innocence.' How seriously can we take this defence?

In one sense, of course, it can be dismissed at once. Sterne is a very conscious artist, especially in *A Sentimental Journey*, the work most relevant to our subject. The pose of the child of nature is a sophisticated literary product. But that does not fully answer the question; we want to know whether simplicity and artlessness of feeling are a serious moral aim informing the art, or whether they are merely a hyper-sophisticated pose.

The most consistent moral imperative in Sterne's writings is generosity. His sermons are full of eloquent praise of generosity and pity. In the Calais episode of *A Sentimental Journey* the narrator is wondering whether to offer the lady a share of his chaise:

> Every dirty passion, and bad propensity in my nature, took the alarm, as I stated the proposition – It will oblige you to have a third horse, said AVARICE, which will put twenty livres out of your pocket – You know not who she is, said CAUTION – or what scrapes the affair may draw you into whisper'd COWARDICE –
>
> Depend upon it, Yorick! said DISCRETION, 'twill be said you went off with a mistress, and came by assignation to Calais for that purpose –
>
> You can never after, cried HYPOCRISY aloud, shew your face in the world – or rise, quoth MEANNESS, in the church – or be anything in it, said PRIDE, but a lousy prebendary.[6]

Here Sterne has managed to rally a collection of deadly sins, united with one or two dubious virtues, and presented them as tempters presently to be routed by the virtue of generosity. In another author we would take this at its face value. Here, we may wonder if it isn't all an elaborate joke, of which the point is that he does just what he wants to do, enjoy the lady's company, with an added intellectual enjoyment of demonstrating sophistically that by yielding to impulse he is resisting temptation.

But if we take that view, Sterne is soon ready with an answer:

> I had then but three sous left: so I gave one, simply *pour l'amour de Dieu*, which was the footing on which it was begg'd.
> – The poor woman had a dislocated hip; so it could not be well, upon any other motive.[7]

Sterne's aim here, as in *Tristram Shandy*, is to follow the unpredictable movements of the mind, to describe emotions almost too transitory to be detected. The following is a good example:

> ... the sun was setting, and reflected through them, [crimson curtains] so warm a tint into the fair *fille de chambre*'s face, I thought she blushed – the idea of it made me blush myself – we were quite alone; and that super-induced a second blush before the first could get off.

There is a sort of a pleasing half guilty blush, where the blood is more in fault than the man – 'tis sent impetuous from the heart, and virtue flies after it – not to call it back, but to make the sensation of it more delicious to the nerves . . .[8]

The word *virtue* is repeated several times in the passage that follows, which is headed *The Temptation*. What does it mean? Obviously the passage is based on traditional ideas of virtue, conscience and temptation.

But its tendency is different from that of all its models. There is not really a conflict of opposed principles. Virtue and temptation are not really disputing possession of the will. Rather there is a delicious mingling of moral sensations. The contrast of virtue and vice are *tonal* – they make an aesthetic chiaroscuro effect or even, more crudely, they could be compared to balancing ingredients in a recipe.

On the other hand, Sterne does not imply that virtue and vice are mere words, and their association with particular impulses merely conventional. The delicate sensibility of the passage quoted actually requires that virtue and vice should be real entities; if the choice were morally neutral, like which way to turn at a fork in the road, the whole structure of feeling and the whole literary effect would be lost. The passage, like much of Sterne's work, equally resists being read as supporting or as opposing traditional moral judgements.

A similar ambiguity persists in apparently satirical passages. At one point we are told that *Le Diable* is the mildest expletive in the French language, reserved for occasions

where small things only fall out contrary to your expectations – such as – the throwing once doublets – La Fleur's being kick'd off his horse, and so forth – cuckoldom, for the same reason, is always – *Le Diable*.[9]

This reads like a typical Augustan attack on false standards, a collocation of ideas obviously incongruous with the implication that the morally blind can't tell the difference, something like Pope's line:

Puffs, powders, patches, bibles, billets-doux.

But it is immediately followed by the famous sentimental chapter on the dead donkey, which must surely be taken, if anything must, as coming directly from the author without irony. Here, we are asked to discard our normal sense of the scale of events and of appropriate feelings about them, and feel more for a dead donkey than we would for a dead friend.

The key point in all this seems to be that Sterne values feeling for its own sake. The object of feeling, or its moral cause, are valued only because they produce the flow of feeling. At times, Sterne speaks of sensibility as a possession. 'O how I envied him his feelings', he says of the Marquis in the Sword chapter.[10]

Sterne is not a solipsist; events and people are necessary to excite feeling. But they are adjuncts, machinery for the production of feelings. And a dead donkey will be, for the moment, more important than a dead man, if it has the power to excite more feeling.

The epicure of feelings, like other epicures, craves two things, subtlety and variety. And in *A Sentimental Journey*, both are remarkable. Temptation, guilt, selfless generosity, poetic rapture, sudden carnal impulse, innuendo and elegant lubricity are all blended. The air of sparkling spontaneity is clearly the product of hard work, just as a well-rehearsed ballet-dancer gives the impression of inventing the steps as she goes along. If we turn to the letters we can see signs of the hard work involved in the single-minded philanderer's trade. Three years before his death he was writing:

> I myself must ever have some dulcinea in my head – it harmonises the soul – and in those cases I first endeavour to make the lady believe so, or rather I begin first to make myself believe that I am in love – but I carry on my affairs quite in the French way, sentimentally – 'L'amour (say they) n'est rien sans sentiment' – Now notwithstanding they make such a pother about the *word*, they have no precise idea annex'd to it . . .[11]

One of his most cunningly contrived effects, and a good example of what bewildered and upset so many of his critics is to be found in the chapter headed *The Rose*, about half-way through *A Sentimental Journey*. Though occasionally suggestive (what exactly, for instance, does the word 'connection' mean in the chapter next but one preceding?) the tone up to here has been mainly sentimental, tearful and generous. Here in a page and a half we have two surprises of quite different kinds. In the first it is hinted that an Abbé sitting in the *loge* at the Opera would either masturbate or put his hand up the skirt of the girl in front of him. Here the narrator acts innocent and has to have the secret whispered in his ear, at which he 'turns pale with astonishment.'[12]

In the second, which has the special emphasis given by its position at the end of volume I of the two-volume work, we have the following:

Of all women, Madame de Rambouliet is the most correct; and I never wish to see one of more virtues and purity of heart – In our return back, Madame de Rambouliet desired me to pull the cord – I asked her if she wanted anything – *Rien que pisser*, said Madame de Rambouliet.

Grieve not, gentle traveller, to let Madame de Rambouliet p—ss on— And, ye fair mystic nymphs! go each one *pluck your rose*, and scatter them in your path – for Madame de Rambouliet did no more – I handed Madame de Rambouliet out of the coach; and had I been the priest of the chaste Castalia, I could not have served at her fountain with a more respectful decorum.

Here the reader is liable to be bewildered. What exactly is the nature of the implied contrast? In the first episode, the Abbé is called an 'illiberal sarcasm' on the Church. If we take this at face value, the point could be 'think no evil'. The Abbé was innocent, and crudely maligned. The lady was innocent in having no false shame at a natural and necessary function. Spontaneity, truth, openness are always right, concealment, shame, suspicion and slander always wrong.

For a moment we may be inclined to reckon Sterne as an early forerunner of the Simple Life advocates of the nineteenth century, vegetarians, nudists, and men like Edward Carpenter and Havelock Ellis who combine a new sexual morality with a rejection of civilized artificialities.

But we soon see that this will not quite do. The point of the second passage is that it is not a scene of simple life, but a very elegant, contrived and artificial picture. Into this delicate blend of mythological refinements and French aristocratic elegance, the blunt phrase 'Rien que pisser' falls with a shock of surprise. The ridiculous ineffective dash in the next sentence, concealing only a single letter, is an invitation to consider the phrase indecent, and the refined feminine lips from which it comes add to the impression of paradox. Stephen's 'filth in a scent bottle' seems near the mark.

'Not so,' Sterne might reply, 'because the function is innocent, and all sense of indecency is the invention of the prurient reader. You are confusing the physically impure with the morally impure.' To this the reply might be that that is precisely what Sterne himself is doing by his Castalian image. His fountain is polluted in the mind, most offensively.

What is clear at least is this. The passage, like Sterne's whole strategy, marks a break from an ancient earthy tradition in English literature. There are lots of full chamber-pots in the novels of Fielding and Smollett, and usually they get upset over people's heads in tavern brawls. Why did readers who accepted this cheerfully so often jib at Sterne's version? Because, just as he refused to separate feelings, he refused to separate facts and styles of life. The lady's innocence and elegance are a titillating factor entirely absent from the crude passages of Fielding and Smollett.

When we see that, we realize that the supposed contrast between the Abbé (if he was justly suspected) and the lady is not the point. Instead, there is a similarity between the Abbé and the narrator. The grisettes were innocent, but the Abbé may not have been; the lady was innocent, but the narrator was inviting the reader to share in the pleasures of the *voyeur*. After all, urination is equally innocent whether performed by man or woman. But we only have to imagine for a moment a chapter ending with a man leaving the coach for the same purpose to see that the literary effect would be utterly changed. What we have then is a very artful illustration of the principle proposed in the passage about the *fille de chambre* quoted above. What Sterne is seeking is the 'pleasing half guilty blush' which can only come from a *mingling* of guilt and innocence. If, instead of watching an innocent act, unusual only in its display, he had been watching some abnormal sexual performance, the characteristic 'sentimental' tone of witty, *faux naïf* indecorum would be lost. The blurring of categories is the unmistakable mark of Sterne's art, and it is enough to explain the impatience with him always felt by blunt men of the world like Dr Johnson and Leslie Stephen, and the contemptuous condemnation of many serious-minded moralists.

To sum up is difficult. Tentatively, and without any great confidence in being right, I would say this. To blur moral categories is always bad; but to show as a psychological fact how inextricably linked in the mind are the diverse parts of our nature is a great service. For all his affectations, Sterne advances the understanding of human nature. Like Rousseau, he shows us what we have always known, but couldn't admit, that every man, saint or sinner, has to think each day about many things that are strangely incongruous with his sense of his own dignity. We are left with the paradox that the great trifler with his over-contrived literary effects is in another sense our first great realist.

CHAPTER IV

Jane Austen

... the perfect happiness of the union.

Last words of *Emma* by Jane Austen (1816)

II Rivalry and Jealousy

Most people, asked to name a literary treatment of jealousy, would mention *Othello* first; and perhaps there is more in this than a simple tribute to Shakespeare's greatness. *Othello* gives us jealousy on the grand scale as a tragic emotion with terrible consequences. As readers of literature this is how most of us may prefer to think of it. Yet a moment's reflection will convince us that this is a little odd, or at least one-sided. Jealousy is, often, domestic, familiar, part of the stuff of daily life, like bad temper, extravagance and avarice. Jane Austen is one of the few who insist that jealousy is not necessarily grand and terrible, nor a contemptible meanness affecting other people, but an emotion to which decent people are liable.

When Fanny Price realizes that Julia Bertram is jealous of her sister for being preferred by Crawford as partner in the play-acting, she ... 'could not think of her as under the agitation of *jealousy*, without great pity.'[1] I doubt if I am very unusual in having read the word 'pity' with surprise. Yet it is the right word. Jealousy is intensely painful; its onset may be so sudden that it would be hard to say how the sufferer could have guarded against it. And, in this case, Fanny has, or will have, good personal reasons too for pitying Julia. She is to suffer similarly over Edmund's preference for Mary Crawford; and, like Julia, though less obviously, she will deceive herself about the character of the emotion. Jealousy is one of the most humiliating of all accusations to bring against oneself.

That jealousy produces dissensions is obvious; and Jane Austen, of course, allows for it. But her cool eye does not see these as irreparable. Being an unpredictable, and often transient emotion, it is hardly strong enough to undermine the family structures of her world. Though Maria and Julia have never felt strongly their mutual bond as sisters, they are not made enemies for ever. When Crawford leaves, Julia is 'cool enough to dispense with revenge'. Jane Austen focuses our attention much more on jealousy as a threat to inner truth, to fair dealing with oneself, to self-knowledge and proper self-criticism. To be aware of being jealous is to add the pain of self-contempt to the pangs of jealousy. So we find that people in the novels, even good people, are possessed of a terrible inner resourcefulness in attributing their motives to any cause rather than jealousy. Maria Bertram has plenty of good reasons, convincing to herself, for resisting Edmund's plea to give up the part in the play that is the cause of dissension with Julia. Fanny even, a much more thoughtful person, is convinced that it is care for the horse's fatigue, not jealousy, that makes her resent Mary Crawford prolonging her riding exercise with Edmund.

But, of course, Fanny's oblivion to her own motives is partial and intermittent, not complete. Her struggle against the half-understood disease is heroic, just because it is so difficult to know what has to be struggled against. Thus Edmund, also self-deceived, decides to act after all, and gently chides Fanny:

'I thought *you* would have entered more into Miss Crawford's feelings.'

'No doubt she will be very glad. It must be a great relief to her,' said Fanny, trying for greater warmth of manner.[2]

This half-successful attempt to be generous is almost heroic; and it is possible only because now she has pierced through her inner concealments, and understands her own feeling and motive, as her following meditation shows:

Edmund so inconsistent. Was he not deceiving himself? Was he not wrong? Alas! it was all Miss Crawford's doing. She had seen her influence in every speech and was miserable.

Later, when Edmund has become seriously disturbed about Mary's defects of character, and uneasily consults Fanny, Fanny is strong enough to forego any temptation to encourage his doubts. She excuses Mary by attributing all to the effect of education.[3] We have seen enough of Fanny's inner struggles to know how difficult and costing those simple words are.

But Fanny's task here, though hard, is simple. To speak generously and to speak truth are here the same thing. At other times jealousy can be a threat to some of the major moral goals of the Austen world – to see things as they are, to judge justly of their relative importance, to comprehend the inner moral self, and apply self-criticism with rigour and justice. Jealousy, and indeed passion itself seem sometimes to sap the sense of reality, and destroy all common-sense judgement of probabilities. So it is with Maria Bertram, infatuated with Crawford, and spurred by rivalry with her sister:

> . . . for the very circumstance which had driven Julia away, was to her the sweetest support. Henry Crawford's retaining her hand at such a moment . . . was worth ages of doubt and anxiety. She hailed it as an earnest of the most serious determination.[4]

Jane Austen does not need to tell us that Crawford wouldn't have been able to remember, ten minutes later, whether he had held her hand or not.

Maria's jealousy is, of course, thoroughly selfish. But even more severe trials, and perhaps even more dangerous moral quagmires, await those, like Fanny, whose jealousy is mingled with serious intentions and generous feelings. We praise Jane Austen, and very justly, for her moral lucidity. We may exult in the bracing atmosphere after the mists of eighteenth-century sentiment, or as a restorative before descending into the fogs of false heroism and special pleading which envelop us in so many of her successors. But it is a mistake, nevertheless, to suppose that she allows for no inner mystery. As Fanny broods painfully upon Mary Crawford's unsuitability as a wife for Edmund, it is impossible for Fanny herself or the author or the reader to know for certain just where is the borderline between her serious moral judgement, her generous care for Edmund's welfare and her self-centred jealousy. Even though we know she is right, we can never know how right or wrong her *feeling* is.

In *Emma* jealousy, like most other things, is less sombre, because felt by characters of brisker and more active temper than Fanny. Yet it is a strong influence on Knightley and Jane Fairfax, and for a short time takes hold on Emma herself. Its power to distort judgement is no less; it is amusing, and ruthlessly true, to watch the most fair-minded of men allowing his opinion of Frank Churchill to vary with his sense of the damage Emma has suffered:

He had found her agitated and low – Frank Churchill was a

villain – He heard her declare that she had never loved him. Frank Churchill's character was not desperate – She was his own Emma, by hand and word, when they returned into the house; and if he could have thought of Frank Churchill then, he might have deemed him a very good sort of fellow.[5]

Comparing his feelings with those of the other person injured by the flirtation of Churchill and Emma, Jane Fairfax, we find that both Knightley and Jane blame the rival far more than the beloved. For Jane 'an airing in the Hartfield [i.e. Emma's] carriage would have been the rack, and arrow-root from the Hartfield store-room must have been poison.'[6] Knightley hardly indicates a touch of condemnation of Emma's share in the blame. Jealousy has a greater power even than passion itself to deflect the judgement. To apportion the blame correctly is a task beyond the scope of anyone in the book, even with the advantage of hindsight, and even with the burden of suspicion and fear removed by the happy outcome.

But the new function of jealousy in *Emma* is that it becomes a sign of what is hidden. Knightley, who had every reason to mis-understand his own feeling for Emma, and confine it in his conscious thought to the quasi-avuncular, is warned of the real nature of his love by the onset of acute hostility to Frank Churchill. And, hostility being so much less embarrassing to express than love, it becomes an early and delightful sign to Emma of his feeling for her. Emma, despite her own liking for Churchill, experiences a 'flutter of pleasure' to hear him described as an 'abominable scoundrel'. So, in *Persuasion*, does Anne take renewed courage and hope when she perceives Wentworth's jealousy of her cousin. In circumstances like these, jealousy almost loses its proper character as a vice, and becomes one of the subtle signals of a formal society, where expressions of affection are rare and deeply pondered, and universal civility, like a cushion softening a blow, inhibits the anxious detective work of the interested heart.

II The Mentor

It is a commonplace that the families and the society of Jane Austen's world exact high respect for seniority. Though we all know this, we may still, perhaps, experience surprise at some instances. The Crawfords' uncle the Admiral apparently, in the judgement of Edmund and Fanny, forfeits nothing of his claim to respect because his conduct and, worse, even his precepts are subversive of all they hold sacred. ('The Admiral hated marriage, and thought it never pardonable in a young man of independent fortune.') Parents, uncles and guardians are apt to counsel prudence, restraint and an eye for the main chance, and to treat the claims of love as secondary. So a peculiar interest attaches to the series of scenes where a heroine receives advice about marrying or not marrying.

We notice first that the plots are so arranged that the advice usually does not come from its most natural source, a parent. Either parents are dead, like the mothers of Emma and Anne Elliot, or they are remote and uninterested, like Fanny Price's, or unequal to the task, like Emma's father, in his doting pride in her, or like Anne Elliot's in his self-centred remoteness.

Sir Thomas Bertram is the most thoroughly tested of all the mentors, for we see him at work on strongly contrasted cases. He returns from the West Indies to find the preparations for his daughter's marriage to Rushworth well-advanced. In the circumstances, the partial stand that he makes against worldliness is creditable. Rushworth's position as a wealthy, landed neighbour, who will make no difficulty about settlements, his obviously being a young man apt to be guided, both by wife and father-in-law, and the nearness and publicity of the event are all strong deterrents to interference. No one knows better than Sir Thomas that a broken engagement is dangerous to a girl's reputation and prospects. The full extent of the danger is hidden from him because he has been absent when Maria has shown the most obvious signs of her feeling for Crawford. Rushworth has no vices of the kind that threaten domestic peace and prosperity. Sir Thomas's anxiety is free from all worldly motives:

> Her behaviour to Mr Rushworth was careless and cold. She could not, did not like him. Sir Thomas resolved to speak seriously to her. Advantageous as would be the alliance, and long standing and public as was the engagement, her happiness must not be sacrificed to it.[7]

Speaking with 'solemn kindness', Sir Thomas offers to arrange for her release from the engagement. Jane Austen gives only the faintest touch of blame to his ease in being satisfied. But there are ironies here to which she does not draw attention now because they are implicit in the whole book. Why does Maria speak so as to satisfy him, and with such an appearance of frankness? Why does she have only a moment's struggle before assuring him of her esteem for Rushworth, and her confidence in being happy with him? To make the reader's question here more insistent we have, within a page or two, a frightening account of her actual state of mind:

> being prepared for matrimony by an hatred of home, restraint, and tranquillity; by the misery of disappointed affection, and contempt of the man she was to marry.

Sir Thomas believes her entirely untruthful account of her feelings, a little because he wants to, but much more because he really knows her so little. He has been remote, and frightening, and is now a restraint on desired amusements. He has left her to be trained by her aunt, who has exaggerated the worldly element in his own standards, and obliterated everything serious and moral in them. He has mistaken her coldness to him, caused partly by his own inability to express the affection he really feels, for a general coldness and incapacity for passion. As with most decent people who are not saints, (especially those who find it hard to express feeling) the worldly side of his preoccupations is much more obvious to an onlooker than the equally genuine serious side. By his remoteness, by leaving things to Mrs Norris, he has in fact inculcated a degree of worldliness far beyond his own. With surprising logic, we find the expected roles reversed. The father is thinking of the claims of the heart; the daughter of the abiding satisfactions of property and income.

All this is, for us, secondary to Fanny's concerns; and it makes his interviews with Fanny to discuss Crawford's proposal all the more surprising.

At first sight it may seem that now the roles are simply reversed. The daughter was worldly, while the father thought of the heart. The niece now silently and inwardly asserts the absolute claims of love, while the uncle urges a mercenary marriage.

When we state the contrast baldly like this, we immediately see that there are many extenuating factors which render it less complete. Sir Thomas does not know that Fanny is in love, and she dare not tell him. There is a strong contrast in Sir Thomas's mind between the dullness of the man who has married his daughter and the lively attractiveness of the man who wants to marry his niece. He is a man of steady mind and settled habits who feels,

with some justice, that he knows the world. The possibility that
Fanny will not like Crawford enough to marry him does not
occur to him until the moment when it suddenly presents itself
as an undoubted fact. Like all men of his kind, he is at his worst
when coping with the unexpected. And he may well have an
unacknowledged bitterness lurking in his mind, when he finds
that his portionless niece, who seemed until recently an un-
attractive little mouse, has won the devotion of a man so superior
in talents and manners to the man to whom he has married his
daughter. As for Crawford's moral inferiority, which impresses
Fanny so strongly, he is largely ignorant of the evidence for it.
Fanny cannot speak of this without speaking ill of his daughter
too. Then he has always felt some conscientious scruples about
Fanny's future welfare, since it is contrary to his conception of
duty to his children to provide liberally for her in his will. Crawford's proposal, made by a man of means in the knowledge that
the lady was portionless, seems a heaven-sent solvent of this long-
standing anxiety. Fanny has always been extremely obedient and
deferential to him; it would require a man of quicker wits and
more flexible mind not to be honestly astonished that the pliable
child could be transformed into the stout-hearted, determined
woman.

All this must be held in mind as we read his solemn rebuke to
Fanny:

> . . . had Mr Crawford sought Julia's hand, I should have
> given it to him with superior and more heartfelt satisfaction
> than I gave Maria's to Mr Rushworth. And I should have been
> very much surprised had either of my daughters, on receiving
> a proposal of marriage at any time, which might carry with it
> only *half* the eligibility of *this*, immediately and peremptorily,
> and without paying my opinion or my regard the compliment
> of any consultation, put a decided negative on it. I should have
> been much surprised, and much hurt by such a proceeding.
> I should have thought it a gross violation of duty and respect.
> *You* are not to be judged by the same rule. You do not owe
> me the duty of a child. But, Fanny, if your heart can acquit you
> of *ingratitude* – [8]

Jane Austen's way of showing that he does not really mean all
this is at the same time a neat illustration of her general grasp
of the processes of the mind. Only a few pages later, Mrs Norris,
who knows nothing of Crawford's proposal yet, criticizes Fanny

for her spirit of 'secrecy, independence and nonsense'. Then:

As a general reflection on Fanny, Sir Thomas thought nothing could be more unjust, though he had been so lately expressing the same sentiments himself . . .

Fanny has gained on his affections; and no one but himself must now have the right to criticize her.

In the misunderstanding caused by Sir Thomas's ignorance of Crawford's character and Fanny's other love, Fanny is not quite fair to him in her thoughts.

She thinks:

He who had married a daughter to Mr Rushworth. Romantic delicacy was certainly not to be expected from him.

Yet Sir Thomas, if not romantic, has shown much more delicacy than his daughter expected or desired.

On the other hand, Fanny does justice to his good intentions:

Her uncle's kind expressions, however, and forbearing manner, were sensibly felt; and when she considered how much of the truth was unknown to him, she believed she had no right to wonder . . .

Sir Thomas is dominant at Mansfield Park. No decision of his can be gainsaid. Both Lady Bertram and Mrs Norris profess always to be carrying out his policies. Yet they so completely misunderstand him that the only rule of conduct Fanny ever hears from Lady Bertram is 'that it is every young woman's duty to accept such a very unexceptionable offer as this.'

The solemn word 'duty', here so horribly profaned by a woman who has no idea that she is not speaking according to the best moral traditions, brings us to the heart of the paradox. Respectability, as Lady Bertram understands it, and even partly as Sir Thomas understands it, consists in an attempt to attain an enduring synthesis between the claims of religion, of morality, and of worldly prudence. The Augustan tradition, to which, on the whole, Jane Austen remains faithful, tended to soften the contradictions inherent in this aim, even at times to seem wholly oblivious of them. It is a fair guess that few Anglican clergy of the eighteenth century liked to preach on those texts which speak of the need to lose life in order to gain it, or to pluck out the offending eye.

When Sir Thomas begins speaking to Fanny about Crawford's proposal, he dreams that he is living in a world of perfectly harmonious principles. Fanny's obedience, her engrained habit of respect, her wish to be married, her wish for worldly advancement, her sexual instincts – and, at the same time, Sir Thomas's prudence, his avuncular care and kindness, his honest satisfaction in the original generosity that brought her to Mansfield – all seem in harmony. Once again we shall see how, in true Augustan style, the requirements of the soul, of the heart, of the conscience, and of worldly ambition are all reconcilable in a perfect happy ending. There is piquancy and paradox in the thought that it is left to Fanny, of all people, to burst the bubble. Fanny, the most timid and conventional of all Jane Austen's heroines, whom so many inattentive readers have denounced as prig and prude, is a very reluctant destroyer of family harmonies. But she is compelled by a force rising from the depths of her being, too strong for habit and fear to counter, which tells her 'how wretched, and how unpardonable, how hopeless and how wicked it was, to marry without affection.'

So much for Lady Bertram's idea of duty. And though *Mansfield Park* has a happy ending, it is important, I think, to feel this moment, as Fanny feels it at the time, with no hope of ever winning Edmund, with nothing to look forward to but a dull and disagreeable life among relatives who will always resent her failure to remove from them, in so easy and creditable a manner, the burden of her support. Like Mr Elton, Jane Austen knew the value of a good income as well as anybody, and she allows Fanny, among the disorders of Portsmouth, to regret the stately ways of Mansfield, which the poor are unable to imitate. More important, she refuses to question the prevailing high view of the degree of respect due to parents and guardians. But she is far too clear-sighted to imagine that the comfortable reconciliation of conflicting principles, which it is the interest of the respectable in every age to put faith in, will always be feasible. The time comes when principles conflict, and each person has to decide which is higher and stronger. Fanny decides for herself, for the author, and for us, and, in doing so, issues a silent but stinging rebuke to those who believe themselves equally zealous in the service of God and Mammon.

Her vindication by events duly follows (a little too neatly perhaps) and Sir Thomas will in due time be a wiser man. But we are not permitted to doubt that she would have been just as right if Crawford had left Mrs Rushworth alone, and Edmund had married someone else.

In *Emma*, the mentor appears in an entirely new light. The natural inheritors of the role, parents and guardians, have abdicated. Emma's father thinks her perfect, and Harriet's is unknown. Instead, the mentor is the person with will and influence strong enough to seize the role. And, a new and surprising touch, Emma herself has a double role; she is both mistress and pupil. Jane Austen achieves much of her subtle effect by silently contrasting her methods with Knightley's. Knightley, as adviser to Robert Martin, is judicious in combining realism about facts (incomes and prospects) with respect for autonomy of feelings. Thus, there is a clear contrast between his own thoughts about Harriet as a bride for Robert Martin and his words to Martin himself:

I felt . . . that as to a rational companion or useful helpmate, he could not do worse. But I could not reason so to a man in love, and was willing to trust to there being no harm in her, to her having that sort of disposition, which, in good hands, like his, might be easily led aright and turn out very well.[9]

Knightley would not lie; but he is prepared to select from his various thoughts about Harriet those acceptable to Martin. This is because he instinctively knows the proper limits of the mentor's role. He knows that to pre-empt another's proper sphere of decision is to court failure. Real advice is given for another to use, in his own way.

What Knightley really does with Martin, Emma only pretends to do with Harriet when she receives the proposal. Her words about not wishing to influence Harriet raise a smile in every reader. But it is important to notice that Emma is not really deceived about Harriet's imaginary superiority to Robert Martin:

'A woman is not to marry a man merely because she is asked, or because he is attached to her, and can write a tolerable letter.'

'Oh! no; and it is but a short letter too.'

Emma felt the bad taste of her friend . . .[10]

Emma knows very well that this inane comment is not an aberration, but characteristic of Harriet's mental processes. And she is continually giving indications that she knows how fond Harriet really is of Martin, and how much stiffening from her own stronger will is needed to prevent yielding. But she constantly employs all her cleverness and all her wilfulness to avoid facing the simple question, if Harriet is really not too good for him, and if she really likes him, why shouldn't they marry? Her ingenious arguments about Harriet's supposed class superiority have an air of desperate clutching at reasons she half knows are not there.

Emma does all this, of course, because she cares more for the role of mentor than she does for Harriet; she even cares more about it than she does about being right. Here the contrast with Knightley is plain and direct; he wants to guide her because he cares for her (how much he does not yet know); she cares for Harriet because she wants to guide her. And here, another and more disturbing parallel appears. We are reminded of Mrs Elton's patronage of Jane. How strange, and yet convincing it is that Emma should be found at this point so much more like Mrs Elton whom she detests than Mr Knightley whom she reveres. Startling, too, for the reader who detests Mrs Elton as much as Emma does, and, probably, despite the author's doubts, likes Emma very much.

There is a general point here about Jane Austen's nature and art. Most novelists, like most people in general, intertwine their moral judgements and their sympathies, so that it is hard to distinguish them. To separate them is a painful and testing process that many novelists simply funk. Jane Austen shows her own likes and dislikes as clearly as others, and is more successful than most in influencing us to share them. But she is ruthless in separating feeling and judgement.

The paradox of the contrast between Knightley's conduct as mentor and Emma's is that Knightley really suffers the pull of personal motives much more fiercely than Emma does. Emma's affection for Harriet is a weak thing in comparison with Knightley's for Emma. As we have seen, Knightley is not immune from the prejudice resulting from these banked fires of love. But that merely shows how insidious are the forces that deflect right judgement and honest dealing. There is a frightening *a fortiori* implied. If Knightley cannot be perfectly just, who can?

III *Rational Passion*

Knightley and Emma, though in very different degrees, are inhibited from exercising their rational judgement both of morality and of facts by egoism. And egoism is presented as a distorting force thrusting up from below. The subject is unaware of it.

Emma could give a dozen good reasons why Harriet should not marry; but a long schooling from experience will be necessary before she catches a glimpse of the real reason, her wish to be in control.

We have arrived now at the most difficult, paradoxical and most easily misunderstood aspect of Jane Austen's moral psychology. It might seem that she is advocating complete detachment from all personal considerations, and complete suppression of all impulses, intuitions and personal likes and dislikes in the interests of reason and objectivity.

As soon as we put it like this, we see that it is not so. There is a contrary movement, which not only treats love as the highest earthly value, but suggests that the deepest love may be a burrowing unconscious force, influencing the depths of the heart before the thinking mind is aware of it. Knightley and Emma really love each other from the first. But what a long, painful and dangerous process is the emergence of this deep reality into consciousness. All the while they are disagreeing and almost quarrelling over Harriet, Martin and Elton, little signs are appearing to us, but not to them, of a concurrence both of their judgement and their feelings.

Emma thinks that there is a sort of parade in Elton's speeches which 'was very apt to incline her to laugh'.[11] A little later, Knightley is thinking:

I never in my life saw a man more intent on being agreeable than Mr Elton. It is downright labour to him where ladies are concerned.[12]

And eventually Knightley is driven to agree that Emma has chosen better for Elton, in designing him for Harriet, than Elton himself has in the marriage he has made.

As R. W. Chapman wisely said, in a note on a passage in chapter XXX, 'Mr Knightley comes unbidden, and sometimes unrecognized into Emma's thoughts.' See, for example, her criticism of Mr Weston's excessive openheartedness . . . and of Frank's dissimulation.*

But the unconscious is very cunning, and is capable of offering false bait.

An obvious case is the plausible reason it offers Emma,

* Chapman supports this, most convincingly, with quotations from chapters XXXVIII and XLVI.

in her solicitude for her nephew's prospects as Knightley's heir,
for her really personal and jealous opposition to his marrying.
But a subtler, and yet more instructive case is the following inner
tirade of Emma against Mrs Elton:

'Insufferable woman!' was her immediate exclamation.
'Worse than I had supposed. Absolutely insufferable! Knightley!
– I could not have believed it. Knightley! – and discover that
he is a gentleman! . . . I never met with her equal. Much beyond
my hopes. Harriet is disgraced by any comparison. Oh! what
would Frank Churchill say to her, if he were here? How angry
and how diverted he would be! Ah! there I am – thinking of
him directly. Always the first person to be thought of! How
I catch myself out! Frank Churchill comes as regularly into
my mind! – '13

Emma has talked herself into this imaginary obsession with
Frank Churchill, aided by the friendly expectations of the
Westons. Lest Emma should suspect why a slight (really not a
serious one) to Knightley drives her into such excitement, her
unconscious seems here to have the power to send out false
signals. And they bear about them little signs of their falsity.
Would Frank Churchill be angry? He seems never to be angry.
And why should he have such extreme solicitude for Knightley
who takes such a low view of him?

Emma, of course, is too easily satisfied to pay attention to
these little signs. But we see them, and they can help us to resolve
the contradiction, which can be stated thus: if we have the power
to deceive ourselves both about our egoism and about our best
and deepest affections, how is it possible to judge?

Though she might have been surprised to be told so, Jane
Austen's answer to this dilemma, implied in the masterly crafts-
manship of *Emma*, is reminiscent of the procedures of the Catholic
Church in discriminating between true and false inspirations
and ecstasies. Since they cannot be studied and judged directly,
they must be judged by their effect on the ordinary daily life of
the subject. And the criteria are the same as in judging those who
do not profess to have inspirations and ecstasies. So, in Jane
Austen, it is impossible at the time to tell the difference between
the best and the worst impulses from below. The difference will
appear gradually, when it is seen whether the influence led to
true or false judgements of character, to true or false understanding of events. The subjective is shown as a formidable

power, which cannot be ignored, but the canons of judgement
are general and impersonal.

Contrasted with this gradual emergence of passion, which is
also a self-realization, we have the susceptible Harriet. ('It really
was too much to hope even of Harriet, that she could be in love
with more than *three* men in one year' Emma thinks, when
wondering how to cure her infatuation with Knightley.) Just as,
when Fanny confronts Sir Thomas, Jane Austen ruthlessly
separates moral duty from respectability and obedience, so here
another powerful and influential cliché of thought is under
attack. It is a cliché often implied by Jane Austen's immediate
predecessors in the novel, and revived by many in the twentieth
century. To summarize complexities briefly, one might say this
cliché depicts passion and duty as eternal opposites.*[14] Passionate
people are supposed to ignore duty, and dutiful ones are supposed
to lack passion. This is a very agreeable doctrine. It suggests to
the respectable that they have little passion, and it suggests to the
wayward that their moral deviations are due to an excess of passion,
that is to an intenser life. Jane Austen shows that often, and
perhaps typically, the reverse is true. Strong characters in her books
generally have strong feelings. Weak characters have weak feelings.
Who can doubt that Knightley can *love* more than Churchill or
Emma than Harriet? Harriet's susceptibility is due rather to weakness of feeling than to strength. Because she does not feel very
strongly she can be *talked* into and out of a series of temporary
deathless passions.

Thus it is that there are two quite different kinds of constancy
in Jane Austen's novels. There is the kind represented by Lady
Bertram, which comes from comfort and habit and an even
pulse; and there is the kind where a strong character is passionately committed, as are Knightley, Wentworth and Anne Elliot.

In these cases, there is no conflict between passion and duty,
because the whole personality is integrated. Conscience and
passion are allies; moral admiration for the beloved is part of
the food of love. But love does not therefore become, as it is
so easy to assume, cool and moderate. It is a force all the more

* As Marilyn Butler says: 'In the three comparable novels by Rousseau, Goethe, and
Mackenzie, the marriage is seen as somewhat cold and formal compared with the
generous, irresistible passion of the unmarried lovers. The latter are innocent
because their feelings are involuntary. They are even superior to more conventional
people, because they act according to their "true", i.e. intuitive, natures rather than
in obedience to forms imposed from without.'

powerful for not having to conflict with the claims of conscience, reason and intellect. In contrast, we have not only the weak victims of a shallow and transient susceptibility, but also the vain, silly people, like Sir Walter Elliot, who are too engrossed in self to know passion at all.

Jane Austen's finest, most touching and final portrait of rational passion is in the person of Anne Elliot. It has always been felt by Jane Austen's admirers that a new, more tender note is heard here than in the stories of previous heroines. The autumnal scenes are justly famous, and they partake just a little of the pathetic fallacy, suggesting the yearnings of an apparently hopeless love. Here, of course, Anne's love is clearly known to herself from the first; and the reader follows and shares her inner sensations. He is not required to repeat the detective work demanded by close attention to Emma's self-deceptions. Even so, Anne does not completely understand her own feelings when Wentworth's long absence is ended. She thinks at first that she wishes to avoid meeting him, and in chapter XI she welcomes a change of domicile which, she thinks, will reduce the number of their meetings. Yet, even then, it may be significant that she mentally adopts the word 'stationed' of her stay at Uppercross – a natural word to apply to a sailor, but an odd one to apply to a young lady staying with friends or relations. She does not need to be told that she loves Wentworth, but she would be startled to have pointed out this little indication that she is identifying with him, when her conscious conviction is still that he has no interest in her.

Anne's more meditative, intensely passionate nature does not prevent her from sharing her creator's robust realism. She splendidly triumphs over the combined wound to love and vanity offered by the discovery that Wentworth thinks her beauty lost.

> 'So altered that he should not have known her again!' These were words which could not but dwell with her. Yet she soon began to rejoice that she had heard them. They were of sobering tendency; they allayed agitation; they composed, and consequently must make her happier.[15]

If there is another passage in an English novel where a girl rejoices at having her looks slighted by the man she loves, I do not recall it. To combine this with a character capable of the most intense, constant, and apparently hopeless attachment to a great passion is an emblem of the author's impatience with the stock opposition between passion and good sense. Anne, without strain on our credulity, remaining, just as much as Emma, a person we feel we have known intimately all our lives, effortlessly combines an extreme of passion with an extreme of detached good sense.

In her sensibility to nature and the *genius loci*, Anne is allowed to transpose into something acceptable, and not in the least absurd, the romantic vapourings of Marianne Dashwood about leaving home. We smile indulgently and remember that the speaker is seventeen when Marianne apostrophizes Norland:

> Oh! happy house, could you know what I suffer in now viewing you from this spot, from whence perhaps I may view you no more! – And you, ye well-known trees! – but you will continue the same. No leaf will decay because we are removed, nor any branch become motionless although we can observe you no longer . . .[16]

Anne's thoughts are more restrained and less histrionic, as we should expect, but they have a touch of sentiment that Emma would not have shown:

> though desirous to be gone, she could not quit the mansion-house or look an adieu to the cottage, with its black, dripping, and comfortless veranda, or even notice through the misty glasses the last humble tenements of the village without a saddened heart. Scenes had passed in Uppercross, which made it precious. It stood the record of many sensations of pain, once severe, but now softened; and of some instances of relenting feeling, some breathings of friendship and reconciliation, which could never be looked for again and which could never cease to be dear. She left it all behind her; all but the recollection that such things had been.[17]

Prose rhythm is notoriously difficult to analyse. But there is, it seems to me, a 'dying fall' in the last sentence, particularly appropriate to Anne Elliot, and inappropriate to our sense of the other heroines.

The reader's sense of the intensity, the purity and the constancy of her feeling for Wentworth is heightened by telling contrasts. Her father and her elder sister belong to the vast crowd of the worldly, unfeeling and insensitive. But it is a typical Austenian touch that it is the worldly, conventional father whose extravagance leads him into debt, while it is the 'romantic' Anne who

level-headedly points out that he who contracts debts must pay
them. Her other sister has accepted a man Anne refused, without
perhaps caring more for him than Anne herself did; and her
affection for her husband is not only self-centred; it is tempered
by rivalry, so that she regards it as a point of honour that her
own sister should be 'better' married than his.

Her cousin Mr Elliot is little more than a sketch, and it may
be thought that the account of his villainy lacks the naturalness
we expect and nearly always get from Jane Austen. But from
Anne's point of view, the salient point is that he is the heir to
her father's honours. When he hints at marriage, Anne has before
her not only the prospect of an advantageous marriage to a
man of ability and address, but also attractions more charming
to the tender side of her character. She would restore the family
to its traditional place, and repay her sister's neglect with benefits.
She would become the lawful successor of her dead mother as
mistress of Kellynch – the mother whom alone among her near
relatives she has had cause to love.

It is a delightful picture, and it would have been easy, in a
novel of different tendency, to make Mr Elliot's attractive façade
a genuine expression of his nature, and so to allow these dreams
to come to happy fruition. Instead, they are harshly dispelled,
by Mr Elliot's unworthiness, and by Wentworth's crushing and
memorable words; 'to see your cousin close by you, conversing
and smiling, and feel all the horrible eligibilities and proprieties
of the match.' On the other side, there is the amusing sketch of
Benwick. When first introduced, he seems set to be a touching
figure of 'patience on a monument'. A sensitive man, steeped in
romantic poetry, but also a brave fighter, who is mourning the
untimely death of the great love of his life – surely, we feel,
there can be no irony here. But there is; he is very soon consoled.
What does this mean?

It certainly does not mean, as perhaps it might in some other
novels of the time, that reading romantic poetry saps the founda-
tions of character. We find that Anne reads it too, and matches
his enthusiasm in argument about it. But it does seem to mean that
a dreamy indulgence in vicarious feeling is no certain guarantee
of constancy. It may contain a wry comment on the cynical
selfishness, not of Benwick himself, but of some of the passionate
poetic lovers he liked to read.

By contrast Anne's passionate love is disciplined in many

different ways. It is disciplined by hardship and waiting, and apparent hopelessness, by the unkindness of home, by the seeming uselessness and aimlessness of genteel spinster lives, and by the requirements of courtesy.

Jane Austen's treatment of this last point is interesting. Several times Anne is prevented by the ordinary customs of politeness from following her inclination to be with Wentworth. But she is not above a little scheming that might well be thought forward:

> In re-settling themselves, there were now many changes, the result of which was favourable to her. Colonel Wallis declined sitting down again, and Mr Elliot was invited by Elizabeth and Miss Carteret, in a manner not to be refused, to sit between them; and by some other removals, and a little scheming of her own, Anne was enabled to place herself much nearer the end of the bench than she had been before, much more within the reach of a passer-by.[18]

Similar accounts in other novels (especially those written by women) generally imply a condemnation of silly flirts. Once again Jane Austen's ruthless realism will not conceal the petty corollaries of grand passion. Her triumph in *Persuasion* is that, in a way that convinces us completely, she dissolves the supposed opposition between the grandly passionate and the mundane, and between the grandly passionate and the exigencies of duty. Anne Elliot is the great lover, the sensitive, romantic spirit, the respecter of society's conventions, the reckless despiser of her own material interests and the deeply dutiful, principled soul all at once.

CHAPTER V

The Realists

... 'all the horrible eligibilities and proprieties of the match!'
Wentworth commenting on the possibility of Anne's
marriage to her father's heir in *Persuasion* by Jane Austen
(1818) chap. XXIII

'I'll ask her to marry me, once more. I will. No one shall
prevent me.'
'What, a woman who spells affection with one f? Nonsense,
sir.'
    Arthur Pendennis and his uncle, the Major, in *Pendennis* by
W. M. Thackeray (1848–50) chap. XIII

'The difference between Miss Brontë and me is that she puts all
her naughtiness into her books, and I put all my goodness ...
my books are so far better than I am that I often feel ashamed
of having written them and as if I were a hypocrite.'
    Mrs Gaskell in letter to Lady Kay Shuttleworth of 7 April
1853.

As to being in love, frankly, I don't believe in it. I believe
that stimulant drinks will intoxicate, and rain drench and fire
singe; but not in any way that one person will fascinate another.'
    Lady Midhurst, letter to Lady Cheyne (No. 9) in *Love's
Cross-Currents* by A. C. Swinburne. Anonymously published 1877.

It is sweet to protect her in the intervals of business, sweet to
pay her honour when she has cooked our dinner well. But
alas! the creature grows degenerate. In her heart there are
springing up strange desires.
    E. M. Forster, *A Room with a View* (1908), chap. IV

THACKERAY

Thackeray's strategy in *Vanity Fair* depends directly on the stock ideas of sexual types that he assumed his readers to have. Amelia Sedley is the good, pure girl, faithful unto death. Becky Sharp is the more or less respectable demi-mondaine of the French novel or of the English tourist's simple vision of Paris. George Osborne is the ordinary, vain youth torn between two views of himself, as the faithful husband and as the irresistible Don Juan, and, because the two roles are incompatible, feeble and ineffective in both. Rawdon Crawley is the sensual man of the world, who, in his progression from one mistress to another, finally meets a woman who is too strong for him, and knuckles under to her completely. Dobbin is the patient, faithful adorer who wins the princess in the end by his very persistence.

The difficulty in reading and judging Thackeray, and the uneasiness which he characteristically produces, are due to this: there is a gap between these simple models and the complex characters which the story gradually reveals. This gap is variable, obscure, hard to measure. Sometimes, for many chapters, one of them will behave as if absolutely true to type. And yet, a reader who took them all as typical Theophrastian portraits would miss most of what Thackeray has to offer.

This disturbing gap between the accepted type and Thackeray's individuals can be seen even in a bare summary of the plot. George Osborne, against his father's stern command, marries his childhood sweetheart Amelia Sedley. He is a little reluctant, and has to be talked into it by his friend, and Amelia's devoted admirer, Dobbin. After a brief marriage, during which he begins an intrigue with Becky Sharp, now married to Rawdon Crawley, he is killed at Waterloo. Both Dobbin and Amelia knew or suspected the intrigue. Amelia bears a posthumous son, and settles down to widowhood, living only for her spoilt and greedy son and for the memory of her weak and inconstant husband. She remembers him, not as she knows he was, but as irreproachable and adoring. Dobbin goes abroad with the army and maintains year after year his love for Amelia. Finally, middle-aged and disillusioned, he determines to break free, and tells Amelia he has had enough. Whereupon, distressed by his sudden change to contemptuous coolness, and fortified by Becky's evidence about her dead husband's infidelity, she decides to marry him. He agrees wearily, and she comes to realize she has forfeited his love before gaining him as a husband.

Meanwhile, Rawdon, a younger son of a landed family, with little money and expensive tastes, sets up house in London on 'nothing a year', making money by gambling, with his wife's charms as an attraction for the gambling victims. Released unexpectedly after an arrest for debt, he comes home to find Becky with Lord Steyne, hurls his present of a diamond ornament at his head, bitterly condemns his wife, and separates from her for ever.

At every stage, each character behaves according to the model up to a point and then strangely diverges from it. Dobbin is true to his self-sacrificing type in hastening the marriage of the woman he loves to another man, but his motive is not what the reader has learnt to expect of such men.

Why had not George's marriage been delayed? What call was there to press it on so eagerly? . . . It was his counsel that had brought about this marriage, and all that was to ensue from it. And why was it? Because he loved her so much that he could not bear to see her unhappy: or because his own sufferings of suspense were so unendurable that he was glad to crush them at once – as we hasten a funeral after a death . . .[1]

In fact, a good man is by no means the same thing as a saint. He is concerned with doing his duty, his honesty is beyond question, but is concerned also with his own welfare. Thackeray may be held to have performed here a greater service than he knew. In an age that tended to muddle various concepts of goodness, the saint, the gentleman, the good citizen, he pointed sternly to the difference. And this is the more striking because there can be no doubt of his real admiration and liking for Dobbin. His ambivalence about Amelia is very much stronger.

The novels which Thackeray's readers knew, both contemporary and earlier ones, are full of secrets catastrophically revealed in the final chapters; the early novels of Dickens, the rivals of which he was most particularly aware, especially so. Thackeray takes the stock situation, of a supposedly faithful husband, suddenly proved after long years to have been unfaithful, and characteristically alters it. The 'good' woman owes her release from a fruitless, pining widowhood to the 'bad' woman, when

Becky, with a sort of exasperated generosity, comes along with incontrovertible proof of George's infidelity. But the difference from the usual revelation of the past is considerable. It is necessary to Amelia's self-deception to have proof of what she really knew all along. She has for years resolutely expelled from her memory the time when in jealousy of George and Becky she 'was making a fool of herself in an absurd hysterical manner, and retired to her own room to whimper in private.'[2] She needs Becky's revelation for two reasons: if she recalled her own knowledge of her husband's infidelity she would be admitting that the intervening years had been spent in a prolonged, culpable, self-delusion instead of honest mistake. But more urgent than this need is the need to find a reason for submitting at long last to Dobbin's importunity. At all costs her self-respect requires that she hide from herself the real reason, that she has suddenly realized that if she does not submit now, he will leave her for ever. The marriage then depends on each calling the other's bluff. Amelia has always despised Dobbin because he adored her, and, feeling herself to be a poor creature, she can only admire someone who also feels her to be a poor creature. George Osborne fulfilled this requirement, and now at last, when the worm turns, Dobbin fulfils it too. Amelia calls Dobbin's bluff by requiring him to turn a painful but morally luxurious 'selfless devotion' into the actual care of a husband. The transition is not easy; and it is not clear that a moderate degree of domestic bliss is preferable to the agreeable comforts of a romantic bachelor officer in an India where even private soldiers had personal servants. Dobbin calls Amelia's bluff by threatening to leave her for good, and thus bringing home to her how necessary he is to her.

Amelia is pictured always as the timid creature who is inclined to be a bully when she has the chance. Her insensibility to Dobbin's feelings, as when she shows him one of his own presents to her, and calls it George's gift, contrasts disagreeably with her exaggerated admiration for her son's mediocre qualities, and her tremulous schemes to please him. She has the monomaniac's conviction that only the matter that most concerns herself can interest others. At times this verges on the ludicrous, as when she cuts short Dobbin's heartfelt farewell before going away for years with 'I'll write to you about Georgy.'[3] So did Lear, confronted with Poor Tom, ask if his daughters had brought him to this.

Yet all through the time when Dobbin is thus neglected and despised, he is really the stronger of the two. He is a man and is free, he could break away and marry, he could stay a bachelor and forget her; he is somebody in the world, and she is nobody. His life has variety and interest, hers is a dreary round of sub-servience to a son who will think less and less of her as he grows older. Moreover, and this is the strongest point of all, he has it in his power to destroy her idol at a blow; he could let her know that her hero-husband had been a low intriguer whose fidelity hardly outlasted the honeymoon.

In all this, Thackeray seems characteristically ambiguous. Are we to think Dobbin's sense of honour in keeping the secret over-strained? Are we to think of him as a true martyr, sacri-ficing his dearest hopes to principle? Or, remembering the anti-climax of the marriage when it eventually occurs, are we to credit him with a subconscious understanding that his wish to marry Amelia was much less keen than he supposed? Are we to think that he luxuriates in the dignified bleakness of his solitary exist-ence? Perhaps more than any other of our leading novelists Thackeray prefers to leave his readers puzzling over such questions. There seem to be several different reasons for this. First, and most obvious, is his peculiar stance as storyteller, of an onlooker remembering. He says in effect, 'If this had all really happened, and you had seen it, you would have had to guess about motives. I offer you the same sort of evidence that you might really get, with my extra talents as an observer thrown in. Take it and be thankful.' And this, of course, is no mere *trompe l'œil* effect. Like all art of more than passing interest Thackeray's is not self-contained, but reflects back on life. The consequence of reading *Vanity Fair* as the author hoped it would be read is to raise questions and doubts about the real people we thought we understood. Here his subtle version of type-casting* is especially effective. For, we may think, if I had known these people I might have noticed only the type and not the subtle variation from it.

But that is not all. Thackeray's ambiguity is more than an effective technical device. Its source was deep within him. There was something negative in the whole cast of his intelligence. He was not only sceptical of other people's explanations, he was

* see first paragraph of this chapter

sceptical of his own. He was happier with a suggestion than with a statement, and often happier with a doubt than with a suggestion. His adverse criticism, even blandly insinuated, always seems more telling than his praise, even loudly trumpeted. (We shall see the clearest example when we come to *Esmond*).

All this may help us to focus better the famous contrast between Amelia and Becky Sharp, which has always been felt to be central to the book's meaning. Seeing what serious doubts the author has raised about Amelia, in some ways so true to the type most admired by the men of the 1840s, we might expect that he intended to speak up on behalf of Becky, the kind of woman everyone agreed to despise. To some slight extent, perhaps, he does so. He shows her courage, spirit and resource; and in one great ironical scene, when she reveals her husband's infidelity to Amelia, he reverses the roles of the 'good' and 'bad' woman as other novelists presented them.* He makes the good woman desperately need the bad woman's help. But this irony of plot, this defeat of normal expectations, hardly extends to a revaluation of Becky's character. Her kindness here is contemptuous; and due, in part, to the ageing charmer's wish to boast of her early conquests.† And he denies Becky some common female virtues, such as maternal love, which she might well have been expected to possess. Most striking and characteristic of all is his account of the two women after the revelation which is of so much service to Amelia. Amelia, who has up to now been trying to help Becky, cuts her dead, and Dobbin seizes his daughter in his arms as if fearing contamination from Becky, or even kidnapping. A rather absurd attempt is made to suggest that she may be a murderer. The more he hints doubts about Amelia's goodness, the more determined Thackeray seems to be to insist on the reality of Becky's badness. But his long, leisurely tale, covering in all some twenty years, has one great advantage. It enables him to show long-delayed consequences. And his narrative presents one character after another with the question, 'Did you really mean it?' And for all of them it proves an uncomfortable question. Amelia is forced to ask herself, did she really mean it when she vowed her whole life to the solemn pieties of widowhood? When Dobbin threatens to leave for good, she finds she didn't. Dobbin

* See, for instance, *Oliver Twist* chap. XL, the meeting of Rose and Nancy.
† Thackeray was keenly aware of this need, and exploits it much more crudely in the case of the Dowager Lady Castlewood in *Esmond*.

has to ask himself, did he mean it when he constantly vowed that marriage with Amelia would be the greatest of all delights? He finds he didn't, but characteristically soldiers on just as if he had. Rawdon Crawley, released from prison, and surprising Becky with Lord Steyne, is forced to see the ugly consequences of his own system of using her charms to attract men from whom he could win money. Becky, surprised with a lover who (she knows very well) is capable of no feeling stronger than a temporary lust, is forced to ask whether she really meant to prefer him to a husband who was devoted to her in his crude way. In each case, the fundamental point is the same: our choices and preferences are not what (influenced by the conventions of society) we say they are. They are often not even what we inwardly tell ourselves they are. Convention influences our inner life as well as our public professions.

To set off these teasing questions, and subtle, but sometimes intangible, criticisms of accepted norms of conduct, Thackeray gives also a broad burlesque of conventional sentiment. The most amusing and the most instructive episode of this sort is old Sir Pitt's proposal to Becky.[4]

'I'll make you happy, zee if I don't. You shall do what you like; spend what you like; and 'av it all your own way. I'll make you a zettlement. I'll do everything reglar. Look year!' and the old man fell down on his knees and leered at her like a satyr.

Rebecca started back a picture of consternation. In the course of this history we have never seen her lose her presence of mind; but she did now, and wept some of the most genuine tears that ever fell from her eyes.

'O Sir Pitt!' she said. 'O sir – I – I'*m married already.*'

At first sight this looks like a very crude parody of a conventional love scene. The absurd, near-illiterate, lustful, filthy old baronet, and the girl prudently making a career out of her sexual attractions are presented in the posture adopted in other novels by high-minded pure young lovers, preparing for a long and virtuous marriage. A fairly good joke, we may think (or perhaps we may think, rather a poor joke) and no more.

But it is rather more. The passage combines this hearty burlesque with a key point in the plot, which, like other key points is worked out over many chapters and many years. Becky has married Sir Pitt's younger son. On the book's very last page, we are told that this younger son, Rawdon, died six weeks before his brother. Had he survived him by a day, Becky, though long since separated from him, would eventually, after many tribulations, have acquired the title of Lady Crawley that she could have had now for the asking with wealth to match. She fails to win all this and the prospect of an early and opulent widowhood because she is too clever in attracting and taming Rawdon, and too quick to follow up her success. Thackeray may smile at simple goodness, and at times his praise of it may hardly sound sincere. But he is a true realist in his demonstration that in this uncertain world the clever calculator usually calculates wrong. That the doves are wiser than the serpents *sub specie aeternitatis* was a truth to which he tried to cling, and it may sometimes have eluded him. But here he is telling us that, judged by results, the doves are wiser in this world. They may suffer, they may fail, but at least they do not contrive their own downfall.

It looks rather as if Thackeray's burlesque of conventional lovemaking has a tendency opposite to its first appearance; it seems to bring needed support to the very convention it appears to be decrying. Is this so? No one who has the feel of Thackeray's mind will be very confident in giving a rapid assent. And there is something in the tone of the passage itself which also raises doubts. These become stronger as we read the first words of the next chapter.*

Every reader of a sentimental turn (and we desire no other) must have been pleased with the *tableau* with which the last act of our little drama concluded; for what can be prettier than an image of Love on his knees before Beauty?

It seems there is another – eminently Thackerayan – point. Ludicrous burlesque as the passage is, it describes two people who *really meant it*. Sir Pitt was really prepared to spite his heirs to get possession of Becky's body; and Becky really did wish that she had been single and could have obliged him. The other and better characters in the book, as we have seen, often did not really mean what they professed. Nor, perhaps, did those couples who enacted, whether in life or in novels, the little sentimental proposal scene here parodied.

Here, perhaps, we come as close as we ever can to Thackeray's most fundamental attitude. The conventional truisms about

---

* It has often been pointed out that, since the book was published in parts, the first readers had to wait some time for this sequel.

marriage, love, fidelity really are true, but they are false in the mouths of many, perhaps of most, through lack of that burning sincerity needed to match their grandeur. For all his cynical-sentimental air there is an austere and deeply serious core to his sexual morality.

Vanity Fair (1847–8) is far and away Thackeray's most valuable statement on all these questions. *Pendennis* (1850) and *Esmond* (1852) seem crude and often dull in comparison. There is only one point, relevant for us, on which they add anything important. Both touch on a vexed question that is absent from *Vanity Fair*, the nature of the connection between maternal and sexual love. The disturbing ambiguity we have already found is once more visible. Pendennis lies ill nursed by Fanny Bolton. His mother, and the 'good' loving Laura, who is waiting for his foolish youth to end, and keeping her love for him in good repair, come to visit him. They assume at once that Fanny is his mistress, which she is not:

> What could Fanny expect when suddenly brought up for sentence before a couple of such judges? Nothing but swift condemnation, awful punishment, merciless dismissal! Women are cruel critics in cases such as that . . . and we like them to be so . . .[5]

Thackeray's point here is that in passionate female hearts, like Helen's (the mother's), and to a less marked degree, Laura's, principles, conjectures, passions, jealousies are all so confused that they are indistinguishable. One can make a theoretical analysis, distinguishing possessiveness, class-feeling, respect for chastity, maternal devotion, feminine rivalry. But Helen herself is aware only of a burning love for her son, and a desperate hostility to Fanny. So it is that moral principles become discredited in the world. For it is easy to see that Helen's amalgam of contra-dictory feelings is largely selfish; therefore it is easy (but mistaken) to conclude that the moral element in it is hypocritical; and even more mistaken to conclude that all serious concern with chastity is hypocritical.

Laura is a little calmer than Helen, and less unfair. She too is majestically cool to Fanny, but she is analytical enough to perceive that Helen's maternal love has a tendency to spread over into an all-devouring passion, which can stand no rival. Thus she says, at one point, to the woman with whom she lives, and who treats her as an honorary daughter:

If Pen had loved me as you wished, I should have gained him, but I should have lost you, mamma, I know I should; and I like you to love me best . . .[6]

This is a statement of great interest and some subtlety. The key words are 'as you wished'. The jealous and possessive mother is capable of resigning her claim. Her inherited assumptions, her instincts and her experience tell her that it is right that a man should marry. She may want to keep him to herself for ever; but she cannot approve of her wish to do so. So, in Laura's case, she can suppress her sense of rivalry, at least temporarily. Laura hints that it might flare out again uncontrollably, when Laura had actually won him.

But again, we have the characteristic Thackerayan ambiguity. Was Helen's willingness to surrender her son to Laura a genuine sacrifice, or was it a prudent cutting of losses? Since most men marry sometime, it is realistic of the jealous and possessive mother to accept this, and to try to direct him to a girl over whom she has influence, whom she has befriended, and who would, perhaps, invite her mother-in-law to live in the same house. And how much of the contrast between Helen's treatment of Laura and her treatment of Fanny is to be ascribed to the (false) assumption that Fanny has seduced Pen? How much to class-feeling? How much to her hope of controlling Laura, a hope she could not entertain about Fanny? Very interesting questions, and disturbing questions; but they lack the penetrating force of the questions posed by *Vanity Fair*. The psychology here is distinctly slacker; Helen is not real enough to provide enough evidence for the answers.

What *Pendennis* does show is that the starker, stranger and much more thoroughly expounded issue in *Esmond*, where the hero actually marries the woman he has put in the place of his dead mother, was no isolated quirk, but an extreme version of one of Thackeray's lasting preoccupations.

The first thing to notice about this extraordinary story is that it created a quite unusual flurry of disagreement among contemporaries. The *Spectator* said:

The relation between Esmond and Rachel Viscountess Castlewood is of that sort that nothing short of consummate skill could have saved it from becoming ridiculous or offensive, or both. In Mr Thackeray's hands, the difficulty has become a triumph, and has given rise to beauties which a safer ambition would not gave dared to attempt . . .[7]

John Forster said simply: 'The thing is incredible, and there an end on 't'.[8] George Eliot called it the most 'uncomfortable book you can imagine'.[9]

Here we have in germ the three conflicting views which have persisted and developed ever since, that it is strange and surprising but beautiful and convincing, that it is impossible, and that it is probable enough but aesthetically displeasing. This will be enough to prevent more thoughtful critics from leaping in with routine denunciations of the early Victorians for their misfortune in not having read Freud. These can, in any case, be answered on their own level, by pointing out that they *had* read, more often than most of their successors today, the *Oedipus Rex* of Sophocles.

Esmond's feeling that Lady Castlewood is his second mother is entirely credible and convincing. Esmond has been led to believe (wrongly) that he is illegitimate; his mother died deserted by her husband when he was very young. With a tactful restraint that he does not always show, Thackeray keeps this tender spring of filial feeling for the dead in reserve until his story is more than half told. Then as Esmond, already a man, sees her grave in Flanders for the first time, he conveys the hidden purity of feeling in one of the most eloquent passages he ever wrote:

A bird came down from a roof opposite, and lit first on a cross, and then on the grass below it, whence it flew away presently with a leaf in its mouth: then came a sound as of chanting, from the chapel of the sisters hard by; others had long since filled the place which poor Mary Magdalene once had there, were kneeling at the same stall and hearing the same hymns and prayers in which her stricken heart had found consolation. Might she sleep in peace; and we, too, when our struggles and pains are over! But the earth is the Lord's as the heaven is; we are alike his creatures here and yonder. I took a little flower off the hillock and kissed it, and went my way, like the bird that had just lighted on the cross by me, back into the world again. Silent receptacle of death; tranquil depth of calm, out of reach of tempest and trouble! I felt as one who had been walking below the sea and treading amidst the bones of shipwrecks.*[10]

---

* The setting is a cemetery near a house of penitents. Although Esmond was not actually illegitimate, his mother's marriage had been a secret, and occurred late in her pregnancy.

The long-delayed eloquence of this helps to convince us that Esmond's feeling for Lady Castlewood will be ambivalent from the first. When he says to Lord Mohun, in answer to the taunting suggestion that he is in love with her, 'I never had a mother but I love this lady as one'[11] he partly means it. But not wholly, because the hidden feeling for the real dead mother is potentially so very powerful. It is natural that a lonely boy, with no fixed home or position in the world, should respond gratefully to feminine kindness. As she is older, and the kindness begins when he is very young, it is natural that his feeling for her should be vaguely filial. She, who is in love with him long before he knows it, has equally natural reasons for dressing her passion in maternal guise. She is married, she is too old for him, and before long she sees him infatuated with her daughter.

The daughter, for all the elaborate rhetoric that is poured out in her honour, is nothing more nor less than a sexy piece. Esmond is a sober, serious young man, who might be expected to delight in domesticity. Why does he remain so long at her mercy? Once again, as so often, Thackeray's psychology is suggestive and interesting rather than clear. Are we to think that Esmond set his heart on a girl he was sensible enough inwardly to despise, and one he had no hope of winning, because he was unconsciously saving himself for her mother, when she should finally become free? As the rightful heir to the title, supposed to be illegitimate, and willingly surrendering his honours to his young cousin, he might well think it imprudent to marry at all.

This seems a promising line of thought. But Thackeray does not really endorse it. Indeed, by making Beatrix captivate the Duke of Hamilton, presented as a sober man of middle age, he seems rather to be overstressing to an almost absurd degree the power of the sexy piece over sensible men. By doing so, he removes the need for any subtle explanations for Esmond's long slavery. He almost seems to say that no one could have resisted her.

So we have a respectable hero who is a kind of double Oedipus, since he not only marries the woman he has treated as his mother, but transfers his love to her from her own daughter. It is tempting and plausible to say that this was less shocking to the book's first readers than to their successors because they chose so largely to ignore the element of sexual satisfaction in virtuous and happy marriage.

In their general celebration of the chaste, dutiful, affectionate woman, the uniqueness of relationships became blurred. Mother, wife, sister all appeared to have nearly the same function. Of the many examples that could be quoted in support of this, the ending of *Bleak House* is one almost exactly contemporary with *Esmond*. Here a prospective bridegroom steps down almost at the altar steps to offer the bride to young Prince Charming, and to revert himself to the role of affectionate and confidential uncle.

Before we give too much weight to this, we must remind ourselves that some contemporaries, like Forster, called the ending of *Esmond* incredible. Moreover, we may well say that in judging thus, he incautiously ignored the great skill with which the catastrophe is prepared. The Lady Castlewoods of this world are adept at concealing their true feelings most of the time, and hers do break out plainly enough at times. As for Esmond, would he not surrender eventually, out of gratitude, out of weariness, out of a gentlemanly disinclination to give pain, out of fellow-feeling for unrequited love from which he, too, has suffered so long through Beatrix's coquetry?

Are we then to agree with those who found it touching and beautiful? Are we to take Esmond's paean of praise from his mother-wife at the book's end as Thackeray's verdict and our own?

This will not do, because it is not really Thackeray's verdict. Lady Castlewood shows a jealousy of her daughter's power over Esmond that might well be called vicious. She even goes to the length of taunting her with her failure to capture the Duke in marriage before a violent death overtook him.[11a] She is repeatedly shown as conquering her jealousy only with a terrible effort. Nor is it true, as may be incautiously assumed, that Esmond himself can see no fault in her:

> 'Do you leave this too, Beatrix?' says her mother, taking the miniature [of her recently dead betrothed] out, and with a cruelty she did not very often show; but there are some moments when the tenderest women are cruel, and some triumphs which angels can't forgo.* . . . If my mistress was cruel, at

---

* This remark shows how unjustly and contemptuously even the best of men will sometimes judge of our sex. Lady Castlewood had no intention of triumphing over her daughter; but from a sense of duty alone pointed out her deplorable wrong. R.E. (This note is part of Thackeray's text and is supposed to be written by the daughter of Esmond and Lady Castlewood.)

least she never could be got to own as much. Her haughtiness quite overtopped Beatrix's; and, if the girl had a proud spirit, I very much fear it came to her by inheritance.[12]

We have here mother and daughter fighting for a man's love, and the mother dead to all shame about the weapons she will use in the struggle. And we have the man over whom they are fighting aware of this. What then are we to make of the daughter's soothing note and of Esmond's own final judgement: 'To have such a love is the one blessing, in comparison of which all earthly joy is of no value; and to think of her is to praise God'?

What Thackeray seems to be doing here, with all his usual artfulness and indirection, is drawing attention to something we all know: that it is impossible to judge one's nearest and dearest. By making the daughter exonerate her mother, and the husband (momentarily) blame her and then praise her to the skies, he opens for the reader other possibilities. He makes us wonder, if the daughter could be so blind to her mother's clearly-revealed passions, perhaps the husband's moment of insight was a brief flash. Perhaps the picture of Lady Castlewood as cruel, designing and jealous was the true one after all? Does that mean we are to dismiss Esmond's final tribute of unlimited praise and adoration as part of the author's irony? The text will hardly support that, and it would in any case be uncharacteristic. Thackeray does not push his irony, or his satire, or his scepticism or his reforming zeal to the limit. One man who did so was Jonathan Swift; and Thackeray wrote in fiercer condemnation of him than of any other. No; Thackeray was a realist. A sensible man always tries to be more keenly aware of his wife's virtues than of her faults. Esmond was a sensible man. If his wife was not perfect, she really loved him; and she had been very patient and long-suffering. And she was infinitely preferable to her daughter.

There will never be universal agreement about the ending of *Esmond*. If everyone must stand up and be counted, I would say, first, that Thackeray convinces me completely that the marriage would really have occurred. I agree that the mingling of maternal, filial and sexual feelings is unpleasant, but it is the unpleasantness of truth. Thackeray's triumph here, and what makes the novel, for all its tedious 'period' trappings, still of high interest, is that he showed how the normal and the abnormal, duty and egoism, truth and delusion meet and mingle. He refuses to show them rigidly separated as the world likes to think they are; but he also

refused to show them almost indistinguishable, with respectability only a mask for appetite, as the cynical railers at the world
like to think they are. The happy ending is of the mixed, flawed
kind that the world really offers to some; and they are sensible if
they give thanks, remembering how easily it could have been an
unhappy ending.

Most important of all, he shows the adaptability, or what might
be called the *hospitality*, of conventional marriage. It can absorb
dangerous passions, Esmond's exhausted lust for Beatrix, Lady
Castlewood's fierce jealousy and possessiveness. It is a very
strange case, but what case is entirely ordinary? There is a kind
of cautious boldness in Thackeray, or even a brave timidity. He
shows us these disturbing things, which are also enlarging and
heartening things, about Victorian marriage. But he is careful to
pretend that he is only speaking about the reign of Queen Anne.

2. MRS GASKELL

I Ruth

If we are to classify Mrs Gaskell as a realist, it is necessary to
make some concessions. She was not always or instinctively a
realist; she developed gradually towards realism. In *Ruth* (1853)
there is a most instructive conflict between the demands of a
penetrating and shrewd observer, who was also a generous and
sensitive judge of human nature, and the demands of a thesis.
The thesis was that the 'fallen woman' was or might be inwardly
pure.

There are always great technical difficulties when a novelist
combines satire on a great public question with the traditional
novel of plot and character. It may be that the two are best kept
separate; and that if satire is to be cast in fictional form, its proper
mode is the fable, where the characters derive their interest from
what they represent, not from what they are. Thus, *Candide*,
Rasselas, and *Animal Farm* are successful works of art, while the
American section of *Martin Chuzzlewit* and *1984*, aiming at the
novelist's and the satirist's target at the same time, miss both.

However this may be, we must take books as we find them;
and we must first ask, 'What is *Ruth* satirizing?' It is satirizing

what the author takes to be the comfortable stock views of the
average sensual man about female virtue. They can be summarized
as follows:

1. Sexual purity is *the* great moral principle for women.

2. Men in contrast have a rich and varied moral life, in
which sexual ethics, though never unimportant, take a subordinate place.

3. Women who fall from sexual purity fall completely, and
become irresponsible, untruthful, unfeeling, unfeminine and
promiscuous.

4. There is, however, one exception to (3). Sometimes
seducers most generously agree to marry the girl, in which case
she gratefully accepts.

Ruth is in many ways a touching and beautiful book. But it
constantly suffers from the effect of the author's generous indignation against these propositions. Consequently the characters
sometimes do not act as they would, and as the author, being a
true novelist, really knows they would, but as is required to
refute the assumptions of the world. Thus, when the seducer,
Bellingham meets Ruth again, acting as respectable governess in
a wealthy family, he does not at first recognize her. But he is
reminded of the woman he has not seen for several years, and he
thinks:

Poor Ruth! and, for the first time for several years, he
wondered what had become of her; though, of course, there
was but one thing that could have happened, and perhaps it
was as well he did not know her end, for most likely it would
have made him very uncomfortable.[13]

He means, of course, that she is on the streets. Yet only a
few pages later, when he has learnt that the governess really is
Ruth, he is penitently asking her to marry him. She rejects him
with scorn and indignation. Obviously, we cannot believe in a
man who, without any spiritual crisis or process of development,
is at the same time so worldly, so conventional, so callous and
then suddenly so generous. It is clear that he is merely being used
to refute in quick succession the third and fourth propositions
above.

Mrs Gaskell's attack on the worldly code fails, however
generous and right-minded we may feel its motives to be. She is
rather more successful in dealing with the uncharitable attitudes of
serious and religious people who do not subscribe, at least con-

sciously, to the assumptions of the world. Thurstan and Faith
Benson, the brother and sister who befriend Ruth, have an interesting disagreement when they learn, after Bellingham has deserted
her, that she is pregnant:

'Faith, do you know I rejoice in this child's advent?'

'May God forgive you, Thurstan! – if you know what you
are saying. But surely it is a temptation, dear Thurstan.'

'I do not think it is a delusion. The sin appears to me to be
quite distinct from its consequences.'

'Sophistry and a temptation' said Miss Benson decidedly.

'No, it is not,' said her brother with equal decision. 'In the
eye of God, she is exactly the same as if the life she had led had
left no trace behind. We knew her errors before, Faith.'

'Yes, but not this disgrace – this badge of shame.'[14]

Mrs Gaskell was learning her trade as a novelist when she wrote
this, and the dialogue is not quite convincing. Moreover, Ruth
makes Thurstan's task of persuading his sister easier than it
would probably have been by the holy joy and resignation with
which she accepts the role of unmarried mother. Nevertheless,
the essence of the conflict between brother and sister here is true
and important and mirrors some of the hardest dilemmas of a
society which professes to be guided in its ethics by religion.
There is a constant conflict, largely unconscious, between Christian ethics and the respectability of the law-abiding citizen. And
this conflict is most acute and perplexing when Christian ethics
and respectability appear to be saying the same thing.

Faith Benson is not worldly; she is perfectly sincere in her
desire to be guided by Christian principles. But she cannot, at
first, grasp the distinction her brother is making. Chastity as a
moral principle, and the harsh social disciplines which aim to
deter girls from having illegitimate children are confused in her
mind. Her brother is engaged in the difficult task of disentangling
the Christian principles (not chastity only, but, more important,
charity and forgiveness, too) from the utilitarian ethics of society.
Faith Benson, influenced a little, as Mrs Gaskell knows, but she
herself does not, by suppressed jealousy, influenced, too, by a
sensible woman's wish to draw a line under an unhappy episode
and forget it, has strong resistance to being convinced. Only
those who have no power of entering imaginatively into a past
period will fail to see how difficult it was for her to accept her
brother's rational argument.

Later, we have a less subtle portrait of the pharasaical indignation of Bradshaw, the wealthy pillar of Thurstan Benson's
congregation, when he finds he has been deceived. Benson has
persuaded him to employ Ruth as a governess by falsely stating
that she is a widow. Mrs Gaskell's generous indignation is too
strong to allow her to enter calmly into his feelings about being
deceived, and about the contamination of his own children.

And what of Ruth herself? At the story's opening she is young,
friendless, inexperienced, timid. Her naïvety almost exceeds what
is credible. Even in the nursery, one would think, little girls
know the difference between a plain statement and a compliment.
But Ruth says that she could not help knowing she was pretty
'for many people have told me so.' At this time she is nearly
sixteen. She has a strong but quite untrained aesthetic sensibility.
Employed in the drudgery of long hours of needlework, she
prefers the darkest and coldest corner of the room, because from
it she has the best view of some beautiful paintings, and she is
similarly sensitive to the glories of nature. Bellingham appears at
first in her eyes as the kindly, disinterested friend who can stand
between her and the harshness of her employer and can take her to
see fine scenery on Sundays. He begs her to regard him as a
'brother', and excites her lively gratitude by offering to take her to
see her old home, which she has imagined she might never see
again.

Thus far we have a perfectly credible and a very touching
picture. But now the author has to turn to the difficult task of
explaining how much she understands about her sexual nature.
The passage is of great interest:

She was too young when her mother died to have received
any cautions or words of advice respecting *the* subject of a
woman's life – if indeed, wise parents ever directly speak of
what, in its depth and power, cannot be put into words –
which is a brooding spirit with no definite form or shape that
men should know it, but which is there, and present before
we have recognized its existence. Ruth was innocent and
snow-pure. She had heard of falling in love, but did not know
the signs and symptoms thereof . . .[15]

One must admit here that intelligent, sensitive, shrewd as she
is, Mrs Gaskell is here somewhat confused. Her entirely genuine
awareness of mystery in the forces of life and in the developing
personality seems to mask any respect for the importance of

facts, and of knowledge of facts. Yet the passage, confused as it is, is at the same time a superb unconscious tribute to the author's honesty. How easy it would have been to ascribe all Ruth's misfortune to the early loss of her mother. But this would not have been quite honest, unless the author was clear both about what the mother ought to have told her, and what she really would have told her. She didn't quite know either, and did not pretend that she did. And her uncertainty is a humane one. There is no reason to say that she was afraid of the facts; but she was puzzled by the inadequacy of cold facts in matters that excite deep feelings. Therefore we are left uncertain just who was to blame, and how much and why, apart from the obvious culprit, Bellingham.

Ruth's timidity is well deployed to make the success of Bellingham's scheme of seduction seem more plausible. Having startled her by proposing that they go together to London, he leaves her alone in an inn without money and with a small un-paid bill for tea. She wishes to run away and avoid Bellingham's return:

> She put on her bonnet, and opened the parlour-door; but then she saw the square figure of the landlord standing at the open house-door, smoking his evening pipe, and looming large and distinct against the dark air and landscape beyond . . . She feared that he would not let her quit the house without paying. She thought that she would leave a note for Mr Bellingham, saying where she was gone, and how she had left the house in debt, for (like a child) all dilemmas appeared of equal magnitude to her; and the difficulty of passing the landlord while he stood there . . . appeared insuperable . . .[16]

One wonders how deliberate was the author's decision to place the brief, deceptive idyll of Ruth's life with Bellingham not, as announced, in London, but in the mountains of North Wales. She may perhaps have felt that the associations of a London hotel bedroom were too squalid for the picture she wished to give of an innocence only just tarnished:

> . . . they settled down to a week's enjoyment of that Alpine country. It was a most true enjoyment to Ruth. It was opening a new sense; vast ideas of beauty and grandeur filled her mind at the sight of the mountains, now first beheld in full majesty. She was almost overpowered by the vague and solemn delight; but by-and-by her love for them equalled her awe, and in the

night-time she would softly rise, and steal to the window to
see the white moonlight, which gave a new aspect to the ever-
lasting hills that girdle the mountain village.[17]

The common-sense comment would be that no girl would
find mountains or moonlight half so absorbing as her first
experiences of sexual intercourse. But perhaps that would be to
miss the point. It may be that the real function of the passage is to
provide an equivalent in visual images of the awakening of the
senses. If so, it is slightly misleading; the images are Words-
worthian, redolent of spiritual grandeurs half-glimpsed. But that
is not really what the author desires to convey. She wishes to
make every excuse for Ruth, to show her cruelly frightened and
deceived, a forlorn waif. But she certainly does not mean that
the episode was innocent even on Ruth's side.

Perhaps we have here rather a rare case. *Ruth* was written in
the middle of the period of most extreme sexual reticence that
the English novel has ever known. It is a stock critical idea today,
but nevertheless in my opinion a mistaken one, that this reticence
on the whole inhibited the true purposes of art.* Here, perhaps,
we have an exception. Mrs Gaskell did not have to ask herself,
probably did not wish to ask herself, what Ruth really felt in
bed. We cannot therefore know what she felt; but at least she
must have responded in some way to the absolute unfamiliarity
of the experience. But North Wales, fine as it is, is not *so* different
from the landscape she had previously seen.

Nor is it merely idle curiosity that makes the reader ask the
question. It is central to the book's main theme, and relevant also
to its chief weakness. Mrs Gaskell wished to make Ruth sympathetic, to show that the 'fallen woman' could be a sweet, affectionate person and much more sinned against than sinning. But she
never quite settled in her own mind the question, 'Do I want to
make her a noble penitent, or do I wish to show her purity
unsullied throughout?' She knew very well that the second
alternative was sentimental and unreal. However deceived, Ruth
is a consenting party, no victim of rape or abduction. But she
does not really show the upheavals of repentance. Ruth is much
the same all through, except for growing up a little. One can only
speculate about the reasons for this; but I think it is worth doing
so, for they seem to lie near the heart of some of the deepest

* See chapter I, for a fuller discussion of this question.

dilemmas of the age.

The Evangelical ethic, which was so dominant at this time that it affected all public communication, and influenced many of different religious schools or of none, conceived repentance as a prelude to religious conversion. It was not usually regarded, as in the Catholic tradition, as a lifelong necessity, the fruit of a regularly repeated self-examination, and affecting both great sins and petty faults. It was rather a grand, unique event, determining the whole future of the soul. So there was the strongest possible contrast between the state of the soul before and after it. To show Ruth's repentance in any but the most muted terms, therefore, would be to suggest that her sin was grave, deliberate, momentous. In fact it was nothing of the kind.

Moreover, Mrs Gaskell half shares the general view of her contemporaries that, for women, sexual conduct is much the most important of all forms of conduct, the supreme testing-ground of the soul. (This is indicated, for instance, in the quotation given above, which speaks of *the* subject of a woman's life.) So it was very difficult for her to convey the degree of blame rightly attaching to Ruth without exaggerating it, and without confusing it with the far heavier guilt of Bellingham. So it is that Ruth has a deceptive air of total purity at all times; and it was this, perhaps, more than the indelicacy of the subject which led to the fierce criticism of some reviewers, who caused the author so much pain.* And, of course, she was writing under the generous conviction that fallen women were gravely wronged by a cynical society; such feelings naturally lead to over-correction of the view being attacked.

Wives and Daughters

I pass over *Sylvia's Lovers* (with some regret), because the demands of a melodramatic plot and the historical form prevent it being successful as a whole. It does, however, have an excellent courting scene where the difference between what is said and what is felt is conveyed with sensitive truth.[18]

In *Wives and Daughters* (1865) there is no thesis, and we find

---

* For Mrs Gaskell's pained reaction to some of these see *The Letters of Mrs Gaskell*, Ed. J. A. V. Chapple and Arthur Pollard. (Manchester U.P. 1966), especially Nos. 148–154.

what is lacking in so many studies of love and marriage, a sense
of causation, a regard for probability, and a subtle awareness of
the slow erosions of time. On the subject of love most novelists
from the eighteenth century to the twentieth have been sadly
limited by the cult of youth. Mrs Gaskell begins with a middle-
aged widower with a daughter approaching seventeen. Gibson
is the kind of active, shrewd man of the world, who is a little
ashamed of the strength of his feelings, and often succeeds in
suppressing them. He is bothered and irritated by the calf-love
of a young apprentice for his daughter. Reading the young man's
high-flown poetical effusion to Molly, he vows to replace the copy
of Shakespeare in the surgery library (from which the young man
took his quotations) with Johnson's dictionary. He thinks:

'Why, she's only just seventeen – not seventeen, indeed, till
July; not for six weeks yet. Sixteen and three-quarters! Why
she's quite a baby. To be sure – poor Jeanie was not so old,
and how I did love her!' (Mrs Gibson's name was Mary, so he
must have been referring to someone else.)[19]

We learn nothing more about this Jeanie, but she is mentioned
occasionally when Gibson's thoughts are in this retrospective
vein. The dead wife is even more shadowy for the reader; but
there is an occasional hint of her influence and remembered
presence in the Gibson household, as when Molly, the daughter,
is seen softly stroking another girl's hand:

A mode of caressing that had come down to her from her
mother – whether as an hereditary instinct, or as a lingering
remembrance of the tender ways of the dead woman, Mr
Gibson often wondered within himself as he observed it.[20]

By judicious use of memories like this, Mrs Gaskell establishes
Gibson as a man with an inner life of which he never speaks. He
would never *mention* this point of likeness to his daughter, would
hardly disturb her by speaking of a mother she scarcely remembers.
And not only is there a barrier between Gibson and the world in
which he is an energetic, kindly and respected figure; there is also
a barrier within himself. He remembers Jeanie for a moment, but
does not allow the memory to have practical influence. It does not
alter his view that Molly is absurdly young to have young men in
love with her; it never occurs to him for a moment that there can
be the faintest parallel between the love-sick young apprentice
and what he himself had been when Jeanie was sixteen. And Mrs
Gaskell neatly stresses this incomprehension – which is a decision

of the will, not a failure of intelligence – by parodying it only a
few pages later in the mouth of a much duller man, Squire Hamley,
who is proud of his ancient lineage, and conscious of a kind of
notional superiority (unrecognized by the world) both to the
neighbouring earl, and to *nouveaux riches* generally. Being poor
he is sensitive about any attempt to enrich the family by marriage:

'. . . if a boy of mine, with only two hundred a year . . . goes
and marries a woman with fifty thousand for her portion, I'll
disown him – it would be just disgusting.'

'Not if they loved each other, and their whole happiness
depended upon their marrying each other,' put in Mrs Hamley
mildly.

'Pooh! away with love! Nay, my dear, we loved each other
so dearly we should never have been happy with any one else;
but that's a different thing. People aren't like what they were
when we were young. All the love nowadays is just silly fancy,
and sentimental romance, as far as I can see.'[21]

One of the most important functions of stupidity in the world
is to reveal the core of absurdity in ideas which cleverer men
conceal and adorn with parades of logic.

By this time the reader is in a position to understand the curious
web of mixed inadequate motives for Gibson's second marriage
to an affected, snobbish and tedious hanger-on of the earl's
family. He thinks that his daughter needs a new mother to guide
her through the years before her marriage; a friend has suggested
it; he is dissatisfied with the style of his housekeeping, and
ashamed when a friend does not get a decent lunch in his house;
there only seems to be one eligible lady in the neighbourhood.
He is unsure of himself, and acts impulsively in one of those
moments when circumstances seem to conspire to make decisions
for us. He feels trapped when he finds that the lady's aristocratic
patrons have been planning the match. He comforts himself by
reflecting that at least he has done well for his daughter, whom he
loves tenderly.

But he is sharply disappointed to find that Molly dislikes the
marriage. The way in which he reconciles himself with her, after
leaving her to avoid a scene immediately after telling the news,
is characteristic:

'I wish you and Hyacinth to become better acquainted – to
learn to love each other.'

'Hyacinth!' said Molly, entirely bewildered.

'Yes, Hyacinth! It's the silliest name I ever heard of; but it's hers, and I must call her by it. I can't bear Clare, which is what my lady and all the family at the Towers call her; and Mrs Kirkpatrick is formal and nonsensical too, as she'll change her name so soon.'

'When, papa?' asked Molly, feeling as if she were living in a strange, unknown world.

'Not till after Michaelmas.' And then . . . 'And the worst is, she's gone and perpetuated her own, affected name by having her daughter called after her. Cynthia! One thinks of the moon, and the man in the moon with his bundle of faggots. I'm thankful you're plain Molly, child.'[22]

It is not enough for the doctor to call his future wife's name silly, for that is a misfortune. He must establish a league of connivance against her with his daughter by accusing her of an affected choice of name. To combine this with perfect firmness in his decision, and with the precept that the daughter must learn to love the new wife, is typical of the man. He is governed by a sense of duty, but will always allow feeling its sway within duty's framework. From now on, the daughter will really know, though she will be tempted to forget, that her father loves her more than he will ever love his new wife.

Mrs Gaskell avoids another of the endemic weaknesses of the literature of love, even more damaging, perhaps, than an exclusive concentration upon the feelings of youth. She never forgets that no one's feelings are fully apparent to anyone else, that no one is simply a passive object of love, like the *Julias* and *Delias* of innumerable lyrics. There is a sharp comedy, and pathos as well, in the proposal scene, when the apparent sensibility which makes Mrs Kirkpatrick burst into tears is due merely to relief at the thought of having a man to earn her living. And there is comedy of a broader kind when Gibson goes to inform some old spinster friends of his engagement, and one of them is explaining to herself that Gibson is the only man who will be able to persuade her to marriage, and the desertion of her sister: ('if he ever proposed she should feel bound to accept him, for poor dear Mary's sake; never explaining what exact style of satisfaction she imagined she should give to her dead friend by marrying her late husband.')

Neither *Ruth* nor any of Mrs Gaskell's other works prepare us for the rich variety of forms love assumes here. Cynthia, the doctor's stepdaughter, is the kind of girl who loves to attract admiration and always does so effortlessly. But she is far from being the stock character of the vain little flirt. She is shown as impressed, in spite of herself, by the depth of feelings she cannot share, and slightly irritated at idealization of herself involved in the admiration she cannot help seeking. Preston, the first man with whom she has been involved before the story opens, has a curious and entirely convincing mixture of feelings for her, possessive, slavish, touchy and potentially hostile and vengeful. The influence of the dead on those who loved them is constantly present, not only in the doctor's memories, but in the masterly account of long, dreary days in Squire Hamley's house when he is mourning his dead wife, and he and his two sons feel their shared masculinity as a poison of dullness and dissension. The blighting effect of lady-like affection on a household is shown in the second Gibson marriage. The doctor is engaged in a constant inner struggle to avoid realizing consciously that his marriage has been a mistake, both for himself and his daughter. Mrs Gibson is a portrait of feminine affectation less brilliant, of course, than Mrs Elton, but fuller; we see what the doctor is up against in a passage like this:

'I quite agree with mamma, who always says you have done very well for yourself; and Mr Gibson too! What an agreeable, well-informed man!'

'Yes he is,' said his wife slowly, as if she did not like to relinquish her role of a victim to circumstances quite immediately. 'He is very agreeable, very; only we see so little of him; and of course he comes home tired and hungry, and not inclined to talk to his own family, and apt to go to sleep.'[23]

Cynthia is more honest than her mother, and more aware of her own limitations, but they are very alike in their reactions to anger, praise and blame. They are both incapable of grasping that they can deserve praise or blame. Gibson is seriously angry with his wife when she makes a base use of confidential medical information, obtained by eavesdropping. But, however forcefully and clearly he explains his criticism, she can never understand that she has been guilty of anything but a failure to *please*. To her, men have moral tastes, just as they may like or dislike their wives' hats, or the dinners provided. The woman's function is to please, and, by doing so, get her own way. The bitter frustration of a man, who has to abandon the hopeless attempt to explain the difference between a principle and a personal idiosyncrasy, is poignantly conveyed. And the author makes effective use of Gibson's profession, which involves lonely hours on horseback, to show us his long, tender memories, his sensibility to scenery and the only half-suppressed sense of the consequences of his hasty decision to marry.

Family likeness, one of the most familiar observations in the world, is also one of the rarest to appear convincingly in books. Here mother and daughter have it; and we see clearly that it is their likeness that makes each irritating to the other. This household of four, the Gibsons and the two stepsisters, Molly and Cynthia, is one of the most vividly presented in the whole English novel, because we are equally aware of their life together and of the hidden feelings of each. So the moments of climax, such as that in chapter XXXIV, tell, as such moments do in life, because all the feelings and circumstances, when the climax comes, are well known already.

Molly, in her steady, diffident way has long been in love with Roger Hamley, the squire's second son. Now, about to leave the country for years, he comes to propose to Cynthia. Molly returns from a walk to find the matter settled. Roger leaves to catch the London coach, and turns to wave, in the hope of catching a last glimpse of Cynthia. Cynthia is not watching, but Molly is; and, as he waves she shrinks back from the window. Then anxious to be alone, Molly finds Cynthia inclined to be talkative; and she reveals the shifting vagueness of her feeling for the man she has just accepted:

He's well enough, I daresay, and a great deal too learned and clever for a stupid girl like me; but even you must acknowledge he's very plain and awkward; and I like pretty things and pretty people.

And she goes on to indicate her doubts about his constancy, and more especially her own during his long absence. Molly's complex feelings here are beautifully conveyed. She does not want to be jealous, she wants to feel that her hero is worthily loved. She sees that he is not, but is afraid to admit it to herself, both for his sake, and because doubts would lead to forbidden and agonizing longings that he should love her. Her fondness for Cynthia, in so many ways complementary to herself, is genuine, her wish that Cynthia should be constant is genuine; and yet inevitably there is a concealed hostility; and her attempt to convince herself that she has a sisterly feeling for Roger is a failure too. So, when her father asks Molly in his forthright way whether Cynthia is worthy of Roger, she is unable, in the rush of contradictory feelings, to answer at all.

Eventually, Cynthia breaks off the engagement, for the characteristic reason that she knows she has behaved badly and refuses to be forgiven and tolerated instead of idolized by her future husband. The scene between the two girls that follows is a rare triumph in conveying unspoken feelings through the medium of ordinary words:

She [Molly] took Cynthia into her arms with gentle power, and laid her head against her own breast, as if the one had been a mother, and the other a child.

'Oh, my darling!' she murmured. 'I do so love you, dear, dear Cynthia!' and she stroked her hair, and kissed her eyelids; Cynthia passive all the while, till suddenly she started up stung with a new idea, and looking Molly straight in the face, she said –

'Molly, Roger will marry you! See if it isn't so! You two good – '

But Molly pushed her away with a sudden violence of repulsion. 'Don't,' she said. She was crimson with shame and indignation. 'Your husband this morning! Mine tonight! What do you take him for?'

'A man,' smiled Cynthia.[24]

How well the unusual, almost excessive tenderness of the first part of this scene conveys her profound, unadmitted relief, coupled with a genuine pity for the girl who has lost what Molly thinks such a great prize; and how sincerely shocked she is to hear her own secret dream expressed in cool, practical words. Such a scene, the culmination of a long and convincing story of friendship between the two girls, makes most accounts of jealousy look melodramatically unreal. We need not be surprised, in the face of subtlety like this, that one of the more brash and imperceptive of our well-known critics should call *Wives and Daughters* insipid.

Mrs Gaskell obtains her effects by patient accumulation of detail; consequently, a critical summary must be particularly inadequate. But I think it is possible to pick out one or two salient features. Less brilliant and subtle than Jane Austen, she is like her in showing that love is as various as personality, while many novelists write as if it were something like influenza that reduces everyone to the same level. She is like Jane Austen, too, (especially in *Mansfield Park*) in showing how a web of different love-feelings affects domestic life among near relatives. But she is unlike Jane Austen in giving in masterly fashion the sense of the passing of many years with all their patterns of continuity and change in sentiment, courtship and marriage.

CHAPTER VI

The Pessimists

'I don't know how it is, Will; but you know women better than I.'

'Perhaps, Colonel,' answered Booth, 'I have studied their minds more.'

'I don't, however, much envy you your knowledge,' replied the other; 'for I never think their minds worth considering.'

> Henry Fielding, *Amelia* (1751) Book IV, chap. VI

The rarest offerings of the purest loves are but a self-indulgence, and no generosity at all.

> Thomas Hardy, *Far from the Madding Crowd* (1874) chap. XX

He [Sergeant Troy] had been known to observe casually that in dealing with womankind the only alternative to flattery was cursing and swearing. There was no third method. 'Treat them fairly, and you are a lost man,' he would say.

> ibid., chap. XXV

. . . she added in a whisper, 'it makes you so cruel to other people when you love anyone.'

> Thyrza in *Thyrza* by George Gissing (1887) chap. XXIX

I J. A. Froude

A variety of motives may cause a novel to be published anonymously. With Scott, it was perhaps a wish to begin a new literary career in middle-age, coupled with an instinctive understanding that with *Waverley* he was embarking on something far greater than all his previous poetic efforts. With the Brontës and George Eliot, it may have been a shrinking from publicity and adverse criticism, coupled with a dislike of being typed as female authors.

Trollope's curious deviation into anonymity in the middle of a successful career seems to have sprung from a wish to test his reputation, and discover whether reviewers had begun to praise his books out of mere habit without really reading them. In none of these cases was the decision to publish anonymously so significant as in that of Froude's *Shadows of the Clouds*, published in 1847 as the work of 'Zeta'.* The volume contains two short novels, and the motive for anonymity in each case may not have been the same. The first and less remarkable novel, *The Spirit's Trials* is largely autobiographical, and recounts Froude's unhappy love for Harriet Bush. True, it ends with the hero's death, and Froude himself lived till 1894. But that, perhaps, is merely a way of writing a double line under the balance sheet of early troubles. The wish for anonymity here was natural. Shame and an honourable respect for the privacy of Harriet's family and his own make a sufficient motive.

The story is a simple one. Edward Fowler, a clever, sensitive boy, who has suffered from a dominating and suspicious father and has been permanently scarred by bullying at school, falls in love in the high, romantic fashion with Emma Hardinge. The status of the two families is similar; Fowler is well-liked and quickly accepted by the girl's family as her future husband. Having previously been an idle spendthrift at Oxford, he is inspired by his love to reform, spend little and study hard. But he is still troubled by debts, incurred earlier. His fear of his father makes him prevaricate; when his father discovers the truth he is more angry about the deception than the debts. Emma's father, hearing the story, peremptorily orders her to break off the engagement, which she does:

Day and night, summer and winter, were all alike to her. Her sun had set for ever, at least this side of the grave, and

---

* Zeta is the Greek zed. Froude was the younger brother of Hurrell Froude, one of Newman's closest friends and associates in the early part of the Oxford Movement, but Hurrell died in 1836, a few months before his brother came up to Oriel as an undergraduate. Newman naturally took an interest in his friend's young brother, and for a time James Anthony felt, strongly, but as it proved superficially, the pull of the Movement's ideas and the attraction of Newman's personality. Hurrell had been in the habit of referring to people he considered useless and worldly, such as Erastian bishops, as Zeds. Froude, writing in the aftermath of unhappy love and of painful disillusionment with the principles of Newman and of his dead brother, may have chosen his Greek letter ironically, meaning, 'These are the subversive and worldly reflections of one whom my brother would have considered a useless outcast.'

would never rise again; the soul had gone out of her; she moved about like an automaton; except when a spectral life would seem to flit for a moment through her as she was dreaming of the past . . . His unworthiness had not affected her love for him; it was the disease of which he had died . . . What lovers see in one another is not the real being but their own ideal of a perfect being which they attach to one another; and this is why a second real love is always impossible, that such ideal when once fastened round a person can never be called back again; it follows and clings to him for ever, and if he changes it goes down with the memory of what he was to a grave from which there is no resurrection.[1]

From this state Emma emerges with an unstable, hyper-sensitive conscience, which makes her as wayward in her acts as the most self-willed, passionate and inconstant girl. She engages herself to marry Henry Allen, an ordinary, likeable young man, who understands and respects her passion for Edward Fowler. She breaks this engagement in a fit of high self-sacrificing wilfulness to marry a devoted clergyman, Barnard, who is physically repugnant to her. She breaks down just before the wedding with a terrible fear of sexual union in marriage, a fear which to the last moment she does everything possible to repress and deny. Her father sends for Henry Allen once again and she marries him, and is later found ministering at the deathbed of her only love, Edward Fowler.

Strange and rather improbable stuff; but its interest for us does not lie in its merits as art which are slight, but in its implied comments by a very intelligent man, in a disturbed and wounded state, upon the received doctrines of the day.

The salient point is that, throughout, everybody does what seems right. Emma is right to love one at heart really worthy of her. She does her duty by obeying her father. Her father, too, acts for the best, both in originally approving and then in forbidding the match. True, he comes in for a little mild criticism, and the grounds of it are interesting:

He forgot that he should have learnt more of Edward before he permitted her to entrust herself so completely to him; that where she could so passionately love there must be real good . . . What I think his error was, that he absolutely cut off all hope. Not only did he not say Edward's future conduct might influence him: but he distinctly declared, and with the whole passion and energy of his nature, that it never should.[2]

Here we see Froude, for all his bitterness, heartily concurring in a very strange consequence of the current idealization of women. Because girls like Emma are pure, therefore their love is pure; and because their love is pure, therefore the object of it is pure. The reasoning is breath-taking in its simplicity and its manifest disregard of the most ordinary lessons of experience. And if we ask, did not Froude know that good women sometimes love the most worthless men, and love them for their faults, the answer is that he knew it very well, and, indeed, showed in the same volume that he knew it. But there is no subject more effective than sex in creating separate compartments in the mind.

Then, Henry Allen does right in forgiving Emma for not loving him as much as Edward and in generously coming to her rescue in the end. Mr Barnard is not to blame for wanting to marry or for putting religion in a higher place than love. Emma in all her vagaries is trying to follow the true light. The result of all this conscientious behaviour is complete disaster. Froude seems to suggest that the consequences could not have been worse if everybody had acted with complete selfishness. Yet no alternative code of conduct is offered. The book ends very enigmatically, by giving some letters of Edward Fowler, written not long before his death. He has a great and terrible religious vision in Magdalen chapel. He feels excluded from heaven, not like the 'scorner, the voluptuous and the fool', because he could not taste its high pleasures, but as the penalty for heretical doctrines:

The vision past. I heard the priest's last blessing thrill around the heads of the favoured ones . . . the white worshippers past slowly out among the profane . . . They mingled in the crowd, and became like the crowd. Close by me one surpliced figure whispered under a deep overhanging bonnet. I caught the words – they were an assignation.[3]

I know of no other Victorian novel that ends in the least like this. But what does it mean? Does it mean that all high-flown feeling, both religious and romantic, is mistaken and sensible men know this, and use religion as they use the marriage customs of society and the facts of sex for their own advantage? Or does it mean that in a corrupt world the honest and pure are always doomed to fail, and be laughed at, and yet are right all the time? Perhaps Froude did not quite know himself, but in any case there can be no doubt of the extreme pessimism of his fable.

One other point is of interest. When Emma is about to marry the excellent clergyman, Barnard, who sincerely loves her, her physical revulsion is of an extreme intensity. It is comparable in its strength, though not in detailed analysis, with Sue Bridehead's revulsion from Phillotson. The man is young, healthy, and in no obvious way repulsive. One may be inclined to see in this a kind of nemesis. Perhaps the early Victorians were not inwardly convinced at all times of the truth of their own assumption that good women lacked carnal desire, even in marriage. Here it takes a negative form, that seems altogether excessive, as if the forbidden passion had returned to plague – not the girls themselves, who may have had feelings the novelists did not know or could not admit – but the romantic male. It is as if a feminine capacity for passion, vaguely sensed, issues in a terrifying version of its opposite.

The second novel, *The Lieutenant's Daughter*, has more obvious reasons for being anonymous. Like many eighteenth-century novels, but like very few of its own time in England, it contains a brothel scene. It is subversive and, arguably, cynical. The plot is one of the oldest stories in the world retold. A trusting, high-minded, passionate girl is seduced under promise of marriage, then abandoned, becomes promiscuous, despairs and kills herself. There are two unusual features, which, between them, show Froude's purpose to be entirely different from that of the many others in his time (including Mrs Gaskell and Trollope) who treated a similar theme, though with less gloomy endings. The first is that an alternative ending is provided. In the main story, Lieutenant Gray and his wife, the girl's parents, are dead before the story opens, and she throws herself histrionically on their graves before taking a dose of poison. In the second version, added as a brief but very telling and thought-provoking afterthought, her father lives a few years longer. Catherine had been married from her father's house, and is shown at the end as a happy wife and mother. Froude is saying that we gravely underrate the influence of luck not only in earthly destinies, but in moral choices. It is the last point that makes the book particularly subversive. Froude's contemporaries were very ready to admit that society treats the fallen woman unfairly, that the man, who usually escapes scot free, is really more to blame. They were not averse from a good deal of high-toned sentimentalism about raising the

Magdalen from the gutter. The meeting of Rose Maylie with Nancy in chapter XL of *Oliver Twist* may be taken as typical of the models from which Froude was, most deliberately, diverging.* The whole point of this tender scene depends on the assumption that the girls are utterly different, not only in their history and destiny, but in their nature. They meet by bridging a great gulf; and to bridge that gulf, even for a moment, is a kind of moral miracle. Froude asks the awkward question, 'Supposing Rose and Nancy were really much the same sort of girl, with a roughly similar equipment of conscience, self-control, passion, vanity and tenderness?' In that case the virtuous history of one, and vicious life of the other culminating in despair may be due to chance. But Froude's point is a dangerous half-truth. To say that all moral destinies are determined by luck alone is not only morally subversive, but opposed to the plain facts of experience. 'Tis one thing to be tempted, another thing to fall'. But there are times when a half-truth is salutary; they occur when the other half of the truth has been reiterated incessantly as if it were the whole truth. Froude knew very well that his respectable readers would not easily bear to be told that their wives and daughters were made of the same essential feminine stuff as Catherine Gray and Nancy. One cannot wonder at his choice of anonymity.

The second unusual feature is the telling of the story backwards. We begin with the suicide, go back to the seducer's desperate interview with the brothel madam, back to the promise of marriage, and the passionate, high-minded Shelleyan letters which show marriage to be an unnecessary formality in a relationship of perfect lifelong devotion and trust. At first sight, the tactics of story-telling seem strange; such an arrangement must tend to increase the reader's sense of inevitability which the alternative happy ending is designed to undermine. But that is precisely Froude's point. He presents us with two alternative sets of inevitable events, the difference being due simply to the different facts from which they start.

The other marked effect of the time-reversal is to accentuate the irony of the tremulous early love-passages, which come last in the actual narrative. Henry Carpenter, the seducer, writes to a friend long ecstatic letters in this vein:

* See quotation on pp. 20-21.

Our lips have touched each other; how long they hung there, God knows, I know not. It was but one thrilling moment of extacy.[4]

But the following is decidedly more interesting:

Catherine is a true child of passion, she has no idea of duty where she does not love, and no sacrifice is too great for her when she does; she has known her fellow creatures only to despise them, because she has only found heartlessness, when there was the greatest pretence of respectability; and it is easy to teach her that the forms of society, which men make so much fuss about, are but modes of legalized selfishness, built together upon the theory that all mankind are trying to over-reach each other . . . Love knows no law, because it fulfils all law.[5]

Here we have, perhaps only half-sincerely put forward, the idea of love as absolute value. It is not often, in reading nineteenth-century novels, that we are reminded of Rousseau. And, so far as Froude's own narrative goes, the strictures on the hypocrisy of the respectable are entirely justified. Carpenter's uncle odiously uses the threat of disinheritance to ensure Catherine's dismissal. The journalists who report her death speak with open cynicism of the pretences of virtue they have to observe in print.

But Froude is not merely pointing a lesson of feminine prudence, by saying that the girl who listens to Rousseauish outpourings may easily find herself deserted and lost. He is saying something much more interesting. He is drawing attention to the paradoxical similarity between Carpenter's two opposite attitudes. At first he was an ecstatic lover; he ends as a weary sensual cynic, anxious to get the girl off his hands at any cost. Both attitudes, Froude's story implies, are the same ultimately. They are merely different phases of feeling. In each a man makes his own desires into a law above all other law. Where there is no concept of fidelity, love becomes a mere sensation; and it is the nature of sensations to vary.

Taken together, Froude's two short novels are complementary in their gloomy verdict. If everyone acts for the best, as in *The Spirit's Trials*, disaster and misery follow. If everyone follows his inclinations, and treats moral principles with contempt, as in *The Lieutenant's Daughter*, the result is even worse. It is as if Froude had said to the public from behind his mask of anonymity, 'I will show you how hollow your sexual conventions, how unjust, how hypocritical, and unfitted to human nature; and I will show you at the same time that the alternatives are, if anything, worse.'

II *Emily Brontë*

It is a commonplace that Emily Brontë takes us into a world unknown to her contemporaries; there could be no more striking illustration of this than the facts that *Shadows of the Clouds* and *Wuthering Heights* were published in the same year, 1847. (Almost exactly contemporary, too, are *Vanity Fair* and *Dombey & Son*; the lot of the generalizer about the early Victorians is rather tougher than is sometimes realized.) Froude speaks only of society, its agreed conventions, and the consequences of accepting or rejecting them. We come now to Emily Brontë as the first of a group who attempted to penetrate to the heart of the mystery. My treatment of her will necessarily be sketchy and concentrate on the few points which are directly relevant.

All readers of *Wuthering Heights* are aware that the book presents two different kinds of love, the love between Heathcliff and Catherine, and the ordinary love of which the world knows as it goes about its business of marrying and giving in marriage. We need to ask, what is the nature of the love between Heathcliff and Catherine, and how in the end does the story value it in comparison with more ordinary feelings? Famous and familiar as they are, we need to look again at Catherine's crucial words to Nelly when she is contemplating marriage to Edgar Linton:

It would degrade me to marry Heathcliff now; so he shall never know how I love him: and that not because he's handsome, Nelly, but because he's more myself than I am. Whatever our souls are made of, his and mine are the same . . .

and a little later:

If all else perished, and *he* remained, *I* should still continue to be; and if all else remained, and he were annihilated, the universe would turn to a mighty stranger: I should not seem a part of it. My love for Linton is like the foliage in the woods: time will change it, I'm well aware, as winter changes the trees. My love for Heathcliff resembles the eternal rocks beneath: a source of little visible delight but necessary. Nelly, I *am* Heathcliff.[6]

Catherine is able to enter into two separate exclusive relationships. Her love for Heathcliff is not sexual, and does not conflict
with her love for her husband. At the same time it is far more
powerful than her love for her husband, just as, when the two
men confront each other in chapter XI, Heathcliff's superiority
is effortless. The husband has every advantage of law, custom,
property and position; and all Heathcliff can be brought to say is
that he is sorry he is not worth the trouble of knocking down.

But the love between Catherine and Heathcliff, though not
sexual, is not in the least ethereal either. It is a matter of intense
moment that they should be buried together, as if a kind of
mingling of bodies and souls, infinitely more complete and lasting
than any sexual union, will alone satisfy them. They are not
guided by any sense of duty, but neither are they governed by
a search for pleasure. Their identity is treated as if it were some
great natural law. To deny its reality, or attempt to thwart it,
is like trying to prevent the waters flowing to the sea. Before this
personal embodiment of natural law, society, morality, inclination, happiness must all give way.

Catherine is so sure of Heathcliff that she may well be thought
sincere, rather than slyly jealous, when she tries to dissuade her
sister-in-law, Isabella, from marrying him. When Isabella calls
her a 'dog in the manger' she replies:

> It is impossible you can covet the admiration of Heathcliff
> – that you consider him an agreeable person . . .

and, on being told by Isabella of the strength of her passion for
him,

> I wouldn't be you for a kingdom then . . . Nelly, help me to
> convince her of her madness. Tell her what Heathcliff is: an
> unreclaimed creature, without refinement, without cultivation:
> an arid wilderness of furze and whinstone . . . Pray, don't
> imagine that he conceals depths of benevolence and affection
> beneath a stern exterior! He's not a rough diamond – a pearl-
> containing oyster of a rustic: he's a fierce, pitiless, wolfish
> man.[7]

Naturally enough, Isabella regards all this as shameless hypocrisy. But we do not; because we are forced to take seriously
Catherine's statement that she is Heathcliff. No amount of self-
criticism or self-disgust can destroy self-love.

If we do take this idea seriously, what does it mean? The
nature of love, high and low, spiritual and sensual, constant

and inconstant, as known to all the authors treated in this book, is a reaching out to the other. And they agree, too, on the whole in showing self-love, self-absorption and loneliness as painful and constricting. Emily Brontë alone presents us with the paradox, that in its deepest and strongest form, this reaching out culminates in re-finding the self. And thus it is not surprising that it has many of the painful features of self-absorbed loneliness. It is tormenting, unchangeable, unavoidable, like the self. That one should be for a time on the hither and one on the far side of the barrier of death seems like a hideous anomaly that cannot last. Thus, the ghost, for all its pseudo-Gothic trappings becomes a perfectly serious metaphorical statement of the idea of unity of two personalities. We are reminded, perhaps, as each, living or dead, torments the other in the shared conviction that they are really indistinguishable, of Hopkins:

Selfyeast of spirit a dull dough sours. I see
The lost are like this, and their scourge to be
As I am mine, their sweating selves; but worse.

On the other hand, Heathcliff and Catherine are also unlike. Though their love is sexless, he is intensely masculine, she intensely feminine; and each is effortlessly attractive to members of the other sex. From one point of view, Heathcliff is an interloper in Wuthering Heights, the cuckoo in the nest, destined to dominate and oust the rightful heir. It is, so to speak, as a successful and tyrannical cuckoo that Lockwood first sees him as the story begins. But, in another sense, Heathcliff is Catherine's adoptive brother; their relationship is rooted in nursery memories. He came into the house so early that he cannot know from his own memory that he was not born there.

Incest between brother and sister is an idea of great power in nineteenth-century romanticism. It combines the forbidden and monstrous with the familiar and ordinary. It is a symbol of that search for origins, that glorification of childhood, that deep conviction that the familiar somehow contains the mysterious and transcendental which informs so much romantic literature. Are we to say that the relationship is, in all but name, incestuous? In one sense since it is sexless, it cannot be. But perhaps there is a subtler sense, too, in which the label does not fit. The sense of the unnatural, which usually pervades incest stories, is absent. Society's assumptions are evaded rather than challenged. A strange, child-like purity in the writing, even when violent and terrible things are to be recorded, is felt by all readers. Incest stories are as a rule either stories of a terrible doom, like the story of Oedipus, or stories of revolt. This is neither; and for a parallel, we may turn perhaps from literature to life – to Wordsworth's feeling for Dorothy, or Macaulay's for his sister. Yet these will only be rough parallels, since they lack the very important element of mutual torment.

What is the relation of all this to normal life? Had the novel been conceived as a pure glorification of a new kind of love, it might have ended soon after the death of the first Catherine. Instead, we have to watch Heathcliff's long revenge on the next generation. We find that his love for the dead Catherine inspires him with hatred and contempt for most others, for his wife Isabella, his son Linton, whom he uses as a senseless instrument of his dynastic ambitions, and his beloved Catherine's daughter. But a partial exception is young Hareton Earnshaw, whom he has kept in a state of ignorant dependence in the house of his fathers, now usurped by Heathcliff. Near the end, he says:

Five minutes ago, Hareton seemed a personification of my youth, not a human being.[8]

and he goes on to say that he is so obsessed with the dead Catherine that he cannot rouse himself to interest in the budding affection between Hareton and his cousin, her daughter, who eventually marry after Heathcliff's death. The younger Catherine, though kept in Heathcliff's house as a dependant, and almost a slave, after the death of her first husband, Heathcliff's son, yet speaks to him 'with a kind of dreary triumph' as she exults over his misery and loneliness.[9]

Hareton reminds Heathcliff of his early self, and the young Catherine cannot but remind him of her mother, however different his feelings towards her are. But, of course, there is the cardinal difference that Hareton is a normal man, for whom love will lead to marriage. In a certain sense there is a happy ending. The love of Heathcliff and the dead Catherine is consummated in the haunting and death of Heathcliff, followed by this union in burial upon which so much stress has always been laid. The abnormal thus removed, the normal takes over. The marriage of Hareton and young Catherine restores the property to the Earnshaw family and can be seen as the restitution of normality, social and sexual, to the scene. One may ask, is it right to call Emily Brontë a pessimist?

Yet there can be no real doubt of the answer. The young couple and normality have the last word, but it is far from being the most powerful or memorable word. Heathcliff and the first Catherine must remain central in the reader's mind. Their love is not only by its nature barren. It also leads both of them, and especially Heathcliff into a mania of destructiveness. The strongest love, in Emily Brontë's world, is a love without kindness or forbearance. The loved one's death, instead of inspiring regret and gentleness, inspires Heathcliff with feelings of hatred and revenge. Earlier, too, it incited him into a marriage of hatred. Heathcliff's son is begotten in hate on an abject and despised woman. The deeper love is not incompatible with marriage to others, but it is a wrecking force upon those marriages. Above all, Emily Brontë must be called a pessimist because at the end normal marriage, normal love are dwarfed – dwarfed by the memory of the tremendous things that have gone before. We are left with the impression that ordinary passion, ordinary marriage, ordinary fidelity are only half alive – their triumph is dreary. She is more pessimistic, really, than Froude. An ill-arranged world is preferable to a dead one.

III Swinburne

Swinburne was much given to superlatives in his literary criticism. In his essay on Emily Brontë* there is a special note, rather unusual in him, of admiration for moral purity. He speaks of her 'Christlike longsuffering and compassion'. The essay is not specific enough to tell us how he interpreted *Wuthering Heights*. But it is clear that he felt it as a work equally removed from conventional morality and from conventional revolt. There is a kind of surprised admiration that a novel of passion should be so far removed from sensuality. Perhaps (though this cannot be demonstrated) he was both puzzled and entranced by her power to adumbrate the incest-theme, and yet leave us in the end with something other. A fiery purity in the midst of passion was for Swinburne unattainable; but he could worship it from afar.

In Swinburne himself the love of brother and sister is unavoidable and insistent; and it is unequivocally sexual.

---

* A. C. Swinburne, *Miscellanies* (1886).

The first and less interesting of Swinburne's two novels, *Love's Cross-Currents* was published anonymously in 1877, and acknowledged in 1905. It is a neatly-plotted epistolary story, owing more to the French tradition than to *Clarissa*. The dominant personality, who appears again in the more powerful, unfinished *Lesbia Brandon*, is Lady Midhurst. She is a mask of what Swinburne in certain moods chose to fancy himself, but with his persistent, passionate weakness and naïvety, never was. She is old, bored, weary, cynical, and takes a delight in shocking the moralistic young. She has a certain family resemblance to those worldly early Victorian figures (Palmerston, for instance) who seemed left over from a more aristocratic, less upright eighteenth-century world. 'As to being in love,' she writes, 'frankly, I don't believe in it. I believe that stimulant drinks will intoxicate, and rain drench, and fire singe; but not in any way that one person will fascinate another.' And later in the same letter: 'I hate the very word "sentiment". The animalist and the moralist I can appreciate.'[10]

In *Lesbia Brandon*,* this cynical note is secondary; dominant is a medley of confused torments and ecstacies, incestuous, masochistic and lesbian. A tone of lyrical joy runs through it all, even the most sombre passages, as if the normal and the conventional, who make terms with the world and even enjoy it, were infinitely pitiable to these proud, tortured spirits.

The most tiresome part of the book, of course, is that devoted to flogging fantasies. But one must concede that these were so perpetually present to the author's mind, that they would never be excluded from a lengthy piece, except when the author was on his best behaviour before the public. And, tedious and perverted as they undoubtedly are, it is perhaps not sophistical to find in them some shadowy positive value. The really disturbing feature of Swinburne's work, and what distinguished this novel from pornography, is his ability to convey sensuality as something affecting the whole personality; and this despite some languorous romantic pessimism. Pain cannot but be felt; for Swinburne, dreamy and full of illusions and megalomaniac fantasies, it was at times an anchor to reality.

---

* Apparently written in the 1860s, the imagined time being 1850–2. Published in 1952, with a thorough textual analysis by Randolph Hughes. Introduction and notes, though exceedingly scornful and unbalanced, are helpful to the understanding of a text full of lacunae and never properly revised.

Herbert, the hero, placed as the young Swinburne was, in an aristocratic milieu, and a wild Northumbrian landscape dominated by the sea, is passionately devoted to his much older married sister, Lady Wariston. His tutor, Denham, is in love with her, resents his love, and tries to exorcize it by flogging the boy. Herbert hardly needs the flogging to encourage him in a higher, more romantic, incestuous masochism. To his sister he talks like this:

> Oh! I should like you to tread me to death! darling! . . .
>
> I wish you would kill me some day; it would be jolly to feel you killing me. Not like it? shouldn't I! You just hurt me, and see.[11]

Then she pinches him until he 'laughed and panted with pleasure'. In the enigmatic fifteenth chapter *Via Dolorosa*, in which no names are used, but only pronouns, it seems that Denham and Lady Wariston have become lovers, and also, by some odd trick of plot that cannot be taken seriously, that they too turn out to be brother and sister. Swinburne, imagining his own masochistic temperament transposed to a woman enjoying an incestuous orgasm, is a formidable conception; and formidable too is the prose he produces for the occasion:

> The horror of her sudden want and intense love seemed to beat upon her nerves, and inflict rapid running strokes or cuts of conscious sorrow. Now dulled and now sharpened, her sense of grief seemed to come and go as in a fierce fluctuation of soul. The whole vision of her spirit was broken and blinded by pain . . . She lusted after death with the violent desire underlying violent fear . . .[12]

and much more.

But it is characteristic of Swinburne, as of so many immoralists and antinomians, to make his moral disapprovals all the more intense for having limited their scope, and rejected so many agreed moral positions. Here his satire is reserved for Linley, Lady Wariston's uncle by marriage. At first, this is a little surprising, since his cynicism seems similar to that of Lady Midhurst, who is almost regarded as an oracle. But there is a difference. Instead of Lady Midhurst's weariness, there is a definite cruelty behind Linley's mask. Urging Denham to flog Herbert, we find:

> His eyes devoured the boy's drawn face and twisted hands; he seemed to inhale his pain and shame like a fine and pungent

essence; he laughed with pleasure as he saw how the words burnt and stung.[13]

It is Linley who arranges, and presides over, a scene in which a courtesan, with 'a hard dry smile, compound of conscious fun and repellent lust',[14] fails in an attempt to seduce Herbert. Swinburne approaches the subject gingerly and with obvious distaste. There is a strong contrast between the boy's innocent chivalry, his half-developed, half-understood sexual desires, and a world of dead lust and cynicism. The chapter, alone in the book, is not greatly different from a similar scene in Thackeray. It is startling to remind ourselves that the implied contrast here is far other. Where Thackeray would be setting sterile lust against the innocence and fruitfulness of family life, Swinburne's version of innocence is a compound of masochism, flagellation, incest and romantic death-wish. Swinburne in his way (and we see this too in his literary criticism) was a great moralist. The instinct to moralize is quite as difficult to control, and as impossible to extirpate, as the sexual instinct:

Naturam expellas furca, tamen usque recurret.

But Herbert has another and stronger love than his love for his sister, his love for Lesbia, the name which Swinburne, with less than his usual tact and subtlety, chose for his lesbian heroine. The plot is so arranged that when Lesbia first sees Herbert, he is dressed as a girl for some amateur theatricals. When she is dying she refers again to this moment and says:

> I should like to see you as you were that first time. You couldn't go and dress up now, though I have seen women with as much hair about the lips. I should like to die acting: I've heard of people dying on the stage.[15]

Just before this Herbert says:

> 'Lesbia – my dearest and first love in the world – if you could love me at last – you need not die at once surely – and I will go with you – Oh, only try to love me for five minutes.'

(*Love* is here, presumably, a euphemism.)

> . . . but as his arms fastened upon her she broke from him sideways, trembling terribly, with widened eyes and repellent hands.

> 'No, no, Herbert! Let me go! let me die! will you?' There was a savage terror in her voice and gesture.

and she goes on to speak of her 'repentance' for her birth. When

she tells him of his physical likeness to his beloved sister, and
thus excites him once again to a dangerous level of passion, she
warns:

'No, not again; when I am dead if you like.'

All this is neatly emblematic of Swinburnian pessimism at its
most intense. The only two moments when the girl he so much
loved could have tolerated his approach were – when he was
disguised, and when she was dead. We are not, however, led to
suppose that Herbert is actually capable of violating a corpse.
His masochism can be, and at times is, transposed into a high
sacrificial key. Offering his life for hers, he says:

I know it's not worth taking, but it might be worth giving –
though it's not worth keeping either.

In a few passages like this Swinburne attains to a pure and
simple eloquence, reminiscent of the finest moments of his
beloved Jacobean dramatists. He was, after all, a very much better
writer of prose than he was a poet.

In the earlier chapter, entitled *On the Downs* when Herbert
makes his declaration of love for Lesbia, he offers to die for her,
in a manly, knightly way (rather than a masochistic way) though
in Herbert, as in Swinburne himself, the two impulses cannot be
entirely separated. It is then that Lesbia makes a reply which is
perhaps the most ironical in the whole canon of Victorian love-
literature:

I don't know if you would like it or not, but I should like to
feel thoroughly that we were not less than brother and sister.[16]

How many correct young ladies in how many thousand novels,
good, bad and indifferent, made just that reply. But Lesbia, a
stranger as it were in Swinburne's world (for her creator obviously
finds lesbianism impossible to imagine) does not know what she
is saying. She is speaking as if she were in Trollope's world, or
in the ordinary world of most of us, in which the relation of
brother and sister is the least carnal of all kinds of affection
between people of different sex. But she is not; she is in a world
where the relation of brother and sister is the most carnal,
tormented and deadly of all. But Herbert is an Etonian* and a
perfect gentleman, and he does not draw attention to her mistake.

One thing that will certainly surprise readers who come fresh

---

* Almost all the male characters in Swinburne's novels, except servants, were
educated at Eton, like himself. Perhaps Wodehouse is not the first author that

to Swinburne as a novelist, knowing him only as a poet, is the convincing social milieu in which these bizarre torments find their setting. It is a very narrow aristocratic world, contemptuous or unaware of the life of unknown compatriots. But it has a surprising solidity; Swinburne is in this like his great contemporaries, Dickens, Trollope, Mrs Gaskell, just as much as he is unlike them in his sensations and moral concepts.

But we may ask, why, if he knew little and understood less of the lesbian condition, did he choose to endow his heroine with it? Because he had a fellow-feeling for all sorts and conditions of those outside the ranks of respectability. His work combines a strong social conservatism with a bitter contempt for traditional moralities. He was fond of talking of de Sade as 'the divine Marquis' and took pleasure in the fact that the most subversive of all writers on sexual questions was an aristocrat too. And he could find a link between his social conservatism and his moral revolt. Both were equally opposed to the respectable, liberal, progressive, middle-class men of the sixties whom (from such very different points of view) Ruskin and Arnold castigated. Defeat, being halfway to death, had a lasting appeal, and he had a tenderness for his family's Jacobite traditions quite as strong as his admiration for Italian nationalists, revolutionaries and anarchists.

Puerile, perverted, disgusting and grossly inconsistent in argument – Swinburne is all these. Yet in a curious way, he demands to be taken seriously for two reasons, because his fantasies spring from his depths of his being, and are never just amusements, and because a strange beauty mingles both with the absurdity and the horror.

IV *Thomas Hardy*

Hardy's tone, we know, varies. Perhaps the most difficult question that can be asked about him (and one of the most important) is this: do his ideas vary with his tone? Is he, fundamentally, saying the same thing in the semi-pastoral of *Far From the Madding Crowd*, as in *Tess* and *Jude*? Is the effect on him of the changes in

---

comes to mind as a parallel to Swinburne. But he is a bit like the Wodehouse character who said (I quote from memory, and no doubt inaccurately): 'Genghis Khan? never heard of him – Harrow man, I expect.'

his personal experience between 1874 and 1895 deep enough to cause a revolution in his thinking on the relation of the sexes? In an attempt to answer, I shall dwell especially on the earliest and the latest of his major works, since, by common consent, the first, *Far From the Madding Crowd* is the most cheerful, and the last, *Jude*, is the most sombre.

The rather vague term, semi-pastoral, which has just been used is intended to suggest the contrast of which every reader is aware in *Far From the Madding Crowd*. There is a strong sense of the richness of country life and its satisfactions, yet the book is full of setbacks and disasters. Gabriel Oak is an archetypal shepherd, whose love endures through all vicissitudes, yet his response to his first impression of Bathsheba's charm reminds us more of Mr Guppy than of Theocritus – he drenches his dry, sandy hair in hair-oil. Graceful traditions, like the sending of valentines, end in violence and madness. Bathsheba is both naïve and coquettish.

Reading with the hindsight denied to the first readers, we can easily find light-hearted adumbrations of themes later to be tragic. This is how Hardy introduces us to the idea that the marriage-bond kills love by commanding it to endure:

'Coggan,' he said, 'I could never wish for a handsomer woman than I've got, but feeling she's ticketed as my lawful wife, I can't help my wicked heart wandering, do what I will.' But at last I believe he cured it by making her take off her wedding-ring and calling her by her maiden name as they sat together after the shop was shut, and so a' would get to fancy she was only his sweetheart and not married to him at all. And as soon as he could thoroughly fancy he was doing wrong and committing the seventh, a' got to like her as well as ever, and they lived on a perfect picture of mutel love.[17]

Yet, of course, there is more than a difference of tone between this and anything in *Jude*. The comic point here lies in man's sly power of adjustment of his wayward, wilful nature to the moral requirements of society. Here, no one stops to wonder what happens when the adjustment is beyond people's strength.

Before Troy appears on the scene, we have got to know Bathsheba. The interesting and unusual thing about her, for the readers of the 1870s, was that she was an independent, modern woman, entirely her own mistress, confidently giving orders to men, and yet remote from all feminist issues of the time. She might come under moral criticism, but it would certainly be criticism of a traditional kind. She could be called 'forward', 'capricious', 'unreasonable', 'vain'. She could not be supposed by anyone to be unfeminine. With unconscious cleverness she blends the role of the woman in charge of a business, giving orders and paying wages, with an old-fashioned feminine 'imperiousness' more like that of the 'cruel fair' of the seventeenth-century poets. Like them she is commanding to men, not because she is really independent of them, but because she feels she would be nothing without them, and had better make the most of the brief opportunities granted by youth and beauty. Until Troy appears, she betrays a touch of surprise that strong men can be so obedient to a woman's caprice and so easily cowed by her displeasure.

The power of the scenes describing her encounter with Troy springs from a happy blending of three different modes of writing. Hardy is at the same time particular, general and symbolical. He is particular, since Bathsheba has attained the status of a full feminine portrait, and general since Troy is not a true portrait, but a typical masculine presence, felt by the woman as answering to her yearning to submit. It is symbolical, perhaps almost by accident, since Troy's military accoutrements, the spur and the sword, become types of masculine dominance, and hence by implication, of feminine submissiveness.

Troy and Bathsheba meet on a narrow path at night:

. . . a figure was apparently on the point of gliding past her when something tugged at her skirt and pinned it forcibly to the ground. The instantaneous check nearly threw Bathsheba off her balance. In recovering she struck against warm clothes and buttons.

'A rum start, upon my soul!' said a masculine voice, a foot or so above her head. 'Have I hurt you, mate?'

'No,' said Bathsheba, attempting to shrink away.

'We have got hitched together somehow, I think.'

'Yes.'

'Are you a woman?'

'Yes.'

'A lady, I should have said.'

'It doesn't matter.'

'I am a man.'

'Oh!'[18]

In that brief passage of dialogue is contained much of their subsequent story, and much of Hardy's general thinking about men and women. 'We have got hitched together somehow' is a wry epitome of the way these two (and people in general in Hardy's world) blindly marry in the dark of passion and thoughtlessness, at the bidding of chance. The spur is an emblem of power and control with a secondary suggestion of cruelty. But this suggestion is in the background, since it is the lady's dress, through which she cannot feel pain, which is held by the spur. This cannot, however, obliterate altogether the ordinary associations of spurs. The idea of a woman as ridden and mastered like a horse, and able to be wounded by a mere movement of a man's muscles, is lurking near the reader's mind, neither definitely summoned, nor firmly dismissed.

The last part of the exchange is an extraordinary neat and economical comment on a parallel and an antithesis to which Hardy's contemporaries among novelists devoted many long chapters. Gentleman: lady = man: woman or, alternatively, gentleman: man = lady: woman. There was much discussion about the problem of defining a gentleman, a word which in the eighteenth century had seemed so definite in meaning.* But it was not, as a rule, in dispute, that, if one did succeed in defining *gentleman*, or, if perhaps that was unfortunately impossible, in learning how to recognize one, one had *ipso facto* solved the problem of the lady. Thus Trollope often admits his inability to define the words, but says, in effect, 'We may not be able to define a horse, but we all know one when we see one.' He and his readers would have found it distinctly odd to be told that defining, or recognizing, a mare was somehow a different kind of problem from defining or recognizing a stallion.

This little chapter of social history – one with which novelists of the time were especially preoccupied – needs to be remembered, to understand the impact of these few telling words. The absence of the usual fourth term in the equation, the word *gentleman*, is here an indication of the irrelevance of class differences to male dominion. Because he is a *male*, lady and woman will be all the

---

* The *Gentleman's Magazine* was founded in 1731, and continued throughout the nineteenth century. It seems likely that by Victoria's time, when the worry about gentlemanliness became acute, the name was too much a venerable, customary one to be found offensive. But a magazine so called could hardly have *begun* in the Victorian period, without appearing provocative.

same. In the face of a man able and willing to dominate, both her position as mistress of the farm and her capricious imperiousness become altogether powerless.

This is soon followed by the swordflash scene, and before it comes its significance is underlined by anticipation. Bathsheba says: 'if you only fight half as winningly as you can talk, you are able to make a pleasure of a bayonet wound.'[19] Troy's sword cuts the air all round her still form, and finally cuts off a lock of hair, but there are no wounds. Instead, in one of the most eloquent passages Hardy ever wrote, we are given a strong visual image of female surrender:

In an instant the atmosphere was transformed to Bathsheba's eyes. Beams of light caught from the low sun's rays, above, around, in front of her, well-nigh shut out earth and heaven – all emitted in the marvellous evolutions of Troy's reflecting blade, which seemed everywhere at once, and yet nowhere specially. These circling gleams were accompanied by a keen rush that was almost a whistling – also springing from all sides of her at once. In short she was enclosed in a firmament of light, and of sharp hisses, resembling a sky-full of meteors close at hand.[20]

Reading this, we are not inclined to restrict its application to these two; it reads like a general statement on sexual roles, one in which polarity of male and female is emphasized as much as possible and similarities are forgotten or denied.

And this polarity is so complete that personality is forgotten too, merged in masculinity and femininity. Naturally, this cannot last; in the next important episode, they become, once again, distinct personalities, each with a history, and with mixed, but intelligible motives. The story of the death of Fanny Robin, and of her child, who is also Troy's, is impressive in establishing the unexpectedness of known characters. Hardy achieves the kind of surprise that we sometimes feel about people we know well, when we say 'I would never have thought he would have done that, but I see now it was in character.'

When Fanny Robin is to be buried, Gabriel Oak tries to protect Bathsheba from the knowledge that her dead child is enclosed in the same coffin. A powerful pathos is developed through the incongruities of the situation, as those responsible for delivering the coffin to its resting-place delay for the pleasures of drinking. There is poignancy in the casual identifying scrawl

on the coffin-lid, *Fanny Robin and child*. Out of tenderness for
Bathsheba's feelings, Oak alters this, rubbing out the last two
words written in chalk, with his handkerchief.

This leads on to the chapter grimly headed *Fanny's Revenge*.
Bathsheba, maddened by doubt and suspicion, opens the coffin
and sees the dead baby, and also recognizes the likeness of the
dead mother's hair to the lock treasured by her own husband,
Troy. As she is inwardly debating whether she really hates the
dead woman, Troy enters:

> He sank upon his knees with an indefinable union of
> remorse and reverence upon his face, and, bending over
> Fanny Robin, gently kissed her, as one would kiss an infant
> asleep to avoid awakening it.

> At the sight and sound of that, to her, unendurable act,
> Bathsheba sprang towards him . . . The revulsion from her
> indignant mood a little earlier, when she had meditated upon
> compromised honour, forestalment, eclipse in maternity by
> another, was violent and entire. All that was forgotten in the
> simple and still strong attachment of wife to husband . . .
> She flung her arms round Troy's neck, exclaiming wildly from
> the deepest deep of her heart –

> 'Don't – don't kiss them! Oh, Frank, I can't bear it – I
> can't! I love you better than she did: kiss me too, Frank –
> kiss me! *You will, Frank, kiss me too!*'[21]

Hardy's comment is simple and uncompromising: it was a
'revelation of all women being alike at heart'. The macabre
kissing-scene is the dramatic equivalent of what is conveyed
symbolically by the swordflash scene, woman's sexual role is
to submit. The more she is crushed and humiliated, the stronger
will be her appetite for more submission. Differences of rank and
circumstances, of prosperity, even deeper differences of personality will be revealed at the crisis as superficial only. A woman
is always a woman, and knows her master. Troy brutally under-
lines the lesson for us by refusing to kiss her, by telling her that
Fanny dead is more to him than she is or has been or can
be, and by apostrophizing the dead woman as 'darling' and
'wife'.

These last scenes figure strongly in T. S. Eliot's *After Strange
Gods*, supporting the indictment that Hardy was deliberately
morbid, and satisfying perverse emotions of his own rather than
tracing the real history and feeling of his characters. Morbid or

not, the message is certainly simplistic, and one may be inclined
to ask whether the doctrine that all women are alike is not a
simple logical muddle. Naturally, all women are alike in that
which makes them women; and all men in that which makes
them men. But just as some men, faced with the strange situation
which confronted Troy, would have behaved quite differently,
with tenderness or self-reproach or horror, so, it seems fair to
suggest, would some women have behaved quite differently
from Bathsheba, with anger, hysterical or controlled, with
feigned indifference, with contempt.

But it seems to me that a few chapters later Hardy goes far to
defend himself against Eliot's charge, and at the same time to
throw doubt on his own generalization that woman are all the
same. Alone, deserted by Troy, who is now believed to be dead,
she opens the case of his watch, which contains the lock of
Fanny's hair:

'He was hers and she was his; they should be gone together,'
she said. 'I am nothing to either of them, and why should
I keep her hair?' She took it in her hand, and held it over the
fire. 'No – I'll not burn it – I'll keep it in memory of her,
poor thing!' she added, snatching back her hand.[22]

The surprise we feel here is salutary. The utter oppositeness
of male and female has been stressed throughout. Here we
suddenly move into another realm, one of creative generosity.
Bathsheba is still feminine, and still recognizably in character.
But without forfeiting that, she has reached a place where 'there
is neither male nor female', where forgiveness is blest and
charity is triumphant. To assert the polarity of sex as powerfully,
imaginatively and memorably as Hardy has throughout, and
especially in the swordflash scene, and then to assert, just as
memorably, a deeper level of the soul whose moral grandeur is
essentially human, and as some, unlike Hardy himself, would
say, divine in its origin – this is magnificent, and not morbid
at all. One can only regret that the melodramatic ending blurs
the effect.

At all stages, Bathsheba's history is told by an author oblivious
of all feminist arguments. *Qua* woman, she is predictably like all
other women, yearning, pleading, submissive, even masochistic.
In her great moment, when she treasures Fanny's hair, she is
beyond all sexual differences, acting as Man, *homo*, not as man
or woman.

This leads on to the case of Marty South in *The Woodlanders* (1887). In a book full of flirtations, passions of varying degrees of egoism and carnality, she stands alone. Her love for Giles is sexual, certainly, in the sense that it is essentially the love of a woman for a man. But Hardy takes care to separate it from all other passions by assimilating it to love that is not sexual but filial. There are two moments of sad dignity and repose in Marty's life. In each she is mourning for the dead; in the first, silently for her father, in the second, with eloquent words for her lost love, Giles Winterborne:

... when the moon arrived opposite the window, its beams streamed across the still profile of South, sublimed by the august presence of death, and onward a few feet further upon the face of his daughter, lying in her little bed in the silence of a repose almost as dignified as that of her companion – the repose of a guileless soul that had nothing more left on earth to lose, except a life which she did not over-value.[23]

Long after, when Giles is dead, and the woman he preferred to Marty has forgotten him in another man's arms, this passage is recalled:

... she entered the churchyard, going to a secluded corner behind the bushes, where rose the unadorned stone that marked the last bed of Giles Winterborne. As this solitary and silent girl stood there in the moonlight, a straight slim figure, clothed in a plaitless gown, the contours of womanhood so undeveloped as to be scarcely perceptible in her, the marks of poverty and toil effaced by the misty hour, she touched sublimity at points, and looked almost like a being who had rejected with indifference the attribute of sex for the loftier quality of abstract humanism.[24]

It is a pity that Hardy marred this fine passage with the phrase 'abstract humanism' – one of his occasional touches of auto-didactic pretentiousness, which, in this case, does not even convey the meaning he certainly intended. What he means is something much less chilly, simply charity, a love generous and self-forgetful. But the implications are none the less clear, especially if we bear in mind the contrast with Bathsheba's passionate abasement before Troy in the presence of Fanny Robin's corpse. In order to become unselfish and truly generous, love, for Hardy, must almost cease to be sexual. It must be essentially like filial love. Marty's love is simple, enduring, impervious to change. Sex, in Hardy's world, is inescapably self-regarding. Passionate feminine abasement is as much so, in its way, as the predatoriness and inconstancy of the male. The most startling statement of this view comes when the kind, gentle Tess, whose love for Angel Clare seemed so pure and generous, actually commits a murder in order to achieve her return to him. Venus is a cruel goddess, even in the case of the 'pure woman'. Marty stands apart; she has escaped the clutches of the cruel goddess by 'rejecting with indifference the attribute of sex'. And Giles, the man she loves, perhaps approaches her pinnacle of generosity in the unselfishness of his love for another woman.

The sadness of Marty (and Giles) is in a sense one of the least sad things in Hardy's work. Hardy's worst fear, as can be clearly seen in some of his poems, was not that life was painful (though his sensibility to this fact was exceptionally acute) but rather that it might be meaningless. Marty's grief is self-justifying; it has value in itself. It is also one-sided. No happy, mutual love, either erotic or affectionate, exists in Hardy's work to embody a similar positive value. For Hardy sexual love and moral sublimity are almost strangers; and Marty South has to abandon the turmoils of the one before she can fully attain to the other.

II

Jude the Obscure is a by-word for pessimism; and so it is important to observe that it contains several different kinds of pessimism. The first kind is a permanent feature of Hardy's work, and might be called ballad-pessimism, the experienced countryman's wry corrective to idyllic dreams of the country:

Every inch of ground had been the site, first or last, of energy, gaiety, horseplay, bickerings, weariness. Groups of gleaners had squatted in the sun on every square yard. Love-matches that had populated the adjoining hamlet had been made up between reaping and carrying. Under the hedge which divided the field from a distant plantation girls had given themselves to lovers who would not turn their heads to look at them by the next harvest; and in that ancient corn-field many a man had made love-promises to a woman at whose voice he had trembled by the next seed-time after fulfilling them in the church adjoining.[25]

The second pessimism, perhaps the least convincing one, might be called the pseudo-Greek. There are vague mutterings about a family curse affecting both Fawleys and Brideheads, so that in each generation marriages are unhappy. The idea is never developed or explained, and it really amounts to little more than a desultory justification for some of the more unlikely strokes of bad luck the characters suffer.

The third pessimism might be called social-critical. Hardy attacks, more fiercely than in earlier works, the assumptions of society, the law and the customs of marriage. To do this, he makes a neat reversal of some time-honoured literary conventions. As we have seen, frankness about sexual desire and action had tended to omit marriage. Marriage had to do with 'love', and 'love' came to seem far removed from sexual satisfaction. One could read a lot of novels by Hardy's immediate predecessors, and be led to suppose that sexual desire, even sexual awareness, was something shared out between men and immodest women. Good girls and good wives were exempt. Hardy sets out to undermine these assumptions – which like many very influential assumptions in all periods, were all the more influential for being unstated, and so impervious to rational criticism – by a simple and effective device. He makes the lawful wife, Arabella, full-blooded, fleshy and philistine. He makes the mistress, Sue, ethereal, intellectual and apt to dismiss the realities of sex as crudely animal. And he does this, as he does many things in a book dominated by anger and tending to shrillness, with a heavy hand, associating Arabella from the first with pigs' flesh, provocatively thrown at Jude as he is thinking high thoughts of scholarship and divinity. More, he carries the reversal of literary assumptions into the next generation; instead of bastard Edmund and legitimate Edgar, we have the misshapen, and ultimately murderous and suicidal Time, as legitimate issue, while the illegitimate are innocent victims.

Arabella traps Jude into marriage by a seductive trick, followed by a lie about a non-existent pregnancy. It is Arabella, not Sue who recalls Fielding's Molly Seagrim and Mrs Waters. To a certain extent, all this is telling. The law that wives should be less carnal than mistresses, and illegitimate children morally inferior to legitimate is a law of literary convention, not a law of nature; and an author has a right to subvert such laws. But there are two points that Hardy did not sufficiently consider.

Jude's troubles spring not from following accepted moral principles, but from mixing incompatibles. Had he been chaste, Arabella could not have deceived him into marriage. Had he been a carefree disciple of the wild oats school, her trick would likewise have failed. That Jude should be inconsistent, influenced by lust, by credulity, by a wish to be decent, is credible enough. But Hardy is illogical in attempting to lay blame for the sad consequences of these manifest inconsistencies upon any of the principles which Jude has confused and muddled. If a man is uncertain whether he is threatened by sunstroke, or rain, or snow and ice, and sets out on a journey prepared for all three, he has only himself to blame if he finds his equipment burdensome, or even faints under the weight. But it would not be fair to deduce from this that heavy overcoats do not protect from cold or parasols from sun.

The other point is less obvious. Hardy is more bound than he knows by the convention he is attacking. Arabella's carnality is treated as repulsive. It is not always easy to disentangle the different principles by which she is condemned; but it is clear that dishonesty in tricking Jude into marriage mingles in Hardy's mind with considerations that lack the same moral force. Her open sexual invitation to Jude,[26] of wife to husband, is clearly regarded as an obscenity. Yet, it could well be argued that since marriage is a sexual relationship, Arabella, for all her vices, her lying and coarse insensitiveness, is more in harmony with the spirit of marriage *in this respect* than her rival Sue is. Hardy's argument tends to rebound upon himself. He conceives himself to be showing that marriage is a fraud, since wives may be coarsely physical and sexually provocative. Actually, he is showing that he himself is really very like the literary predecessors he is supposed to be refuting. Like them, he finds it shocking that a wife should have the slightest interest in sex.

Now we come to a type of pessimism which Hardy was the first to voice, and which has an abiding interest. The character and destiny of Sue is Hardy's bitter, intelligent and intensely personal reaction to the fashionable ideas of the nineties about the 'New Woman'. He was quick to form his opinions here, and Sue may be regarded, in part, as presenting a comment on the optimists discussed in the next chapter. There is overlapping in time here; some readers must have read Hardy's refutation of the new ideas before being fully aware of them. One book in particular, published in the same year as *Jude*, and probably not one which Hardy had in mind, may be used as typical of a whole current of new ideas. This is Grant Allen's *The Woman Who Did*. Here we have a young woman, handsome, well-educated, sincere, affectionate and constant, who refuses to marry the man she loves and is free to marry, simply from a preference for free union (conceived to be as solemn and permanent as marriage.) Herminia, in everything except her opinions, is very near to the Victorian ideal womanly type. She is thoroughly maternal, inexorably proper, and prone to blush at the slightest indecency. She treats a proposal of marriage as her predecessors in the high Victorian tradition would have treated an immodest suggestion:

'How soon may we be married?'

At the sound of these unexpected words from such lips as his, a flush of shame and horror overspread Herminia's cheeks. 'Never,' she cried firmly.[27]

Respectability is treated as a 'leprous taint', and the marriage service of the Church of England is accused of 'shameful indecorousness' and treated as a terrible threat to the modesty and purity of English girls. But, at the same time, Herminia is unlike her fictional predecessors in preaching a frank sexual enjoyment, for women as for men. But promiscuity and loveless intercourse are most severely reproved; Herminia's aim is to be a highly moral, frankly enjoying, passionately loving, monogamous mistress.

In some ways Sue is very like this, with the important proviso that a complex being like Sue cannot be wholly like a simple one. She has a similar sense of quasi-religious awe about the supposed joys of sexual union, and the same dislike of the marriage ceremony. ('Somebody *gives* me to him, like a she-ass or she-goat')[28]

But she is much more aware than Herminia of dark and primitive forces. She turns to Greek paganism, just as Swinburne had done, to buttress her rejection of Christianity. To some extent she is aware of the divisions and contradictions in her nature and in her theories. She likes to present herself as a new woman, yet claims to be 'more ancient than mediaevalism'. Her statue of Venus, which she worships secretly, is more than a symbol. It has a fetishistic quality for her. And gradually we come to see why. She has taken the Christian ideas of mortification and self-discipline, and transferred them to the service of her pagan deity.

Just as many a Christian through the centuries has felt a conflict between his sexual desires and his belief in chastity as a religious duty, so does Sue feel a conflict between her belief in the flesh, and her instinctive distaste for it. Admittedly, she finds sexual intercourse with Jude more tolerable than it had been in her marriage to Phillotson. But this is only a matter of degree. She can never be self-forgetfully carnal, as her paganized conscience tells her she should be.

Or rather one part of it does; for she is simultaneously under the influence of quite a different current of ideas, stemming from feminist writers like J. S. Mill. In this vein, she regards sex differences as unimportant, talks of Venus Urania (a spiritualized deity of intellectual companionship), and speaks scornfully of the philosophy of the respectable world as recognizing only 'relations based on animal desire'. In her strange correspondence with her husband, when she is pleading to be allowed to separate from him, the contrasts of her nature are well shown. For a time she writes, with copious quotations, like an excessively priggish, blue-stocking disciple of the high Victorian agnostic tradition. Suddenly her urgent personal fears break in, and she expresses the wish that sex did not exist and that the world could have been peopled by 'some harmless mode of vegetation'.

There is, however, one thread of consistency in Sue's contradictions. She is always in some sense a feminist. Whether she is devotedly praising the joys of a carnal passion from which her own instincts rebel, or attacking the marriage bond, or speaking of a rarefied, intellectual companionship between people of different sex, she is constant to her theme of the slights and wrongs immemorially endured by women, and in her claim that they are equal to men. This is a claim that Hardy cannot admit. Here is his description of the dormitory in the Training School at Melchester:

 . . . they all lay in their cubicles, their tender feminine faces upturned to the flaring gas-jets which at intervals stretched down the long dormitories, every face bearing the legend 'The Weaker' upon it, as the penalty of the sex wherein they were moulded, which by no possible exertion of their willing hearts and abilities could be made strong while the inexorable laws of nature remain what they are.[29]

Hardy decisively rejects the whole feminist argument of the preceding generation, which was the soil for the growth of the idea of the 'New Woman' à la Havelock Ellis and Grant Allen; and this is his final word on the matter. The feminists saw the natural disabilities as trivial compared with those caused by bad traditions and false theories. Hardy reversed this, and he did so feelingly. The phrase 'inexorable laws of nature' was no cliché for him. It represented the slowly-garnered fruits of his deepest meditations on life. It was an epitome of what found full imaginative expression in memorable descriptions, like that of Egdon Heath.* The attempt to turn Hardy into a feminist is altogether vain.

It is not merely deliberate statements like this one that undermine Sue's feminist position. More cunningly, Hardy shows that beneath a veneer of new ideas, and old, rebellious pagan ones revived, Sue is not the New Woman at all, but the Old in disguise. Her sexless coquettish style is as tantalizing and self-centred as the most obvious provocation. Even Jude, who is slow to understand, comes to see that she is jealous of Arabella, and will yield her body to him if he pretends to more interest in Arabella than he really feels. His comment 'Jealous little Sue! I withdraw all remarks about your sexlessness' clearly carries the author's endorsement.

La Rochefoucauld said that women did not understand their own coquetry. Sue's whole treatment of Jude might have been invented to illustrate this saying. The austere feminist doctrines of Mill and the sickly pseudo-pagan deliriums of Swinburne become new weapons in the old game, the game of provoking male interest and desire by refusal. And in case we should miss the point, Hardy has an impartial observer describe her as 'a little hussy' and 'a tantalizing, capricious little woman'.[30]

What are we to make then of Sue's last phase, when under the influence of the shock of finding her children murdered, she returns to Phillotson, her original and lawful husband, though her fear of his caresses is stronger than her fear of spiders? This certainly does not seem to be the act of a heartless and teasing flirt. Nor is it. Hardy's conception of her character includes this but it includes much more. Bathsheba, too, could be a teasing flirt, and yet she was reduced to the abasement of begging for a kiss that was denied her and given only to the dead. Hardy tends to see feminine nature in layers. The flirtatious and provocative

* *The Return of the Native*, chap. I.

is a superficial layer, which is fully in evidence only in a civilized setting when men agree to play the woman's game. Beneath, in all Hardy's women potentially, and in many actually, is an irrational and passionate animal force. It turns Tess into a murderess, Bathsheba into a humiliated slave, and Sue into a creature embracing what is most horrible to her at the bidding of a superstitious guilt.*

Hardy was never likely to go very far along the path marked out by Havelock Ellis and the optimists of the next chapter. However much he sympathized with their criticism of marriage laws and traditional moral views, he disagreed fundamentally with their contention that natural forces are beneficent, and will lead us to happiness if we passively follow them. But the ferocity of his reaction is nevertheless surprising. He combines the idea that 'all women are alike at heart' with an indictment of the new ideas for making them worse. It is something like a secular variant of Sancho Panza's 'Man is as God made him and often a great deal worse.' Woman is as nature made her, but worse if feminism gets a hold on her. By attempting to be advanced, intellectual and rational, Sue suppresses for a time what, in Hardy's view, can never be suppressed for ever, the irrationality and weakness of the female, decreed by 'inexorable laws of nature'. When the long-suppressed feminine forces break out at last, they are more savage and destructive than ever. Sue is both more unhappy and more harmful to others than Hardy's other women.

All this should hardly surprise us. Like most pessimistic people Hardy was intensely conservative. There is not much happiness in his world. Such as there is, is enjoyed by people well-rooted in traditional ways:

> For a moment there fell on Jude a true illumination; that here in the stoneyard was a centre of effort worthy as that dignified by the name of scholarly study within the noblest of the colleges. But he lost it . . . This was his form of the modern vice of unrest.[31]

Sue's form of the same vice consists in denying the natural limitations of the feminine; in attempting to substitute theory for sensation. Hardy ends where he began; the tone varies but the ideas are the same.

---

* I call her guilt superstitious not because I think it superstitious to treat the marriage bond as sacred, but because she regards her children's death as a punishment for her sin.

George Gissing

The reader familiar with the work of the English novelists from Richardson to Hardy comes to Gissing with a shock of surprise. This man, surely not a profound or highly original writer, seems to be a denizen of a different world. We are well accustomed by now to differences of value and moral emphasis. Gissing seems to present us with a new world of facts, which implicitly denies what everyone else seems to have assumed as too obvious to need discussion.

To a large extent, and with the air of a man pointing out the obvious, and indifferent to the charms of paradox, Gissing ascribes to women the characteristics universally supposed to belong to men. In *The Nether World* (1889) we have the cruel, battling East End woman, Clem Peckover. Attacked by Penny-loaf, the wife of her lover:

> It was just what [she] desired. In an instant she had rent half Pennyloaf's garments off her back, and was tearing her face till the blood streamed.[32]

Her domination over the weak husband is quite other than that ascribed by earlier novelists to strong-willed women, a function of determined will and moral influence. It is more like a proletarian version of the dominion exercised in other novels by fierce men over women, by Dickens's Murdstone, say, over David Copperfield's mother:

> his disposition now was one of hatred, and the kind of hatred which sooner or later breaks out in ferocity. Bob would not have come to this pass . . . if he had been left to the dictates of his own nature; he was infected by the savagery of the woman who had taken possession of him. His lust of cruelty crept upon him like a disease . . .[33]

Later we hear of Clem's attachment to Bob being 'fierce, animal.'

Just as we have this female equivalent of the strong, brutal male, so, in a different social setting, does Gissing present us with a feminine version of the *idée reçue* of male superiority in strength, intellect, education, sheer effectiveness in the world. Gone is the old Dickensian and Ruskinian kind of feminine superiority, the moral superiority of the angel in the house. In books like *Born in Exile* (1892) or *The Crown of Life* (1899), it is the woman who is strong, who has an assured position in the world, who can consider the question of marriage coolly on its merits. The men are the fond, weak yearners, who are unspeakably grateful for a smile or a glance. After proposing marriage, Godwin Peake, in *Born in Exile*, is characteristic of a whole group of Gissing's male protagonists when he says: 'Such a piece of recklessness deserves no answer'. Godwin and others feel like despised and useless beggars aspiring to implacable Queen Cophetuas. So the hero of *The Crown of Life* reflects:

> 'Three years of laborious exile were trifling in the balance; had they been passed in sufferings ten times as great, her smile would have paid for all.'

In the same book Miss Bonnicastle discusses a young man's wild oats in Paris with the easy worldliness previously reserved for disreputable uncles like Jane Austen's Admiral Crawford, and dismisses the ensuing qualms of conscience as absurd.[34] And after more than a generation in which novelists had meditated on the problem of the 'fallen woman', we have, perhaps for the first time, the concept of the 'fallen man'. In saying this, I naturally do not mean that all previous novelists treated male chastity as a trivial question. That is plainly not true of Richardson, Jane Austen, Trollope and many others. But here we have something other than moral disapproval; we have a man experiencing a paralysing fear that his lapse from chastity has devalued him for ever in the eyes of decent women. So Otway cries, with an astonished triumph:

> She has mentioned me; that is enough. I am not utterly expelled from her thoughts, as a creature outlawed by all decent people.

and a moment later, after dreaming fondly of an interview:

> I cannot face her without shame – the shame of every man who stands before a pure-hearted girl.[35]

One only has to think of the position in society held by Henry Crawford in *Mansfield Park*, and held to the end despite all misdemeanours, to see that we are dealing here with something quite other than moral seriousness. No one would dream of offering Gissing as a rival to Jane Austen in that quality. We are dealing with a new vision of society, in which sexual roles have been to an astonishing extent reversed.

We shall encounter (in the next section on the optimists) novelists who conceived their role as prophetic, and therefore presented for the inspiration of readers relationships of a new kind. Gissing is at the opposite pole. His ordinary reputation, as a patient observer of detail, a kind of imitation urban Dickens without genius, poetry or humour does not very greatly belie him. And he was, after his early idealistic socialist novels, devoid of faith, impatient of theory, an outspoken enemy of cant (a term under which he included much that might seem to others simple moral decency.) He is tedious in his reiteration of the platitudes of unenlightened common sense, that it is better to be rich than poor, that the educated are more civilized than the uneducated, that a mob is fickle and cruel. The unexpectedness of his dominant women and shrinking men is due to a unique combination of detached observation and intense emotions. For a variety of reasons, he felt the female sex to be dominant over him. Both the violent, drunken shrew and the serene, unapproachable queen were constantly in his thoughts. His deep personal sense of injury, of being denied his rights not just by society, but by life itself, caused him to feel humiliated before all women, both those he considered to be above him and those he despised. Lacking much self-knowledge, he seems to have projected his own feelings on to a variety of fictional characters (some of them in other ways little like himself) without being aware of it. This does not turn his picture of society into a caricature; he is too careful an observer for that. It is more as if a drawing, exact in every outline, had been made on paper of some strange, unearthly colour. The likeness remains exact enough, so long as one discounts the pervasive lurid gleam.

My account so far has been one-sided. A prolific writer, Gissing on other occasions follows a more conventional line, often with an extra twist of sordidness startling to readers long familiar with the points he was making. Thus many of his predecessors had written of unscrupulous husband-hunting, realistically, like Trollope,* or with gay fantasy, like Surtees. In chapter XIII of *The Unclassed* (1884), characteristically headed *A Man-Trap*, Gissing makes the process more crude, and the marital prospects more intensely gloomy. Harriet lures Julian into her bedroom to show him how she has hung an engraving. She lives in a boarding house, and she assures him that the very fact that he has been in

* Trollope's fullest and most memorable treatment is to be found in *The American Senator*.

her bedroom in broad daylight and fully-clothed for a few minutes will be death to her reputation. Respectable conventions (suitably exaggerated for the occasion) and the man's gentleness and credulity are turned in a woman's hand into weapons of ruthless social destruction. It was typical of Gissing's negative cast of mind that he saw the 'old' tricky, husband-hunting woman as destructive, just as much as violent shrews and detached, superior ladies. In the same way, he pours equal scorn on traditional views and on progressive or revolutionary doctrines.

Gissing's cynicism and ruthlessness spring from oversensitiveness about his marriage to a drunken prostitute. His supposed toughness is a façade and his stinging rebukes to idealists read very much like lectures addressed to his dreamy, wayward self. Occasionally, he allows this dreamy self to rhapsodize undeterred by irony; when this happens the contrast with his usual tone is both startling and revealing. Nor is it something he outgrew; it is as likely to occur in his latest books as in earlier. The following is from *The Crown of Life* (1899):

Images of maddening beauty glowed upon him out of the darkness, glowed and gleamed by he knew not what creative mandate; faces, forms such as may visit the delirium of a supreme artist. Of him they knew not; they were worlds away, though his own brain bodied them forth . . . For the men capable of passionate love (and they are few) to miss love is to miss everything.[36]

While in this mood, seldom but powerfully felt in his writings, he is capable of regarding even an unrequited love as a blessing, giving life purpose and meaning, and helping to save a man from mere slavery to the senses.

It is not easy to discern a central point of balance between Gissing's cynicism and his romanticism, between his angry denunciations and his tender musings. Massively unfortunate in domestic life himself, and lacking the highest creative powers to detach him from his own experience, it was hard for him to describe feelingly the ordinary decencies of marriage. Yet at times he does, with some hesitation, feel towards the idea that for many, domestic life, however much marred by circumstances, quarrels, disagreements and incompatibilities, is their strongest comfort in an unfriendly world. Perhaps the most touching example is to be found in what is on the whole his gloomiest book:

'Look Clara, you and I are going to do what we can for
these children; we're not going to give up the work now we've
begun it . . . But I can't do without your help. I didn't feel
very cheerful as I sat here a while ago, before you came down;
I was almost afraid to go upstairs, lest the sight of what you
might be suffering should be too much for me. Am I to ask a
kindness of you and be refused, Clara?'

It was not the first time she had experienced the constraining
power of his words when he was moved with passionate
earnestness.[37]

The scene ends with a grudging promise on Clara's part to try
again, and a shared resolve not to mar the peace and rest of the
coming Sunday. The man, in this case the calmer and less selfish
of the two, feels exhausted with the moral efforts of the dialogue,
following upon his other worries and fatigues. But, 'Never mind;
the battle was gained once more.'

This is not an attractive portrait of the married state. Yet the
home is seen as the place of least unhappiness and greatest moral
possibility in a grim social world. Classifications are arbitrary,
however useful; and this scene is a salutary reminder that even
Gissing was not quite the Platonic idea of the pessimist. Like a
glimmering light seen in the distance in an underground passage,
the high ideal of the family and joyful, innocent domestic life,
is glimpsed by those who will never reach it.

CHAPTER VII

The Optimists

'Men are like the earth and we are like the moon; we turn always one side to them, and they think there is no other, because they don't see it – but there is.'
    Lyndall in *The Story of an African Farm* by Olive Schreiner (1883) Part II, chap. V

There lingered behind her that peculiar fragrance of modern womanhood, refreshing, inspiriting, which is so different from the merely feminine perfume, however exquisite.
    George Gissing, *Born in Exile* (1892) Part V, Section IV

Before the show breaks up, she would like to drop the august title of the Eternal Woman, and go there as her transitory self.
    E. M. Forster, *A Room with a View* (1908) chap. IV

. . . 'you have dressed the unknowable in the garments of the known.'
    The Doctor in *Nightwood* by Djuna Barnes (1936) chap. VII

As Tolstoy said at the beginning of *Anna Karenina*, all happy families are alike, but each unhappy family is unhappy in its own way. The pessimists of the last chapter form no school; their reasons for taking a gloomy view of sex are all different. There is no literary resemblance whatever between (say) Swinburne and Gissing.

Tolstoy's words must not be applied too rigorously to the optimistic school of Havelock Ellis, Olive Schreiner, Grant Allen and D. H. Lawrence. There are, as we shall see, important differences. Nevertheless, we are faced in the 1880s and in the early decades of the twentieth century with a pattern of thought much more theoretical and iconoclastic than before. Sexual morality for these writers ceases to be a part of ordinary morality, conceived in traditional terms. It becomes *the* essential message. Be right about sex, say these writers in effect, and you will be right automatically about religion, politics, education, hygiene, money and literature. Be wrong about sex, and the consequences are too terrible to contemplate – hardness, pharisaism, cruelty, hypocrisy. And this was a primary intuition, which it was considered unnecessary, foolish – almost blasphemous – to try to justify. The very fact that you questioned it, or even asked for reasons before believing it, indicated that you were one of the goats, one of those excluded from the triumphant march onward of a new humanity, and more especially a new womanhood towards – towards what? Well, towards happiness; but that is too feeble a word. Beatitude would be nearer the mark.

Complete revolutions of belief, perhaps still more of sensibility are, we know, rare. What are the elements of continuity between the late-Victorian crusaders and the early-Victorian traditionalists? Can we, for instance, claim Charlotte Brontë as a forerunner? The feature of her books which her first readers found arresting, or exciting, or occasionally shocking, was the tone of uncontrollable passion; and this passion was felt by woman for man. Yet it is only a *tone* of uncontrollable passion; her actual narratives show that it can be controlled.

In chapter XIX of *The Professor* she writes:

 . . . if we rarely taste the fulness of joy in this life, we yet more rarely savour the acrid bitterness of hopeless anguish; unless, indeed, we have plunged like beasts into sensual indulgence, abused, strained, stimulated, again overstrained, and, at last, destroyed our faculties for enjoyment; then, truly, we may find ourselves without support, robbed of hope . . . God, spirits, religion can have no place in our collapsed minds, where linger only hideous recollections of vice; and time brings us on to the brink of the grave, and dissolution flings us in – a rag eaten through and through with disease, wrung together with pain, stamped into the churchyard sod by the inexorable heel of despair.

In fact, the resistance to passion, and the disapproval of allowing it free play are even stronger than the passion itself, and every bit as fiery in rhetoric. Many people, I dare say, reading *Jane Eyre* for the first time have been so swept away by the rhetoric of passion as to suppose that Rochester and Jane were about to ignore as irrelevant the fact that Rochester was married. But the author does not allow them to do so.

In one way, certainly, Charlotte Brontë does seem to be genuinely like the Ellis school. She does appear to think that nothing matters very much compared to love. But there is a difference. In Charlotte Brontë this is not a doctrine, it is only a feeling. She feels this because she is high-toned and accustomed to a monotonous life, because, in fact, she has not much else to think about. From one point of view, despite the startling boldness of her expressions, she is still the traditional woman of Byron's aphorism:

> Man's love is of man's life a thing apart,
> 'Tis woman's whole existence.

But her theory remains that of all good Christian people, that we are here to serve God, and save our souls, and all our other aspirations must be subservient to that. This, no doubt, was what Leslie Stephen, that most firmly orthodox of sexual moralists, though not of religious thinkers, meant when he said: 'her mind . . . never broke the fetters by which the parson's daughter of the last generation was restricted.'[1] The word 'fetters' is tendentious and patronizing, but the judgement embodied is sound enough.

And then there is Kingsley. Equally passionate and rhetorical, he introduces two new features. He does not merely, like Charlotte Brontë, celebrate sexual union (always of course in marriage) as the greatest earthly bliss and highest moral good, but he also speaks with the severest moral disapproval of those who fail to see the self-evident truth of what he is saying. Here he does really remind us of his successors of the Ellis school. Yet still there is a difference. Kingsley was a Christian, though an extremely eccentric and muddled one. He does not mistake sexual union for the *summum bonum*. In my formulation above ('greatest earthly bliss') he would have insisted on the underlining of the word 'earthly'. In a man so muddled and excitable, it is vain to look for coherent ideas. We have to be guided by his emotional tone. And at times it does seem as if he means that those who deny Christ are only subject to an unfortunate mistake while those who question the glory of sex are guilty of the sin against the Holy Spirit. Had the matter been put to him in this form, he would certainly have denied that this was his view. Yet the impression that he half-consciously felt in some such way remains.

In so far as he did, he is a true forerunner of Havelock Ellis.

The other new feature, not to be found in Charlotte Brontë, is his fierce attack on celibacy. This was, on the whole, acceptable to those who read his novels, which were published in the ten years following 1848, and are thus contemporary with Charlotte Brontë's. Kingsley was able to make this attack acceptable to respectable readers, in a time of some severity in public expectations about the morality of novelists, by giving it a bitter anti-Catholic tinge. This, in the time of 'Papal Aggression',* was such a respectable sentiment that perhaps few readers clearly understood how self-contradictory Kingsley's thesis was. It is possible to honour both celibacy and marriage as in traditional Catholic teaching. It is possible to despise both. It is not possible in logic to exalt marriage and decry celibacy, without implying that the unmarried, and especially the large numbers of women who have no prospect of marriage, have no spiritual function, are, in fact, just surplus. But logic was a faculty that never troubled Kingsley's thinking, or rather, for he never really thought at all, his feeling.

Neither Charlotte Brontë nor Kingsley will fit neatly into a pattern. They are not quite in tune with the moral views of the novelists who were their contemporaries, nor are they in tune with Havelock Ellis. But they may have served to some extent to prepare the way for him for this reason: the lovers they describe are chaste, monogamous and morally responsible, but at the same time they glory in a physical passion of unrivalled intensity.

II

But there is another, entirely different, kind of continuity between the early Victorians and the Allen-Ellis school. The early Victorians believed passionately in freedom; and this was a general sentiment that united men of different temperament and opposite political party. It was one of the most conservative among their

---

* 'Papal Aggression' was the term used to describe Pius IX's action in appointing English Catholic bishops of English cities, in place of the old Vicars Apostolic. Lord John Russell wrote an inflammatory open letter to the Bishop of Durham, and the Ecclesiastical Titles Bill, providing for fines against the new bishops, was passed in the Commons by a large majority. It was never, however, enforced.

great men, who wrote to universal nods of satisfied approval of:
a land of old and just renown,
Where freedom slowly broadens down
From precedent to precedent.

The Reform Bill, the Corn Law Repeal and many lesser liberal triumphs were all seen in this way.

The rhetoric of freedom was pervasive; but it was subject to exceptions. It applied to doctrinal tests in the Church of England, but not to Irish nationalism, which was not, of course, held to be inspired by a claim to freedom at all, but only to anarchy and licence. And the greatest of the exceptions was sexual morality. It was so great an exception that it was not noticed as such. From one point of view, the doctrine of Grant Allen might be called the belated application to sexual questions of the grand early Victorian doctrine of *laissez-faire*. It is an interesting and difficult speculation to ask: why was this obvious connection so hard to see at the time? Why did Manchester business men who believed that the maximum public good would result from unrestricted economic individualism never for a moment imagine that their doctrine could be applied to private life? Impossible to do more than suggest a tentative answer. Perhaps one factor was that the liberal economic doctrines were generally presented in close association with ideas of discipline and self-control. Smiles, their most notable publicist, wrote books entitled *Character*, *Thrift* and *Duty*. There was far more stress, in the popular mythology of the Manchester school, on the industrious apprentice about to become a millionaire than there was on the millionaire's exercise of the freedom of choice which his success gave him. Then, it may be that the crux of the matter was the conduct expected of women. And the economic world was a world of men. Wealthy ladies were the wives or heirs of wealthy men. So it did not come naturally to the readers of Smiles to ask whether, if unrestricted liberty was such a wonderful thing, it might be right to apply the doctrine to private conduct.

Grant Allen (1848–99) is one of those figures whose importance is entirely historical; that is to say, when the interest of novelty and the *succès de scandale* are over, they are forgotten except by those who seek to understand the feelings of the past. In his article entitled *The New Hedonism*,* he attempted to apply both the

* *Fortnightly Review*, March 1894.

tenets of early Victorian liberalism and the findings of mid-Victorian biology to moral questions. He is an individualistic utilitarian, sacrificing the grave, impersonal social attitudes of Mill and the old *Westminster Review* to preach an aggressive pursuit of personal pleasure. And pleasure is to be found mainly through sexual experience. He attacks all ideas of discipline and self-sacrifice, and pours scorn on 'asceticism' (a word whose meaning he obviously does not understand). Though he was at one time in his career a professor of mental and moral philosophy, his thinking is very loose. He entirely fails to note the distinction, familiar to all serious moralists at least since the time of Aristotle, between doing as one likes at the moment and doing what will tend towards lasting happiness. And he imitates the Manchester school (unconsciously perhaps) in making an unexplained mental leap from the happiness of the individual to the well-being of society. The idea that self-discipline is needed for the good of society is just as foreign to him as the idea that it is needed to restrain wayward, self-destructive impulses. His doctrine is reducible to a simple and attractive proposition: if everyone does exactly as he likes, all will be happy, so far as the physical conditions of life allow.

He has, too, special theoretical justifications for giving the sexual impulse a uniquely important place. It is not merely, as everybody knows, one of the most powerful impulses, it is also the source of all the higher faculties. 'Everything high and ennobling in our nature' he says, 'springs directly out of the sexual instinct.' The aesthetic sense is presented as a secondary sexual attribute like the female robin's appreciation of the male's red breast:

> To it [the sexual instinct] we owe our love of bright colours, graceful forms, melodious sound, rhythmical motion. To it we owe the evolution of poetry, of romance, or *belles lettres*.

I spoke just now of mid-Victorian biology as a source of Allen's ideas. I did not mean, of course, that they constituted a legitimate logical deduction from the findings of Lyell and Darwin. These keener thinkers would have been quick to see that Allen's development of their theories was illogical. Since sexuality is something common to men and animals, and since animals do not have poetry, romance and *belles lettres*, it must follow that the sexual cannot be the *sole* source of the latter achievements. The

shade of Darwin must long since have become inured to such
mishandling of ideas which have been used to justify (among
other things) American capitalism and Nazi racialism.

Nevertheless, however illegitimate the deductions, it seems
likely that, subjectively, the scientific influence was strong. For
centuries the literature of love had contained the assumption that
the reality of love was in the soul, and that the physical was an
expression of this, or could even be a desecration of it.* Now,
vaguely apprehended notions of biological evolution lead Allen
to reverse this, and to find in the physical the origin of all higher
feelings. It must have been most flattering and agreeable to
those about to satisfy their sexual desires, in any of the various
modes approved by Allen, that they were nobly contributing to
the spiritual and aesthetic advancement of the race.

In Allen's best-known novel, *The Woman Who Did*, the very
pure heroine, who rejects marriage to the man she passionately
loves on high ethical grounds, says: 'To be celibate is a very
great misfortune for a woman; for a man it is impossible – it is
cruel, it is wicked.' There is an important difference between
this and Kingsley's attack on celibacy. The motive of Kingsley's
attack was to glorify marriage, and his view of sexual union was
quasi-sacramental. Now we have something quite different; a
justification of sexual action as a kind of natural necessity, like
food. And, to add to the sense of bewilderment, in many readers,
the doctrine is propounded by a girl, and a young girl, and a
heroine, who is praised for her moral purity.

Though he makes occasional use of words like 'sacred', Allen's
doctrine is pseudo-scientific, rather than pseudo-religious. And
this is one reason why he is a less significant figure than Havelock
Ellis, who was both what would now be called a sociologist and
a kind of serious pagan religious teacher. We might say that the
1880s and '90s saw a frontal attack on traditional notions of sexual
ethics, and that this was divided into a low and a high attack.
Grant Allen was the spearhead of the low attack, Havelock Ellis
of the high. On one point neither of them was perfectly clear.
Were they attacking the theory or the practice of the early
Victorians? We touch here, of course, on a confusion very common
in reforming literature of all kinds. The world is at all times

---

* e.g. Petronius: 'Foeda est in coitu et brevis voluptas' translated by Ben Jonson
'Doing a filthy pleasure is and short'.

corrupt and unsatisfactory; but the corruption and unsatisfac-toriness of today or of the past are palpable. The corruption of tomorrow, which will infect a system not yet tried, is vague and unpredictable.

In the case of sexual ethics the distinction was particularly vital. The ethical ideal of the early Victorians was pre-marital chastity, followed by loving and fruitful monogamy. The reality included less desirable features; prostitution, the double standard which treated male lapses as venial and female ones as unfor-givable, and the right of an unfaithful and brutal husband who refused to support his wife and children to claim all a wife's earnings as his own. It was tempting, but it was idle, to speak here of hypocrisy. There must always be a gap between any high ideal and the world of everyday. But it is clear that the new school of late Victorian theorists regarded the gap as intolerably gaping. Worse, they suspected, rightly or wrongly, that many worldly-wise early Victorians paid lip-service to an ideal, just *because* they found the incidental corruptions exceedingly con-venient.

The most surprising, and the most significant, feature of Havelock Ellis's sexual theory is its intense religious earnestness. A man who spent thirty years in the composition of books of sexual case-histories[2] might be expected to lose some of his early idealistic excitement. Ellis never did; he was one of those rare men who never became familiar with the everyday. He was the sort of man for whom every dawn and every sunset is as wonderful as if it were the first or the last he had ever seen. And so it was with sex. Ellis writes at times in the style of an imprisoned troubadour sighing for a momentary glimpse of a *princesse lontaine*, or like Rudel in Browning's *Rudel to the Lady of Tripoli*. But – and it is a fundamental and astonishing difference – he writes thus of the *function* of sex, not of an idealized person. The ordinary veneer of familiarity about the facts of the matter, which most people develop in adolescence or in early adult life, was never found in him. Aspects which become to most people trivial or shameful or simply uninteresting never became so to him. His first involuntary daytime emission he called 'natural and beautiful'. He was affected all his life by what he called 'urolagnia' – that is, he experienced sexual pleasure from urina-tion, and intense sexual stimulation from the sight or the idea of a woman urinating. He wrote lyrically of this last as a subject

for serious art, and was of the opinion that a masterpiece of
Rembrandt, which originally had this subject, had been spoilt
by overpainting due to false notions of decency. Here he reminds
us for a moment of Sterne; but the contrast is more important
than the similarity. There is nothing titillating in Ellis's treatment
of this subject, so long as his account is read in the spirit in which
it was written. Strange as it must seem to many, he finds something
inspiring, almost holy here.

Ellis's chief complaint against the early Victorians (and
previous ages too) was that they denied intense sexual sensation
to women. Inclined usually to condemn wrong views gently, he
was moved for once to something like indignation when he
quoted earlier writers who said that it was a vile aspersion to
ascribe sexual feelings to women, or maintained that an orgasm
was, in a woman, a sign of a lascivious personality.

Ellis's deep respect for female sexuality was put to a test very
much sharper than most men have to endure. His wife was an
active and extremely passionate lesbian. Ellis took a vicarious
emphatic joy:

> In what the special beauty of that night lay it was not for
> her to tell, or for me to ask, only to divine, but I know that she
> always recalled the anniversary of it as one of the sacred days
> of her life.[3]

The word 'sacred' here is especially characteristic of this
whole school of thought. How easy it would be to present the
situation either in terms of broad farce or of morbid psychology.
Ellis does not so much reject such interpretations as remain
sublimely oblivious of them. Here, paradoxically, we can see an
element of continuity. The early Victorians had idealized women's
power of love, believing it to be far stronger and purer than
men's. Ellis idealizes women for having more exquisite sexual
sensations. The idea that men pay for their superior strength by
a certain moral coarsening remains the same in these two very
different guises.

It would seem that Ellis's tenderness about women was
different from the normal male kind, springing as that does from
an awareness of difference, of polarity. Ellis's tenderness was
much more due to identification. He felt the woman in himself.
Or rather, it might be truer to say that he felt both male and female
sexuality as a wonderful, inspiring *continuum*, in which differences
of gender were secondary. Hence his quite unusual degree of

interest in his own body and its functions; hence also his power of empathy with the raptures of a lesbian wife.

Like many other seminal minds – and Ellis was perhaps more influential than any other Englishman has ever been in changing moral attitudes on sexual questions – he was suggestive rather than dogmatic and open to many different interpretations. His own sexual emotions were so unusual that if his influence had been confined to those capable of feeling just as he did, it would have been slight. Rather, his influence was pervasive in developing a general sympathy in the respectable public for *all* kinds of sexual abnormality and every misfortune consequent upon the weakness of the will to restrain impulse. There was only one proviso; all aberrations and all weaknesses must be such as to touch the heart.

Yeats gives the following most instructive account of the reception of the news that Oscar Wilde had been sent to prison for homosexual practices:

'Wilde will never lift his head again,' said the art critic, Gleeson White, 'for he has against him all men of infamous life.' When the verdict was announced the harlots in the street outside danced upon the pavement.[4]

Plenty of evidence could be adduced to show that Yeats (and White) were substantially correct about public feeling. That is to say, many respectable men of the world, both bachelors and fathers of families, resorted to prostitutes. They felt themselves justified in regarding homosexuals with horror and contempt. Ellis, probably more than anyone else, was responsible for a gradual change in sentiment, so that resort to prostitutes, being a commercial transaction devoid of all respect and tenderness, would be regarded as more shameful than any sexual practice which could make any claim, however tenuous, to the name of love.

The dancing harlots and their clients would probably have justified their sense of moral superiority by some concept of 'natural' and 'unnatural'. A later generation, influenced by Ellis and others, might retort that homosexuality, too, was natural, in that it corresponded to some people's natural impulse. Prostitution, on the other hand, was unnatural, being a commercial exploitation, and being, above all, joyless. Homosexuality here is merely an illustration, a useful one because of the exceptional horror which it excited. It serves as a type of all sexual abnormalities capable of arousing tenderness. Ellis, himself not homosexual in the least, was yet influenced in all his theorizing by the fact that his urolagnia was a much rarer deviation from the accepted norm, and one that most people would have considered as strange (or perhaps repellent).

There remains the difficult question, what kind of religious feeling was it that issued in Ellis's genuine expression of awe, his pervading sense of the sacredness of sexual topics? Ellis seems to have been a 'nature mystic' of the non-religious kind.* He was the kind of person who could lose the sense of himself and feel completely merged into a natural scene, as he describes in the part of his autobiography which deals with his time in Australia. From one point of view, Ellis was a revivalist of a very old religion, the religion of phallic worship, conceived as an expression of the deepest forces of nature.

But this is not the whole story. He is also fond of transferring Christian theological terms into his rhetoric of sexual joy. Nor is this entirely empty rhetoric. When he tells us of the bitterness and the glory of being married to a lesbian, he is very much in earnest when he speaks of the path of Calvary; and he goes on 'as all Christendom has testified, that path of Calvary is not the path of failure.'[5]

If we think of the more militant neo-pagans of the next generation, of E. M. Forster for example, we feel at once that we cannot group Ellis with them. He spoke from the heart when he said:

> I have always instinctively desired to spiritualize the things that have been counted low and material, if not disgusting; and where others have seen all things secular I have seen all things sacred.[6]

In all this, of course, Ellis is the forerunner of Lawrence, who makes an exactly similar application of the spiritual resources of Christian earnestness to the dark gods of the flesh. But there is also, as we shall see, a profound difference. For Ellis sex is polymorphous; the traditional sense of polarity between male and female blurred, almost lost. Lawrence restored and intensified it, and so regarded as perverse and soul-destroying many things that Ellis was prepared to tolerate.† With Lawrence as an artist

---

* For an excellent discussion of the differences between religious and non-religious mysticism, see R. C. Zaehner: *Mysticism Sacred and Profane* (Oxford 1957).
† cf. my remarks on *The Fox* in chapter IX.

I deal later. What concerns us here is rather the *cult* of Lawrence as a purveyor of sexual freedom. It is easy to show that those most enthusiastic in the cult are generally far from agreeing with what Lawrence actually said. The so-called 'permissive' sexual ethic of much post-war fiction tends to claim Lawrence as its standard-bearer, because of his great talents. Actually, that ethic is rather a conflation of some aspects of Lawrence (often minor and rather uncharacteristic ones) with the teachings of Grant Allen and Havelock Ellis. The fact that in some respects these two last preach incompatible doctrines, and that each is incompatible in some ways with Lawrence is seldom noticed. Grant Allen's cheerful hedonism, plus Ellis's tolerance of the unusual, added to the intense pseudo-religious earnestness of both Ellis and Lawrence – this is the mixture often presented to us in publishers' blurbs as the acme of modernity. In reality the ideas are all from sixty to ninety years old.

Or rather, what was new in these ideas was sixty to ninety years old. But much more than was realized, some parts of Ellis's teaching was very traditional. In part, of course, this was simply because, despite his dreamy prose style, he was in many ways a sensible man; and there are certain traditional insights which can never be discarded without a flight into unreality. But there was one very important respect in which Ellis did not either invent anything new or repeat traditional wisdom. He was more influenced than he knew by the very men of his father's or grandfather's generation against whom he supposed himself to be in rebellion. He thought and wrote of sex always with maximum earnestness. He did not allow much for the play of mood and fancy, and for the lewd, light-hearted aspects of love. Now it is arguable that the early Victorians whom, in this, he imitated were themselves aberrant from the traditional wisdom of the race. It is a hard saying for ordinary human nature, whether the subject is religion, politics, literature, sex or anything else, that *no* allowance must ever be made for play of mood, for recreation, for frivolity. He was thus responsible (in part and unwittingly) for a new kind of pharisaism based on a ponderous sexual seriousness. The 'holier than thou' attitude of the new scribes and pharisees of the dark gods has been a tiresome feature of the 'Lawrence' cult. And, as we have seen, the Lawrence cult has only a tenuous relation to what Lawrence wrote, and is derived, in essentials, from the doctrines of Ellis.

III

Ellis was not a novelist; but he was closely associated with two women who were, his wife and Olive Schreiner. The latter's *Story of an African Farm*, first published in 1883, under a male pseudonym, is one of the few novels of merit, before those of Lawrence, which is inspired by new sexual doctrines. The date may seem to us now surprisingly early. Both the author and Ellis were in their twenties when it was written. But there is nothing youthful or transient about its earnestness. This was an unchanging characteristic of Olive Schreiner, who in 1911, in the last decade of her life, was still writing in this style:

Are there not women who, under the guise of 'work', are seeking only increased means of sensuous pleasure and self-indulgence; to whom intellectual training and the opening to new fields of labour side by side with man, mean merely new means of self-advertisement and parasitic success? . . . At the Judean supper there was one Master, and to the onlooker there may have seemed twelve apostles; in truth only twelve were of the company, and one was not of it. . . Judas could hang his Master by a kiss; but he could not silence the voice . . .

There are women as there are men, whose political, social, intellectual, or philanthropic labours are put on, as the harlot puts on paint, and for the same purpose: but they can no more retard the progress of the great bulk of vital and sincere womanhood, than the drift-wood on the surface of a mighty river can ultimately prevent its waters from reaching the sea.[7]

So, in Olive Schreiner, a more tempestuous temperament than Ellis himself, we are confronted for the first time with a vision of the 'New Woman'. A very vague phrase, certainly; what did it mean in the *African Farm*? This is not at all an easy question to answer; though it is obvious on every page that, for the author, the effort to answer it is paramount. The book shows signs of its early date, published in the same year as Trollope's *Autobiography*, and less than three years after the death of George Eliot. The 'New Woman' here, Lyndall, has the great advantage of living in a world where her type is still unfamiliar. She can preach a feminism as fierce and uncompromising as that of her creator in the passage just quoted. At the same time she can appeal at times to male chivalry, as the 'Old Woman' had been accustomed to do.

Like the heroine of *The Woman Who Did*, she refuses to marry the man she passionately loves:

'If you do love me,' he asked her, 'why will you not marry me?'

'Because, if I had been married to you for a year, I should have come to my senses, and seen that your hands and your voice are like the hands and the voice of any other man. I cannot quite see that now. But it is all madness. You call into activity one part of my nature; there is a higher part that you know nothing of, that you never touch. [8]

But her refusal does not lead, as might be expected, to celibacy. On the contrary, she plans to marry someone else; and to achieve this she reverts rather to the 'Old Woman's' traditional appeal to chivalry. To this other, Gregory, she says:

'I remember your words: *You will give everything and expect nothing*. The knowledge that you are serving me is to be your reward; and you will have that. You will serve me, and greatly. The reasons I have for marrying you I need not inform you of now . . .'[9]

A few pages later she explains to the man she loves her decision to marry a man she despises:

'Who is this fellow you talk of marrying?'

'A young farmer.'

'Lives here?'

'Yes; he has gone to town to get things for our wedding.'

'What kind of fellow is he?'

'A fool.'

'And you would rather marry him than me?'

'Yes; because you are not one.'

'That is a novel reason for refusing to marry a man . . .'

'It is a wise one,' she said shortly. 'If I marry him I shall shake him off my hand when it suits me. If I remained with him for twelve months he would never have dared to kiss my hand.'[10]

The fundamental idea of chivalry is, presumably, respect for the fact of feminine physical weakness and for the supposed fact of feminine inferiority in will and intellect. Confronted with Mrs Proudie, chivalry tends to be forgotten, as Mr Crawley showed when he defied her and made her husband, the bishop, jump with admiration.[11] It is a safe guess that the majority of readers, both in the last century and in this, have shared the bishop's admiration. Olive Schreiner's 'New Woman' is here living on borrowed time. She is appealing to the chivalrous male, trained in the tradition of the knight-errant. But she is appealing not as a damsel in distress, but as an imperious and sarcastic school-mistress. It can't last.

Though the 'fool' is submissive, he is not required to come up to scratch. Lyndall is only using the threat of this marriage as a lever against the man she loves. What she really wants is to live with the beloved 'without being tied'. And he says: 'It is better to have you on those conditions than not at all.'

This must have been intoxicating stuff for the early devotees of the 'New Woman'. The love literature of many generations had been based on the assumption that marriage was a triumph for a woman. Decent men were ready enough to concede this triumph to the woman they loved; others were more reluctant. Men who married their mistresses were supposed to be acting generously, though perhaps imprudently. Phrases like 'make an honest woman of her' were emblems of ideas deeply embedded in the consciousness of the race. Now, the 'New Woman' wins all along the line. She reduces the male to anxious wondering about the permanence of the union; and at the same time as she proclaims her freedom, she can still claim a formidable tax on chivalrous traditions, because she knows just as well how to play that game too:

'Poor little thing,' he said, 'you are only a child' . . .

She looked into his eyes as a little child might whom a long day's play had saddened.

It is comforting to learn that her hands and feet were tiny. Lyndall's tactics then are excellent. But if we ask what is her doctrine of love, or what is the author's, the answer is not so clear. She is eloquent against loveless marriages:

A little weeping, a little wheedling, a little self-degradation, a little careful use of our advantages, and then some man will say – 'Come, be my wife!' With good looks and youth marriage is easy to attain. There are men enough; but a woman who has sold herself, even for a ring and a new name, need hold her skirt aside for no creature in the street. They both earn their bread in one way. Marriage for love is the beautifullest external symbol of the union of souls; marriage without it is the uncleanest traffic that defiles the world.[12]

This certainly does not prepare us for her behaviour to the beloved and the fool! But here, in contrast to her later conduct and self-justification, she is not really speaking as a 'New Woman'. This likeness between the prostitute and the wife who seeks only money and position in marriage was a commonplace of early Victorian moral thinking. It is found most fully developed, perhaps in *Dombey & Son* (1846–8), where an extended comparison is made between a prostitute and Dombey's second wife.

Lyndall seems to be entirely free of any authorial criticism. But her inconsistencies, which appear on the whole to be the author's also, give the book its special interest and importance. No other novel conveys nearly so well what it was like to be a serious, passionate, rather muddled intellectual, born in the 1850s convinced that great changes were afoot, despising and pitying the early Victorians, yet agreeing with them in many more ways than one realized. The most striking thing in the end about *The African Farm* is not any character, or its story, or any doctrine it preaches. It is rather the sense of revolutionary expectancy, the diffused awareness of something totally unforeseen about to transform the most familiar physical facts, the most traditional sentiments, the most unquestioned principles. The turmoil and upheaval suggested here lasted in some minds for a whole generation. H. G. Wells's *Ann Veronica* (1909) differs from Lyndall in being a trained scientist; and she finds the hostility of the world fairly easy to conquer. But her older mentor Miss Miniver is still speaking much in the old terms:

Everything, Miss Miniver said, was 'working up', everything was 'coming on' – the Higher Thought, the Simple Life, Socialism, Humanitarianism, it was all the same really. She loved to be there, taking part in it all, breathing it, being it. Hitherto in the world's history there had been precursors of this Progress at great intervals, voices that had spoken and ceased, but now it was all coming on together in a rush. She mentioned, with familiar respect, Christ and Buddha and Shelley and Neitzsche and Plato. Pioneers all of them. Such names shone brightly in the darkness, with black spaces of un-illuminated emptiness about them, as stars shine in the night; but now – now it was different; now it was dawn – the real dawn.[13]

Wells was not exactly a subtle satirist, but he had a good ear.

Still, however 'new' their womanhood, no one could doubt that Olive Schreiner's Lyndall and Ann Veronica were just as different from men as any earlier women had been. (It is one of Wells's most sensible points that it is nonsense to say that learning has the slightest tendency to de-sex a woman.) It was left for Ellis's wife, in her novel *Attainment*, published in 1909, the same year as *Ann Veronica*, to speak of a 'new attitude', which 'contains the virility of true womanhood, the womanliness of true manhood'. This was, perhaps, the logical conclusion of the whole movement; but in such matters many forces are more powerful than logic. Very few were prepared to go to this length. There may have been some who concluded that if this was the logical conclusion, the premisses must have been wrong. Many more remained halting between several opinions, or tried to make a synthesis of incompatibles.

Lawrence

The Lawrence cult has produced its crop of ineptitudes; but one point is clear. Lawrence is, in a literary sense, a far greater figure than our other optimists. Since that is not in dispute, the question for us is not one of literary magnitude, but of continuity. How far is Lawrence the true heir of Havelock Ellis and his associates?

The passage just quoted from *Attainment* will help towards an answer. To speak of the virility of true womanhood, and the womanliness of true manhood is, for Lawrence, as great an absurdity as it would have been for Trollope. Indeed, he rebuts any such merging of sexual roles, any such denial of an inescapable polarity much more strongly than Trollope would do. Trollope's treatment of feminism (for instance, in *Is he Popenjoy?*) is amused and contemptuous. Lawrence constantly attacks the doctrine enunciated in *Attainment* with indignation. And it is easy to see why; not only is he in general a fiercer personality than Trollope; he also feels more threatened. What Trollope could smile at as a temporary hobby-horse of a few cranks had become in the years just before and after the Great War almost a received doctrine in 'progressive' literary circles. Moreover, the polarity of the sexes, with its manifold implications about contrasting roles in the family, in work and in society, was for Trollope simply an obvious assumption of common sense.

For Lawrence it was a sacred mystery; its denial not so much a product of silliness as an act of blasphemy.

Nor is this the only or quite the deepest difference between Lawrence and the novelists of the Ellis school. Lawrence is always uneasy about, and in his best and most characteristic writings tends to reject altogether, a mere quest for experience. In the exchange between Birkin and Ursula Brangwen, in the chapter called *Water-Party*[14] we hear a note never sounded by the Ellis school:

'Aphrodite is born in the first spasm of universal dissolution – then the snakes and swans and lotus – marsh-flowers – and Gudrun and Gerald – born in the process of destructive creation.'

'And you and me – ?' she asked.

'Probably,' he replied. 'In part certainly. Whether we are that, in toto, I don't yet know.'

'You mean we are flowers of dissolution – *fleurs du mal*? I don't feel as if I were,' she protested.

According to the Ellis school, experience was its own justification. Here it is not so; experience is judged, by canons which are obscure indeed, yet peremptory, unanswerable in their mysterious authority.

When we are told that Gudrun could not get beyond Gerald, we are being told about an inner spiritual lack or even a betrayal of the self. And the happy satisfaction of her sensuality is, for Lawrence, no answer at all to the charge. The sinister chapter *Rabbit* suggests the possibility of a demonic sensual satisfaction, or what Birkin, just before the passage quoted above, calls 'the flowering mystery of the death process'.

In the Ellis school, the stress is all upon activity, freedom of choice, or in their fashionable and dated word, *emancipation*. In Lawrence, there is a stress on passivity, on waiting, on obscure adumbrations, of things not yet understood. Thus Tom Brangwen muses:

It was coming, he knew, his fate. The world was submitting to its transformation. He made no move; it would come, what would come.[15]

And there is fear and awe:

When he approached her, he came to such a terrible painful unknown. How could he embrace it and fathom it? How could he close his arms round all this darkness and hold it to his

breast and give himself to it? What might not happen to him?[16]
Ellis, admittedly, shows a certain sense of mystery and reverence. But this Lawrentian fear, experienced by Brangwen, might
have seemed to him a reversion to the primitive world of taboo,
from which he conceived it his life-work to liberate mankind.

It might be instructive to imagine two groups of people
reading that key passage in *The Rainbow*, where the first Mrs
Brangwen advises Anna about her marriage:

'Remember, child,' said her mother, 'that everything is not
waiting for *your* hand just to take or leave. You mustn't expect
it. Between two people, the love itself is the important thing,
and that is neither you nor him. It is a third thing you must
create.[17]

The first group, consisting, say, of Thackeray, Mrs Gaskell
and Trollope, would find, in language somewhat strange, and
perhaps disturbing, a statement essentially familiar. The stress
is on responsibility; perhaps rather more on a cosmic religious
responsibility, and less on a social responsibility than they would
be accustomed to. Yet all of them would have admitted, perhaps
with embarrassment, if pressed, that their social morality had a
religious basis.

The other group, say Havelock Ellis, Olive Schreiner and Edith
Ellis, would have shaken their heads over a return to early
Victorian taboos. The third thing would sound to them unpleas-
antly like a periphrasis for God; they would feel threatened in their
tenderest nerve; they would feel a blasphemy against their sacred
gospel of 'Doing as One Likes'.

If both groups read on, their original reactions would only
be confirmed when Lydia Brangwen's husband dies and she
muses:

'I shared life with you, I belong in my own way to eternity.'[18]
This is not the language of Thackeray, of course. But Lawrence is
at one with the early Victorians and in opposition to the Ellis
school, in being unimpressed by calculations of pleasure, or
even of happiness in any ordinary sense.

Perhaps this is most obvious of all in the passages in *Women in
Love* which meditate on death. Ursula thinks:

What a gladness to think that whatever humanity did, it
could not seize hold of the kingdom of death, to nullify that
... the great dark, illimitable kingdom of death, there humanity
was put to scorn. So much they could do upon earth, the multi-

farious little gods that they were. But the kingdom of death put them all to scorn, they dwindled into their true vulgar silliness in face of it.[19]

And Birkin even goes so far as to suggest that the world might be better without any human beings at all.

Here, of course, Lawrence is equally far from the traditionalists and the progressives. Even if we partly discount the last sentiment as showing a kind of sickness in Birkin, not approved by the author, (and it is by no means clear that we should) we are in any case moving in a world previously unknown in the English novel.

It is equally difficult to place Lawrence fairly in any tradition in his idea of the will. It is a commonplace both of ancient pagan and of Christian wisdom that man's will is weak so that he often prefers the evil he does not desire to the good he does. Where Ovid and St Paul agree, our great English novelists from Richardson to George Eliot are ready with infinitely varied and subtle illustrations and examples. Lydgate did not *mean* to let Rosamund trap him, or to incur a financial obligation to Bulstrode; and this single example will perhaps suffice when every reader can easily supply twenty of his own. And this is especially relevant to our theme because, the sexual urge being very strong, a strong will is needed to control it. But Lawrence seems throughout his work to question this whole traditional structure of thought, which is also confirmed in most people's experience. He seems to say that if you are too weak to do what you intended, it only proves that you didn't really intend it at all. And Birkin says this explicitly in answer to Ursula's objection:

'What they *do* doesn't alter the truth of what they say, does it?'

'Completely, because if what they say *were* true, then they couldn't help fulfilling it.'[20]

Lawrence (or at least Birkin) here is equally far from either tradition. Thackeray and the others knew of impulse, and of the attempt to control it by will informed by duty. The Ellis school blurred the distinction, and came near to saying that impulse *was* duty, though they could allow for a distinction between trivial and transient impulses and those which really engaged the personality.

Lawrence speaks obscurely; but sometimes at least, he actually seems to be saying that the will is not weak at all, that it must press on to its true goal; and that when it appears to be weak, this is only because of a concealed insincerity.

Hence the strange failure to distinguish in the plot of *Women in Love* between what the characters intend and what happens to them. Did Gerald intend to kill his brother? Is his death in the snow his destiny or his intention? Perhaps Lawrence fails to answer clearly because he does not admit the validity of the question.

II

The first Mrs Brangwen proclaimed her loyalty, not just to the husband, but to that 'third thing'. Its nature is unspecified, but it seems clear that its general character is religious, not social. What of social responsibility then? As on so many other questions, it is easy to quote Lawrence on either side of this one. Two cases by their fullness of the treatment, their psychological insight and their obvious literary merit seem to claim priority for us as we consider the question. They are the second marriage in *The Rainbow*, and the case of Birkin and Ursula in *Women in Love*.

Will and Anna, the second pair in *The Rainbow*, try to live as if they were alone in the world. They have no need of a clock.

This then was marriage! The old things didn't matter any more. One got up at four o'clock, and had broth at tea-time and made toffee in the middle of the night. One didn't put on one's clothes or one did put on one's clothes. He still was not quite sure it was not criminal. But it was a discovery to find one might be so supremely absolved. All that mattered was that he should love her and she should love him . . .[21]

How are we to take this? There seem to be two indications, which both point the same way. The first is the contrast with the first marriage which is conceived as far closer to certain deep rhythms, and which receives its final assurance of lasting dignity in the splendid words of the bereaved survivor ('I shared life with you I belong in my own way to eternity'.) The second indication is the tendency of this isolated, irresponsible marriage of Will and Anna to lapse into unfeeling sensuality. Will returns from a feeble, indecisive encounter with a girl in Nottingham, determined to transfer the thwarted sensuality on to his wife. Anna knows that this is his aim and accepts it eagerly:

Very good, if she could not influence him in the old way, she would be level with him in the new. Her old defiant hostility came up. Very good, she too was out on her own adventure. Her voice, her manner changed, she was ready for the game . . . To his latent, cruel smile she replied with brilliant challenge. He expected her to keep the moral fortress. Not she! It was much too dull a part.[22]*

A little later:

He must enjoy one beauty at a time . . . He would say during the daytime: 'Tonight I shall know the little hollow under her ankle, where the blue vein crosses.' And the thought of it, and the desire for it, made a thick darkness of anticipation . . . He wished he had a hundred men's energies, with which to enjoy her.

And later:

All the shameful things of the body revealed themselves to him now with a sort of sinister, tropical beauty. All the shameful, natural and unnatural acts of sensual voluptuousness, which he and the woman partook of together, they had their heavy beauty and their delight. Shame, what was it? It was part of extreme delight.

Now it might be argued here that passages like these should be interpreted in the light of the later and similar passages in *Lady Chatterley's Lover*, which seem to carry the author's full approval. This, in my view, would be a great mistake. The world of Lady Chatterley is so different, the author's literary power so much reduced, that the only safe way is to interpret each book by its own assumptions. And in *The Rainbow* both the general pattern of the work and the detail point to a condemnation here. Isn't it significant for instance, that in the last passage, we have the word *woman* instead of *Anna* or *wife*? Sensuality has deprived him of the sense of her personal relation to himself. And the reader's memory of the impressiveness of the first Brangwen marriage will not incline him to approval of the second.

But in *Women in Love*, in the next generation of the same family, we find a different emphasis. Birkin and Ursula come together again after a ferocious quarrel; and they talk as if the whole world except their two selves was unreal:

. . . 'I'm thinking we'd better get out of our responsibilities as quick as we can.'

---

* It is significant that this passage occurs in a chapter entitled *The Child,* and hints at the responsibilities Will and Anne are trying to forget.

'What responsibilities?' she asked, wondering.

'We must drop our jobs like a shot.'

A new understanding dawned in her face.

'Of course,' she said, 'there's that.'

'We must get out,' he said. 'There's nothing for it but to get out, quick.' . . .

'Where will you wander to?' she asked.

'I don't know. I feel as if I would just meet you and we'd set off – just towards the distance.'

'But where can one go?' she asked anxiously. 'After all, there *is* only the world, and none of it is very distant.'

'Still,' he said, 'I should like to go with you – nowhere. It would be rather wandering just to nowhere. That's the place to get to – nowhere.'[23]

How far we are asked to admire this attitude may be a matter of dispute. Perhaps the change from the stable, rooted first marriage in *The Rainbow* to this is really a change in the society pictured; and that those who desired a true marriage must behave differently according to the different circumstances. This would imply that the social history given us in the two novels, *The Rainbow* and *Women in Love*, taken together, is a history of the decline of civilization, and that true marriage must, in the time of Birkin and Ursula, regard society as hostile and dangerous, while in the early days pictured in the first chapters of *The Rainbow*, it was a possible ally.

Equally, it could be argued that the inferiority of Ursula and Birkin to the first Brangwens of *The Rainbow* is personal. They are more intelligent, they know much more, but they are more superficial. Their loss of calm is a symptom of a loss of spiritual insight. However this may be, it is obvious that throughout the long panorama of the two novels, feelings become more brittle, tempers more irascible, fidelity more difficult, and promises less to be relied upon.

The calm and peace of those early chapters of *The Rainbow*, where a precious equilibrium seems to be achieved between the claims of the universe, of society and of marriage, is never recaptured in Lawrence's work. Instead we have a series of heroes who are angry, self-righteous and irresponsible globe-trotters.

It is difficult, if we read Lawrence's later letters, in which so many of these attitudes of his heroes are expressed personally, to feel confident that the author understood these heroes very well or judged them very fairly. But that question may be left aside while we ask, how does this aspect of Lawrence's work compare with the two traditions with which we have been comparing him, that of the writers here called realists, and those called optimists?

The realists would have seen the anger and frustration of Lawrence's later heroes as the nemesis of their irresponsibility. They would perhaps have said, in their rough common-sense way, that an attempt to turn all the years of marriage into a protracted honeymoon, from which the world and its claims and its work are shut out, is sure to end in misery. The optimists would have recognized Lawrence as one of their school, and might have marvelled at the eloquence of his paeans to the glory of sex. But he would have left them uneasy. They wished very much to believe that their gospel of doing as one likes was not anti-social. In so far as they protested against society, they conceived themselves to be protesting only against its corruptions and injustices. If everyone was free sexually, they thought, there would be more social harmony, not less; there would be more goodwill, co-operation and a livelier sense of the duties of a citizen.

In the later part of *Women in Love*, and in his subsequent writings, Lawrence repudiates all this. He indeed leaves it open to us to say that it is only because society has become more decadent and corrupt that the good man and good husband can no longer even wish to be the good citizen also. Thus, in chapter XXVI ('A Chair'), Birkin says:

When I see that clear, beautiful chair, and I think of England, even Jane Austen's England – it had living thoughts to unfold even then, and pure happiness in unfolding them. And now, we can only fish among the rubbish-heaps of the remnants of their old expression.

and a little later declares 'One should just live anywhere – not have a definite place.'

If we accept this as correct, we are crediting Lawrence with a sentiment that the optimists would have found most distasteful, indeed barely comprehensible. For, in that case, Lawrence would be saying that the dark gods were powerless to improve society, or perhaps that so few would heed their message that the corrupt mass would be unaffected. Havelock Ellis and his friends saw themselves as reformers, pioneers. They were exploring new territory, which would one day be within the reach of all; just as anyone can now buy an airline ticket to places that the first explorers reached less than a century ago. Lawrence does not think like that. His sexual initiates are few, not because they are pioneers, but because, like a band of monks devoted to asceticism and prayer, they are asking more of themselves than ordinary human nature can be expected to give. A few men in each generation have the vocation to be Carthusians. The number may vary, but no one imagines that their life could ever become *usual* among the mass of average sensual men. So Lawrence's divergence from Havelock Ellis is quite as important as any similarity.

In some ways, as we have seen, Lawrence reminds us more of those against whom Ellis and his friends were in rebellion than he does of Ellis himself. Yet, in the end, we cannot help including him here among the optimists. For no one could have a stronger sense than he of the positive spiritual possibilities of the relation between the sexes. His conception of it, for those who can enter into it and are not repelled by its fierce intensity, will make the mid-Victorian wedding-bell chapters seem tame. And yet, there will be others for whom this Lawrentian intensity will seem to be bought at too high a price. There seems to be no forgiveness for those who fail. Gerald Crich and Gudrun seem in the end greater outcasts than any Victorian 'fallen woman'. The tenderness which Mrs Gaskell shows for Ruth or Trollope for Carrie Brattle,* is not for them. The gospel of 'doing as one likes' has never had a fiercer opponent than he.

* In *The Vicar of Bullhampton*.

CHAPTER VIII

The Male Homosexual

'Love to me is a religion. All the examples I've come across
so far seem to me heresies.'

Edith Ellis, *Attainment* (1909)

How awful they were, women!

D. H. Lawrence, *Lady Chatterley's Lover* (1928)
chap. XVII

In 1968, a once-popular novelist wrote in his reminiscences:[1]

Another thing that is a cause of wonder to me as I re-read
[*Tell England*] is the indubitable but quite unconscious homosexuality in it. The earlier part was written when I was 18 or
19, and in those early days 'homosexuality' was a word which,
absurd as this may seem now, I had never heard . . . I did not
know that homosexuality could exist in embryo without even
knowing itself for what it is, or desiring the least physical
satisfaction.

This passage needs to be kept constantly in mind as we trace
the half-invisible threads leading to the full presentation of the
homosexual theme in Forster's *Maurice* – the only major English
novel in which the subject is central.

It is easy to find even in the works of the classic Victorian
novelists passages that are sexually ambiguous. Many a dormitory
seduction may have begun something like this:

'Good night, young Copperfield,' said Steerforth. 'I'll take
care of you.'

'You're very kind,' I gratefully returned. 'I am very much
obliged to you.'

'You haven't got a sister, have you?' said Steerforth yawn-
ing.

'No,' I answered.

'That's a pity,' said Steerforth. 'If you had one, I should
think she would have been a pretty, timid, little bright-eyed
sort of girl. Good night, young Copperfield.'

'Good night, sir,' I replied.

I thought of him very much after I went to bed, and raised myself, I recollect, to look at him where he lay in the moonlight, with his handsome face turned up . . .[2]

Before long Steerforth has given David a feminine nickname, and it is obvious that his interest is potentially homosexual. But it is not actually so. The author's strategy in all this is to prepare us for the seduction of Little Em'ly, and to show the cunning blindness of David's hero-worship, as Steerforth's cynicism becomes more and more obvious. It would be a misreading to see the course of the story as a deliberate concession to the prevailing ideas of what could decently be mentioned in a novel. Nor is there, necessarily, any falsification of probabilities. Many an adolescent sentiment, we may suppose, goes just so far and no further.

The time would come when a new race of propagandists for a homosexual way of life would cash in on this Victorian unawareness of hidden possibilities. In 1902, an anthology of homosexual literature* provokingly included passages from some of the most respected nineteenth-century writers, including Byron, Shelley, Leigh Hunt, Tennyson (*In Memoriam*) and Browning (*May and Death*). With the possible exception of Byron, none of these was constitutionally homosexual, and few, if any, of the passages chosen from them had any homosexual element at all.

Carpenter's most fruitful source, naturally, was the school-story, whether reminiscence or fiction. And some of the passages are indeed rather startling, like this one from Disraeli's *Coningsby*:

At school friendship is a passion. It entrances the being; it tears the soul. All loves of after life can never bring its rapture, or its wretchedness; no bliss so absorbing, no pangs of jealousy or despair so crushing and so keen.

The anthology makes no distinction of types, and it is unlikely that the editor sincerely believed that all his examples were genuinely homosexual. But in his attempt to endow a minority culture with a new respectability, he was glad to invoke a Prime Minister, a Poet Laureate, and a notable romantic monogamist.

Though some important novels, like *David Copperfield* and *The Mill on the Floss*, have schoolroom passages, the school story can

---

* Edward Carpenter, *Iolaus.*

seldom be taken seriously as literature. But the Victorian school story is worth a little attention here, since it was through the school story that the faint beginnings of a new understanding reached ordinary respectable people. There are guarded hints in *Tom Brown's Schooldays*, but they perhaps will have been ignored by most readers. A more notable case, interesting because it is the work of a more talented writer, is Howard Sturgis's *Tim* (1891).

Tim is the story of the devotion of a younger boy to an elder, who responds intermittently and a little half-heartedly. It ends in the death of the younger boy, Tim – a symbol, perhaps, of the fact that such an affection is unlikely to be prolonged into adult life. If it is, it must change its character, and become either openly homosexual, or else much less intense.

When Tim is fourteen, and the elder boy, Carol, is eighteen, Tim wonders whether Carol will ever be in love, or ever marry; and in this 'remote and awful contingency' would they stay close friends? When the story of David and Jonathan is read in chapel, Tim wonders whether any woman could ever love Carol as he does, and the scene is emphasized for the reader by a sunbeam striking the elder boy's curly head 'which seemed transfigured'.

Later Tim sacrifices the friendship in order to shield Carol from the anger of the girl he wishes to marry, since she has declared that she will never marry a man with an intimate friend. This nobility comes as a revelation to Carol, who had never understood the strength of Tim's affection.

When Tim is dying, he says:

'You kissed me that day, Carol [after a shooting accident which occasioned their first meeting]. Will you kiss me now?'

Carol bowed his head without a word and kissed him. And thus their friendship was sealed at either end.

Tim asks for the passage about David and Jonathan on his tombstone, stressing particularly the phrase 'passing the love of women'; then he asks his friend to leave him, because before death he must be alone with his father, whom he has always feared more than he has loved. Without any difficult struggle, duty triumphs over feeling.

From the literary point of view, all this is small beer, though as he showed in *Belchamber*, Sturgis was capable of distinguished work. But its historical importance, as the symptom (if not the

cause) of change is considerable. The ambivalence here is deliberate. Sturgis knows perfectly well that he is writing about
homosexual sentiments, and he is putting up a persuasive case in
their favour. The first readers will generally have found the sentiment less cloying than many now would do. The affection of
which he writes is physically pure and morally responsible.
The highest ethical concepts, charity, self-sacrifice, humility are
invoked. Moreover the background is thoroughly English; the
plot, though a little contrived, contains many probable and
familiar episodes. If you were at Eton, you would find in the book
many things you remembered. And if you weren't, you would be
reminded that the upper-classes were a law unto themselves.
Many readers may have found the death-scene as touching as
their grandfathers had found Little Nell. They will have been
persuaded to accept and approve something really homosexual,
but surprisingly near to their ordinary sentiments and aspirations.
It would all tend to reduce that sense of the monstrous and the
bizarre which had for so long been inseparable from all dis-
cussions of the subject. A whole tribe of less able writers of school-
stories, such as E. F. Benson, will have had a similar effect.

Generally, then, Victorian readers were presented with two
views of the matter, either something tender, innocent, boyish
and sentimental, where a chaste kiss was the ultimate reach of
daring, or else something violently unnatural. The latter type
seldom appeared in serious prose fiction; it was to be found in
poems like Swinburne's *Hermaphroditus*, written in 1863 and
published three years later, in the travel books of Burton and
others, and in certain scientific publications. There was also, as
with heterosexual pornography, an underworld of books like the
anonymous *Teleny* (1890), which has detailed descriptions of
homosexual acts, presented in alluring style.

But there is one major author who is entirely distinct from
the categories just outlined, and though he was only secondarily
a novelist, his unlikeness to nearly all other writers on the subject
makes him an arresting figure.

Walter Pater was entirely homosexual in temperament. He was
also a man to whom restraint, dignity and chastity were precious.
Marius the Epicurean (1885) is primarily the story of a spiritual
quest, and the theme of friendship is subordinate. The hero has
two friends, Flavian and Cornelius, who correspond to two stages
of his spiritual development.

Like many beautiful male figures in Pater's writings, Flavian is compared both to a Greek god and to a fine statue. He is intellectual and sensual, loves dress and is or has been a frequenter of prostitutes.

How often, afterwards, did evil things present themselves in malign association with the memory of that beautiful head, and with a kind of borrowed sanction and charm in its natural grace. To Marius, at a later time, he counted for as it were an epitome of the whole pagan world, the depth of its corruption, and its perfection of form.[3]

Flavian soon dies, and the one happy day of comradeship Pater describes before this occurs under the aegis of Venus, as the young men are singing the praise of love. But, of course, it is the love of man and woman that they are celebrating; Marius and Flavian are apart from the processions and celebrations. Though Marius's attachment is called 'feverish', turning him into an 'uneasy slave', there is no real current of homosexual feeling on Flavian's side. Without being very specific the author leaves us to suppose that Marius is chaste in feeling as in deed, while Flavian has not abandoned his wayward female loves. We understand this better when we have witnessed Flavian's pagan death-bed and are able to compare him with Cornelius. The meeting of Marius and Cornelius occurs in a Christian setting. In the persecution, Marius sacrifices himself (though he is not yet definitely a Christian himself) to secure the escape of his friend, who, we are told, is about to marry.

In each case, then, the chosen friend is heterosexual; in the first case, pagan and promiscuous, and in the other, Christian and virtuous. Marius's feelings for each are not precisely defined. It is clear, though, that each at the time is more to him than any woman could be. It is clear, too, that even in the period of his friendship with Flavian, and still more later, Marius lives mainly in the realm of the intellect, and his affection is of a rarefied, almost ethereal, character.

All this, we can hardly doubt, is a tactful, but perfectly genuine equivalent for the predicament of the author and those like him, homosexual in constitution, chaste either instinctively, or by deliberate moral restraint. Here we are in a different realm from the naïvety of David Copperfield, and the *faux naïf* of *Tim*. There is no concealment and no falsification. Marius's eye is homosexual, like Pater's own, but his conduct is not. Not all Pater's disciples would follow this austere path; but when they did not the master was quick to repudiate them. Six years after *Marius*, Pater wrote a review of Wilde's *Dorian Gray*, and when we recall his habitual temperance of language, and his love of understatement, we may call the condemnation savage:

> To lose the moral sense therefore, for instance, the sense of sin and righteousness, as Mr Wilde's hero – his heroes are bent on doing as speedily, as completely as they can – is to lose, or lower, organization, to become less complex, to pass from a higher to a lower degree of development.[4]

In *Marius*, a homosexual temperament is compatible with an asceticism which controls the heart as well as the body. The decencies (or pruderies) of the age are irrelevant here. Pater said just what he meant.

In Frederick Rolfe (1860–1913) we find for the first time a novelist for whom the homosexual theme was central, and who tried to find in it a spiritual dimension. The literary historian may be tempted to allow Rolfe more significance than he warrants. Had he been a great writer, or even a good writer of the second rank, he would have been profoundly interesting. The inner life of the spirit is, in the main, an absentee from the great tradition of the English novel. The stresses endured by the man of religious temperament and strong faith who is constitutionally homosexual could make a novel of the highest originality. It would be hard to name another topic so important in itself which had been so completely neglected.

Unfortunately, Rolfe is a writer of a grotesque badness, who lacked above all the interest in human nature's variety, which is the novelist's indispensable gift. The only person he was interested in was himself, but he did not understand himself, so the path of serious autobiography was also closed to him.

All the same, *The Desire and Pursuit of the Whole** retains its claim to an extended footnote in the history of the novel, since it has something new to offer. It is a hypnotically concentrated account of the world as it appears to a bitter, lonely egoist, who is craving for a holiness he can never begin to attain, and for a carnal release of his homosexual nature, which will never be satisfying.

* Written about 1909, published in 1934.

The title may be supposed to refer to Plato's *Symposium*; and nowhere, perhaps, in all literature does the idea of sex as the consequence of the splitting of the personality into two separate beings seem more appropriate. The hero is seeking for himself in another; he resents his inability to be self-sufficient. He is incapable, like his creator, of love or friendship; and as for desire, the more keenly he feels its sting, the more he detests its indignity. Aristotle's remark about the man contented with loneliness being either a beast or a god hardly seems far-fetched here. The hero is a failed god, constantly liable to be transformed into a beast.

Zilda, or Zildo, the shadowy other half of the Platonic whole, is so indeterminate in sex that the pronoun 'he' can change to 'she' in the course of a sentence or two. This is not really an extreme example of the well-known homosexual literary practice of translating the desired male into a female for the sake of respectability. Zildo exists entirely as a dream or fantasy in the author's mind; and it may be that in that dream-world, his sex really was indeterminate. For Rolfe had a drive towards purity only less strong than his drive towards carnal degradation; and what he desired most of all was to imagine Zildo as sexless:

the candid wistful visage, the lovely form full of promise, full of joy, the slim, magnificent membrature, all alive, all supple, all indefectible, all without trace of sex. Oh to take! – marry? Rather than anything else in the world. Oh to take the offered bud, which taking would bring to bloom. Buds neglected wither . . . Yes; he must leave it, to wither: because he might not take it against its will.[5]

After many chapters of this kind of thing, the book ends suddenly with a marriage, and the boy-girl unconvincingly but permanently transformed into a girl.

More interesting than all this is the frank running commentary of the embittered homosexual against the world, women and heterosexual institutions. There is often a grain of truth in the prejudiced tirade. For instance:

That is the worst of the human female. She comes brazenly out; and jests and jousts with the male. He lets himself forget how strong he is. Suddenly, unknowingly, unintentionally, he hurts her. She runs back into her stronghold . . . she is a martyr.[6]

On the subject of prostitution, he for once produces an almost convincing piece of dialogue:

'How often have you committed this mortal sin?' It was quite a joke. 'About twice in a month'. 'Since when?' 'About a year.' 'What do you pay?' 'The price is five franchi: but we students pay three . . .' 'Who first took you there?' 'No one, signor: I went by myself.' 'Now why?' 'I had a wish. And one of my friends went when he was thirteen.'

Prostitution has always been a subject that novelists, reflecting in this, society's perplexities, find it difficult to see in any moral perspective. The homosexual's resentment at its privileged status, regarded as an inescapable social necessity, seems well justified. It would be hard to discover any theological, moral or social argument for the idea that a casual homosexual act is infinitely more heinous than fornication. It is more a prejudice natural and comforting to a powerful majority. It is hardly of a more advanced order of ideas than 'Wogs begin at Calais'. For once the frequently absurd Rolfe speaks with persuasive dignity as he tells this truth.

By his failure as a novelist, Rolfe points to what is lacking in the treatment of homosexuality by English novelists. I mean a sense of the condition as a special case of a universal human condition. To find this we must turn to Proust. In an introduction of 1937 to the lesbian novel *Nightwood*,* T. S. Eliot wrote:

> In the Puritan morality that I remember, it was tacitly assumed that if one was thrifty, enterprising, intelligent, practical and prudent in not violating social conventions, one ought to have a happy and 'successful' life. Failure was due to some weakness or perversity peculiar to the individual; but the decent man need have no nightmares. It is now rather more common to assume that all individual misery is the fault of 'society', and is remediable by alterations from without . . . It seems to me that all of us, so far as we attach ourselves to created objects and surrender our wills to temporal ends, are eaten by the same worm . . . To regard this group of people as a horrid sideshow of freaks is not only to miss the point, but to confirm our wills and harden our hearts in an inveterate sin of pride.

This is an eloquent plea for the Catholic moral tradition, and

---

* See chapter IX for my view of *Nightwood*.

for its application to the art of the novel. Unfortunately, the Catholic tradition, which has contributed works of genius in poetry and autobiography, has given little to the English novel. Rolfe, the failed priest, is there to remind us of our loss.

II

Forster

> It's one thing for England and another for Italy. There we plan and get on high horses. Here we find what we are, for things go off quite easily by themselves.
>   Philip Herriton in *Where Angels Fear to Tread*, chap. VI

When a complex subject is regarded as dangerous or embarrassing, incompatible views of it tend to flourish side by side. This is especially true of homosexuality in the later nineteenth century, when Forster was growing up. An ordinary citizen, with no experience and no special knowledge, might have been aware of a number of current views. First, homosexuality was a consciously-chosen perversion, closely associated with a hyper-aesthetic intellectualism, moral irresponsibility and a general contempt for ordinary people, the family, patriotism, work, honesty, fidelity and English traditions. People affected by this perversion (of whom Oscar Wilde was the most celebrated) were members of a small, idle and decadent clique.

This view contrasted strongly with the next, that homosexuality was a form of immaturity. For this there was a persuasive common-sense basis in the acknowledged fact that the adolescent male often forms emotional attachments to men or to older or younger boys, that this tendency is intensified by the segregation of the sexes, and that most men emerge from adolescence firmly heterosexual. Many a solid late Victorian paterfamilias had memories of his public school, sentimental or carnal or both, which he generally did not confide to his wife, and perhaps not, in any frank or direct way, to his sons. It may well be that the attempt to suppress such memories was responsible, in part, for the unusually violent tone of moral condemnations in the field.

But a public school education also confronted men of talent with Greek culture. And the more intelligent kind of schoolmaster, whether or not he had any homosexual leanings, was often an ardent admirer of all things Greek; the intelligent boy's literary sensibility was awakened by Greek literature rather than by English; and if he had a philosophically questing mind, Plato was its chosen nourishment.

The effect of Greek culture generally, and of Plato in particular, in disturbing the assumptions of the surrounding society must have been considerable. To some extent, of course, this is true also of previous centuries. But the education of the seventeenth and eighteenth centuries, much more than that of the nineteenth, gave the primacy to Latin, and the Greek influence was much less insistent. Two points about the Greeks were especially important here. First, Greek homosexuals married, had children and were respected in society. They were often thoroughly masculine and warlike. Second, Plato and Socrates were conceived as lay saints, high-minded, austere philosophers, who, by their deep concern for the things of the spirit, had prepared the way for Christ. It would have strained credulity to say that imitating Socrates, or being influenced by the *Symposium* could lead either to effeminacy or to decadence. Yet the effect of his Greek studies on a sensitive boy must often have been bewildering. How was he to reconcile or even to connect the Greek text expounded in the morning by an enthusiastic (or perhaps embarrassed) scholar with the lubricious intimacies of the changing-room a few hours later? And yet, of course, the contrast would be no more stark than that of the heterosexual world, where monogamic idealism and novels about true love competed for attention with the allurements of the London streets.

Different as was the world of Oscar Wilde from that of public school Platonists, they had one obvious point in common: both were for the few, both were intellectual élites. But the ordinary citizen's bewilderment was to be increased in the eighties and nineties by the appearance of a new kind of homosexual propaganda, whose sources were not Greek but German and American, which was popular rather than cliquey, radical in social tendency, and associated with the open air more than with art and scholarship. The apostle of this new school was Edward Carpenter, and its remote half-understood prophet was Walt Whitman.

Carpenter's general interest lies in his lack of originality and in his frankness. He is a kind of intellectual resultant of different pressures. He presented to an English public for the first time the ideas of German and Austrian theorists, who maintained that homosexuals ('homogenic' was the word preferred by Carpenter) were a third sex, sometimes known as urnings.* The condition was supposed to be innate and unchangeable, and there was a definite suggestion that urnings were on the whole a higher type, superior to both men and women in intelligence, aesthetic sensibility, loyalty and power of affection. The idea that the homosexual was born and not made was used to refute moral disapproval; but its scientific vogue was short. It became less persuasive after Freud had attacked it. But Carpenter was not a scientist and his appeal lay in the fact that he was able to combine this scientific theory with a new form of Anglo-Saxon Puritanism. Carpenter, like his other master Whitman, is a man of the simple life. The absence of servants, a vegetable diet, long walks and hearty wood-cutting would deprive the homosexual relation of all taint of solitary self-indulgence. Democratic or radical views would counter the tendency of all minorities to form themselves into self-conscious élites.† With notable, and probably unconscious skill, Carpenter turned the tables on the complacent heterosexual world. It was *they* now who were self-indulgent, artificial, distrustful of the simple impulses of nature. The noble homosexual, rising early to light his own fire, and willing to sacrifice everything for his chosen friend, was more in harmony both with nature and with conscience. Carpenter presents a new homosexual version of a venerable English synthesis – a synthesis between moral strictness, self-righteousness and doing as you like. It is the system of the seventeenth-century Puritan with nature substituted for God. To follow your own natural impulses is to follow nature itself; but to do this requires courage and self-discipline. It is never an easy option; it is rather the conventional, worldly (and heterosexual) people who never follow the prompting of nature because they care so much for the opinion of the world. Carpenter's *Love's Coming of Age* was published in 1896, the year after Wilde was sent to prison. It is no wonder the public was confused.

---

* *Urning* was a word derived, via German, from the Greek Ouranos (heaven). Thus the implication was that homosexuals were more spiritual than other people.
† Two titles of Carpenter's works are characteristic: *Towards Democracy* and *Civilization: Its Cause and Cure*.

Carpenter's particular importance for us lies in his influence on Forster. But, before considering that, it is necessary to consider the latter's more general intellectual and moral heritage, and to understand how it was that (as he explained in the terminal note to *Maurice*) a moment came when Carpenter's doctrines seemed to be just what he needed. Forster never knew his father, and he received the coddling, suffocating, female kind of upbringing which is a classic influence in the formation of a homosexual. But behind this immediate home influence was a venerable tradition, which perhaps affected him ever more deeply, the tradition of the Clapham Sect. This tradition, honoured by the names of Wilberforce, Stephen, Thornton and Venn is far too complex to be treated here.* But certain features stand out. It was a tradition of deep evangelical piety, of intellectual culture, of personal responsibility, and of energetic public action in great public causes such as the abolition of slavery. And it was the tradition of a self-conscious élite, spiritual and intellectual. The odd use of the word 'saved' in *The Longest Journey* to mean 'one of our set' and therefore free from the taint of the boorish, philistine, uncomprehending world is a secular variant of the curious mingling of the evangelical doctrine of salvation by faith with the social and intellectual superiority of Clapham. Similarly, Bloomsbury was, in some respects, a secular equivalent of Clapham.

The young Forster found himself set apart from the ordinary, busy world in several different ways at once. First, and most important, he was a homosexual in a world oscillating uneasily between incompatible views of the meaning, causes, limits and moral implications of the condition. Then he was a man whose unearned income saved him from any need to work, and he was a fastidious intellectual, and potential artist, who naturally gravitated to an exclusive Cambridge set, the leading vices of which were affectation and intellectual contempt for the ordinary man. Meanwhile, the Clapham sense of spiritual fulfilment, had been transposed in Forster's case into a mild but obstinate *culte de moi*.

Yet he was a very cautious and conventional young man too. No one, reading his early novels, could doubt that love between man and woman was a subject he found boring; yet it is hard to decide how deliberate is the intrusion of the concealed homo-

---

* For a fuller discussion see my *Truth to Life* (Collins 1974).

sexual theme into this time-honoured topic of the novel. It is certainly very uneven in its incidence. Some of the books, like *Howard's End*, show it very little.

In the early novels it is usually an Italian who is seen with the homosexual's appraising or enthusiastic eye. Of this kind are Gino in *Where Angels Fear to Tread*, and the 'Phaethon' driver in chapter VI of *A Room with a View*. The obvious device of employing a spinster lady, like Miss Abbott or Miss Bartlett, to convey the homosexual's feelings for the man is discreetly used. Being an English spinster she will not make any indecorous advances. She will probably be too old and plain to excite the interest of a young Italian male, so a vague yearning will be all. Nevertheless it is a carnal yearning. 'I'm in love with Gino ... I mean it crudely,'[7] says Miss Abbott near the end. Here, as in some other cases, consistency of character and ordinary probabilities are sacrificed to the need to express disguised homosexual feeling. We know Miss Abbott, and she would never have said this.

The function of Italy in these books is curious. In part, indeed, it is traditional; the Italy of the Grand Tour, of Shelley and of Pater, with its perennial message of antiquity, civilization, warmth and beauty to the starved denizens of the north, battered by the English climate, bullied by English Puritanism, grieved by English ugliness. But there are, nevertheless, special features.

Italy is seen as the land of spontaneity; its social traditions and moral restraints are either ignored altogether, or else shown as wonderfully and inexplicably encouraging the free play of impulse. In Italy what you ought to do, and what you are expected to do, and what you want to do mysteriously tend to be one and the same thing. This is very strange; and only in part to be explained by the serene confidence of the moneyed Englishman on holiday in the 'years before the flood'. The lesson is reinforced by those English characters, especially the elder Emerson in *A Room with a View*, who are naturally in key with the Italian spirit. 'To be happy' old Mr Emerson constantly seems to say, 'requires only an act of the will'. Unhappiness is due to convention, stuffiness, respectability, timidity, English hypocrisy. Here, indeed, is a leading source of disharmony in these early books, as important in its way as the disharmony caused by the attempt to express homosexual emotions through heterosexual stories. For the books are, with all their faults, obviously the work of a talented and witty writer, who is a penetrating observer of the comic aspects of the social scene. How intractable, in the midst of them, appears this crude romanticism, this insistent and insidious appeal to ignore all the lessons of experience, to forget that happiness is not, in the real world, a matter of choice; and worse, to forget that the subordination of the will to impulse is one of the surest and quickest roads to misery. Mr Emerson's muddled and contradictory moralizing ('Do you suppose there's any difference between spring in nature and spring in man?')[8] escapes completely from the shrewd appraising glance of the social comedian.

How are we to explain this? Certainty is not possible, but it seems probable that the restraints, social and self-imposed, upon a homosexual of conventional and cautious character are partly responsible. Homosexual fulfilment, because it is difficult or impossible to attain, retains the illusion of being utterly, finally blissful. The heterosexual man knows very well in his twenties that certain scraps of traditional wisdom are true, that passion is deceptive, that desire is unpredictable, that happy marriage requires discipline and sacrifice. Forster, in his twenties, in many respects already an accomplished novelist, is still in this one respect in the cloudcuckooland of the dreaming adolescent girl who has never been kissed. And, as so often happens with sexual fantasies of all kinds, he projects his sexual musings on to his whole world-view. All happiness, not merely sexual happiness is assured, in Mr Emerson's view, tacitly endorsed by the author, to him who makes a determined bid for it.

In some of the early short stories a Pan-figure had been used to link the homosexual musings with a diffused pagan religiosity. The realistic tone of *A Room with a View* makes such a device impossible here. Its place is taken by the now time-honoured and quasi-sacred ritual of the homosexual novel – the bathe. The few pages that describe this[9] are worth close attention, both for the technique of presentation and for their general teaching.

The bathe takes place in a muddy and not very secluded suburban pond. It is obvious from the first that it represents a moral test. He who funks the bathe is tacitly compared to a soldier who runs away in battle; and he who engages in it half-heartedly ('Wetting his hair first – a sure sign of apathy') is convicted of false values. The bathe is a way to communication with some ultimate spirit of nature; man is subsumed into a cosmic dance with 'water, sky, evergreens, a wind'. The piles of clothes left on the pond's edge become symbols of convention, respectability, death.

But if it is a cosmic and pantheistic bathe, it is also definitely a homosexual bathe. The profusion of hints offered to indicate this is almost excessive. One figure is 'Michelangelesque on the flooded margin' (this perhaps may be the twentieth-century equivalent of the 'decent obscurity of a learned language', with art replacing Latin.) Then the three 'gentlemen' are compared to nymphs.

But what happens next is extremely characteristic of Forster, or rather of the books he published in his own lifetime. A scene on the edge of becoming openly sensual is suddenly deflated by a very probable event – the approach of ladies.

How cautious, how tricky, how superficially deceptive, how unconvincing really this is. The whole point of the scene, as of other homosexual bathing scenes had been that the desire of the homosexual to see another man's naked body is one that society, being heterosexual in all its assumptions, regards as harmless, provided the motive is not admitted and indifference is feigned. Propriety imposes its veto precisely at the point where sexual interest, for the homosexual, comes to an end. The frolic has been enjoyed, and propriety is impeccably preserved.

The last words of the chapter gently and tactfully insist on the natural harmony between the pagan-religiose and the homosexual elements in the frolic:

> On the morrow the pool had shrunk to its old size and lost its glory. It had been a call to the blood and to the relaxed will, a passing benediction whose influence did not pass, a holiness, a spell, a momentary chalice for youth.

The Longest Journey (1907) was published a year before *A Room with a View*: but it represents in some ways a later development of Forster's thinking. It is the first book that faintly foreshadows *Maurice*. It is still, of course, inexplicit and at times deceptive. Rickie is in some ways closer to the author than any hero before Maurice, though he is very much less intelligent than his creator. His one moment of vision comes when he witnesses the passionate embrace of Gerald and Agnes. Perhaps the plot requires Gerald's unexpected death immediately after this; otherwise Rickie might have discovered that the man, not the woman, had been the focus of his interest. Deceived about this, he marries Agnes and lives to regret.

Agnes herself is portrayed with a petulant animus, which is mainly absent from the other more high-spirited early novels. Ansell's absurd pseudo-philosophical arguments against her existence are taken seriously in the sense that they point to the conclusion that she is spiritually null; and there is a suggestion, pervasive though imprecise, that her faults are typically feminine. Here, perhaps, more than anywhere else, Forster's limitations as a creative artist are seen. Women henceforth in his novels (except in *Howard's End*) tend to approximate to two types: the boring, self-important, priggish (like Agnes or Adela Quested) and the mother-figure, like Mrs Moore. We may excuse the homosexual for thinking of them personally in this limited way. But, remembering the achievement of Proust, we need not excuse the artist. Stephen is a more elaborate and more tiresome version of Gino, a timid, feminine idea of the over-mastering male at one with nature.* But he is thoroughly English; the Italian vision has been naturalized into the English countryside. Salisbury Plain seems to whisper of Pan, or perhaps of native English gods. Forster is ready now for *Maurice*, with its English setting, and thoroughly English story.

Maurice was completed in 1914 and published in 1971. Without it, this part of our story would be fragmentary. With all its faults (some of which are obvious) it is an outstandingly honest, intelligent and fascinating work. Personally cautious still, since he never published it in his lifetime, Forster as artist now abandoned all evasiveness. The absurdities of *Maurice* (and it has one or two) are not like the absurdities of the bathe just described. They come from a deeper level; they are inherent in the author's vision and predicament.

The first point to stress is the ordinariness of the hero; an ordinary, muddled, second-class brain inhabiting the ordinary, beefy, English-public-school body, with most of the ordinary tastes and prejudices of a rather complacent stockbroker in the days of England's imperial supremacy:

> While paying three guineas he caught sight of himself in the glass behind the counter. What a solid young citizen he looked – quiet, honourable, prosperous without vulgarity. On such does England rely. Was it conceivable that on Sunday last he

---

* I once heard a lady speaking of a bull thus: 'He's very naughty you know. He nearly killed the farmer. I do love him.' I was irresistibly reminded of Forster's attitude to Stephen Wenham.

had nearly assaulted a boy?[10]

This is a tremendous relief. By comparison most homosexual fiction in English appears melodramatic and tawdry, like the voice of prurient schoolboys. And it was sound tactics to centre the story on a man in most respects unlike the author. No doubt some homosexuals are artists and many more are failed artists; but Forster sensibly ignored this fact. He wanted to show the impact of the workaday world on a sexual temperament that is neither very rare, nor restricted to a single class or intellectual type.

A sign of this new artistic confidence, of a man at last saying what he really means, is to be seen in the handling of the one overtly symbolic passage in the book, in which Mr Ducie illustrates his little lecture on the 'facts of life' by drawing with a stick on the sand of the seashore. Mr Ducie forgets to rub the drawings out, and is afterwards bothered by the fear that they might be seen by a lady:

'Sir, won't it be all right?' Maurice cried. 'The tide'll have covered them by now.'

'Good Heavens . . . thank God . . . the tide's rising.'

And suddenly for an instant of time, the boy despised him.[11]

The fine economy of this needs to be contrasted with the often breathless and cumbersome symbolism of the early novels – for instance, when the bookcase falls on Leonard Bast. Here the tide unobtrusively combines its different functions. It represents the transitoriness of the impression made on this boy by new ideas which are of absorbing interest to other boys. Male and female is and will always be an unknown language to him. At this level the image has a grave beauty. But the episode provides also an ironic comment on society's uneasy attempt to combine two ideas, which are both, in a way, true, but which are hard for common-sense to reconcile – that sex is significant and momentous, and that it is private, embarrassing and animal.

Less successful, perhaps, is the little trick of plot in the same chapter. Mr Ducie asks the fourteen-year-old boy and his wife to dine with him 'this day ten years hence.' When that day comes,[12] Mr Ducie and Maurice meet by chance in the British Museum.* Mr Ducie vaguely remembers him, but he muddles his name, and

* An improbable place for Maurice and for the gamekeeper, though not for Mr Ducie. The venue seems to be chosen so that a model of the Parthenon may reflect a French and Greek dignity on the homosexual pair.

has certainly forgotten his invitation. Maurice is engaged in a crucial verbal contest with the gamekeeper, who, if we are to believe Forster's ending, is about to provide Maurice with the equivalent of a lifelong happy marriage.

It is in this happy ending, and in the whole figure of Scudder, the gamekeeper, that we see Carpenter's influence. Carpenter helped him to exorcize the nineties and the precious, over-civilized image of homosexuality. Scudder is presented (a little clumsily, perhaps) as a breath of fresh air. After their initiation into the physical, here called 'sharing', Maurice:

> was not afraid or ashamed any more. After all, the forests and the night were on his side, not theirs; they, not he, were inside a ring fence.[13]

Who are 'they'? Other people in general, the respectable world and heterosexuals. Coolly considered, this is nonsense. Forests do not take sides on such questions; and the animals that live in forests are for the most part heterosexual. But it would be a mistake, I think, to ascribe the muddle entirely to the muddled mind of Maurice. It is the voice of Carpenter, and, for the moment at least, uncharacteristically shrill, perhaps because of hidden doubts about his own logic, the voice of the author.

The obverse of this, that normal, married love is stuffy and airless, is not forgotten either. When Maurice goes to the hypnotist to be cured of homosexuality, he acquiesces at first, and then rebels:

> Ah for darkness – not the darkness of a house which coops up a man among furniture, but the darkness where he can be free! Vain wish! He had paid a doctor two guineas to draw the curtains tighter, and presently, in the brown cube of such a room, Miss Tonks would lie prisoned beside him.[14]

Near the end we find the pure milk of the Carpenter ethos in Maurice's thoughts:

> They must live outside class, without relations or money; they must work and stick to each other till death. But England belonged to them.[15]

A cancelled chapter in which Maurice and Alec Scudder grow old as happy woodcutters is eminently Carpenterian.

And yet, Scudder is a *gamekeeper*. And a gamekeeper, like a valet, belongs essentially to a settled world based on hereditary wealth and social deference. The canniness, the comfortable conservatism of this are pure Forster; and Carpenter, could he have read *Maurice*, would surely have been disappointed at an incomplete discipleship.* Scudder himself remains a puzzling figure. He has two opposite roles, the dangerous plebeian blackmailer, and the honest, faithful 'married' lover. He is fairly convincing in either role, though much less vivid than Maurice himself and his Cambridge friend, Clive Durham. (We must remember here the difficulty usually experienced by highly educated people in understanding and portraying the uneducated; this is a general difficulty, separable from the homosexual theme.) But the trouble is that we can hardly accept that the same man plays both parts. It seems as if Forster needed two different Scudders, and telescoped them for the sake of brevity. The author's attempts to explain that he really meant well all the time he was threatening blackmail are unconvincing.

This simplistic romantic tale is, in the author's intention, the central thing. But the reader may disagree. He may well find Clive the book's most interesting character; and one is surprised to notice how fresh to the novel tradition he is. He develops from sentimental adolescent, fancying himself in love with one of his own sex, to ordinary married man, sincerely horrified to hear of the possible goal of the yearnings he once felt. And this is a very common development, very little understood or explained, imperfectly remembered as a rule, by those who have experienced it. The book's central irony, that Clive, who is really heterosexual, is the first to shock the irrevocably homosexual Maurice with words of love, is effective and true. In the circumstances, Maurice's naïve words in reply are as poignant as they are amusing:

Durham, you're an Englishman. I'm another. Don't talk nonsense. I'm not offended, because I know you don't mean it, but it's the only subject absolutely beyond the limit as you know, it's the worst crime in the calendar, and you must never mention it again. Durham! a rotten notion really . . .[16]

The idyllic bicycling day, which follows later after Maurice has recovered from this shock, is one of the most convincing of the numerous romps in Forster's works – even though, regrettably, it includes yet another bathe – because it is not a pagan experience of mystery, but a simple, carefree, youthful

* It could be argued, perhaps, that Alec's status really works the other way – that both men emerge from the settled, conventional world into freedom, or what the book, rather fancifully, calls the greenwood. I do not find this convincing, since Alec whether as sinister blackmailer or trusted friend retains the tones of a servant. There is no suggestion that class becomes irrelevant here.

day, suggesting to us but not to them a painful contrast with what is to come.

In the first half of the book, Clive is a most penetrating study of a common type of young man – the kind who is growing up intellectually at a much faster rate than he is emotionally. The attractive, innocent priggishness of the condition is beautifully caught. Unfortunately, Forster cannot keep it up. In his *Terminal Note* of September 1960, he wrote: 'Clive deteriorates, and so perhaps does my treatment of him.' This is a revealing half-truth. It would be more accurate to say that because the treatment deteriorates, the character has to be made to. The later appearances of Clive are unconvincing because they are written with personal animus, a concealed dislike and envy of that great world of marriage and babies and ordinary feelings, which, after all, is and must be the world of all of us, even for those who are unfitted for it or opt out of it. This is a pity; and, even if one were willing to concede the whole Carpenter-Forster moral case, it would remain regrettable. Monks generally respect the institution of marriage and admire the best feminine qualities; and if they don't, so much the worse monks they. Almost, we are tempted to bring in against Forster the verdict given against Maurice: guilty of the Englishman's inability to conceive of variety. There are people like the later Clive, but they do not develop naturally out of the Clive we have been shown before. Perhaps we need two Clives as well as two Alec Scudders.

If the carefree Cambridge day is the best, the book also gives a glimpse of the worst:

> His expression aroused the suspicions and the hopes of the only other person in the carriage. This person, stout and greasy-faced, made a lascivious sign, and, off his guard, Maurice knocked him down . . . He spluttered apologies, offered money. Maurice stood over him, black-browed, and saw in this disgusting and dishonourable old age his own.[17]

Unlike all previous fictional studies of homosexuality, the book can claim inclusiveness as well as ordinariness.

It remains to consider the ethical nature of homosexual marriage as Forster conceives it. It is clearly loyal, lifelong and exclusive; it is all the more surprising, therefore, to find it so entirely based on physical attraction. This precedes any mutual understanding of character, and overrides the absence of shared interests. The body is wiser than the mind, and more truthful than the heart. Strange, contrary to all normal experience and slightly crazy. But there can be no doubt that it is what the book says.

III

Satire

Good satire requires understanding, even sympathy with the thing satirized. Open discussion is a necessary condition of understanding. It is not surprising then, that a serious satirical treatment of homosexual culture had to wait until the 1930s. In *The Near and the Far* (1931–40) L. H. Myers gave us something which is, like Forster's work, unchallenged on its own ground. It is the only notable satirical study we have.

Myers's book professes to have as its subject India in the reign of the Emperor Akbar, and the struggle for the succession between his sons, Salim and Daniyal. Though it is oriented and exotic, and though it makes serious use of the ideas of oriental religions, it deals really with things much nearer home. Prince Daniyal, the homosexual and founder and master of the 'Camp' is a complex satirical portrait of the literary homosexual of the Bloomsbury type; and being a Prince he is able to create a whole society round him, and to be courted and admired by many whose spirit is different from his own. Myers is really asking the question, 'Supposing these Bloomsbury men had undreamed-of power, wealth and influence, supposing they were near the mainstream of the nation's life, instead of in a quiet backwater, what would they do and be then?'

The Prince and his entourage are seen mainly through the eyes of two very different men. Prince Jali is an intelligent, wilful, sensual adolescent. His father, Rajah Amar is a wise man of the world with a strong thirst for the spiritual life. As a Buddhist, he is embued with a sense of the nothingness of all human affairs; as a stern moralist he discriminates sharply between different kinds of men. Prince Ali, Jali's cousin and Amar's nephew, is a bemused inmate of the Camp, and a candidate for seduction by Daniyal.

Daniyal professes to be devoted to the arts; the main occupation of the Camp's inhabitants is the writing and acting of plays. The physical appearance of the Camp is designed to convey its spiritual nature:

There across two miles of milky-blue water, shimmered and glittered the pleasure-houses, kiosks, and pavilions of Prince Daniyal's encampment. Seen through the haze of early morning they looked scarcely real – hardly more substantial than their inverted image that trembled upon the lake's pearly surface.[18]

For dynastic reasons, Daniyal is due to marry Princess Lalita. The tone of Daniyal's set is well caught in the following scene:

Late in the evening a certain fair-haired youth, who was sitting next to Daniyal at table, left the room and presently returned dressed in a girl's clothes. Sitting himself down by Daniyal again, he proceeded to mimic Princess Lalita in her speech and manners. Daniyal was evidently prepared for the entertainment, for he played up. He completed the scene by fondling the creature and addressing him as 'Lalita darling'.[19]

This scene with its weak, brainless comedy, its sycophancy, its contempt not only for conventions and decencies, but for people, reverberates through the book. And the author tacitly asks us to bear it in mind while he pauses to rebut three influential views of the Daniyal type. The first is, roughly, the Carpenter view, with which we are already familiar. Not, of course, that Carpenter would have approved of Daniyal, or even of his more tolerable English counterpart Lytton Strachey. But Myers's point is that the uncritical may confuse Carpenter and Daniyal. The bracing, simple type of homosexuality may win undeserved credit for the morally decadent type. Thus we are told that Akbar, who is the plain man magnified to an extraordinary power, might easily be misled about his son:

. . . although it is quite true that Akbar would object very strongly to Daniyal's vices were he to see them as they are, there is not the smallest chance of his doing so. In his mind sodomy is associated with stories of youthful Greek heroes bound together in death-defying friendship; it reminds him, too, of his own early days and of rough, manly loves amongst the young warriors of the Steppes. Sodomy, in his view of it, is at the furthest possible remove from effeminacy or perversion. It is an excess of virility; it is merely the young fighter's peccadillo.[20]

This kind of mistake is, of course, a misconception of the nature of the case. The next is, for Myers, a fundamentally wrong view of moral questions, endemic in our century:

Was it possible [Jali reflects] that Daniyal and his friends were different from what he thought them? Did they possess compensating virtues that he was unable to see? Or, assuming that Daniyal was indeed what he thought him, was it necessary to look upon such a character as vile? Weren't all people very much alike when you got to know them? Wasn't it rather naïve to consider some people very good and others very wicked?[21]

The third, which occurs to the mind of a beautiful and brainless girl, is the one the inhabitants of the Camp would wish the world to take:

. . . homosexuality was at once a delectable piece of naughtiness, a badge of intellectual distinction, and the leaning natural to sensitive and superior personalities.[22]

It is typical of Myers's fierce seriousness to enshrine Lytton Strachey's own view of himself and his friends in the mind of the most stupid, and nearly the most immoral person in the book.

Daniyal's doctrine is that nothing in this world is nearly so important as art. And what is the nature of this art? It professes to be witty and satirical. This means sneering at ordinary humble people for not being enlightened and artistic; and, on the other hand, sneering at the great men of the past. The first Myers sees as a mean triumph over those less fortunate than himself. The second attempt fails more dismally ('The objects of Daniyal's mockery then, indeed, appeared wholly out of his reach; they towered above him like Colossi carved in the face of a cliff.')[23]

It is notable, too, that the intellectualism of this set has nothing to do with reason or with any pursuit of knowledge. Their inconsistency is obvious in combining rejection of all moral categories with a burning moral indignation against those who oppose them. The link between all these contradictory attitudes, of course, is egoism – and the hungry, defeated resentment of the man of talent aspiring to be a man of genius – or rather, to convince himself and others that he is a man of genius. The inner certainty that the truth is otherwise makes men of this sort morbidly sensitive to the public opinion they profess to despise. They are entirely dependent for their inner contentment upon an admiring circle of boon companions, and an awed, shocked and perhaps half-admiring public. The desire to shock and surprise is subject to a very severe law of diminishing returns. Soon, Daniyal has to take refuge in blasphemy, but here too novelty will pall. And all the time, the inner nature is being choked by affectation, so that Rajah Amar concludes: 'the posturer has swallowed up the man'.

Morally, Myers's fundamental point is that triviality is not a trivial thing. Something diabolical, a denial of all life, may appear locally as a petty snigger. To bring this idea home to the reader is a task of great difficulty; and the author's strategy for doing so has two parts. First, the exciting but at times rather shadowy struggle for the succession suggests great world-forces of cause and effect at work behind and through the motives of men. These forces will make use of Daniyal as of other men. Here, it seems to me, he is only successful intermittently; and in the last part of his work, *The Pool of Vishnu*, he seems uncertain of his aim.

The second and more fundamental idea, conveyed mainly through the Buddhist sensibilities of Rajah Amar, is that there is an eternal order of things, alien to all our passionate strivings; in the face of this the triviality of Daniyal is a pitiful impotence. Myers is a member of a long line of classical moralists who end by saying that things are as they are, and why then should we wish to be deceived? In this, when we consider the extraordinary difficulty of making abstract ideas tell in fiction, his measure of success was notable. So it is that the symbolical-naturalistic equivalent of this condemnation of the Camp by reality has in its context a quite surprising force:

> Daniyal's Camp was certainly not permanent, and after its desertion the light wooden structures that composed it would very soon rot away. He could see them in his mind's eye, flimsy ruins without any beauty in their decay; in the end mosses and creepers would spread over everything, willows and alders would sprout up, the site would disappear completely.[24]

It remains to ask, 'How complete is the opposition between Forster and Myers?' – and since they are our only two novelists of distinction who have seriously addressed themselves to the subject, this is a question of importance.*

Morally, the opposition is not as total as it first appears. The nearest approach to Daniyal in Forster's work is Risley in

---

* Naturally, I count Pater distinguished, but for him, as we have seen, the subject is not central.

Maurice; and, for him, Forster obviously has a strong distaste, though he might consider moral disapproval as misplaced. In each man there is a vein of ill-articulated nature-mysticism, though not of the same kind. The message of the caves in *A Passage to India* is that there is no ultimate spiritual order; moral questions do not therefore cease to be important, but they cease to require absolute answers. The morality of *Maurice* is an elegant and civilized version of 'Do your own thing'. Myers, confronted with a homosexual of a more sincere kind, might have been prepared to modify his criticisms. Daniyal, like Pope's Sporus, is meant as an extreme case.

But when all allowances are made, the two powerful artistic statements remain irreconcilable. One is eloquently advocating, the other is beautifully denying, that man is the measure of things. As will always happen, when its implications are energetically sought, sexual morality confronts us with ultimate questions.

CHAPTER IX

The Lesbian Theme

'I'm getting tired of men; they're so selfish and unreasonable.'
Patty Ringrose in *Eve's Ransom* by George Gissing
(1895) chap. XI

'Ah!' he said. 'Love, that terrible thing!'
She began to beat the cushions with her doubled fist. 'What could you know about it? Men never know anything about it, why should they? But a woman should know – they are finer, more sacred: my love is sacred and my love is great.'
The Doctor and Jenny in *Nightwood* by Djuna Barnes
(1936) chap. IV

If the burgeoning of the male homosexual topic in the novel was slow, half-hidden in swirling, deceptive mists of schoolboy sentiment, it yet assumes an appearance of relative clearness and simplicity, when compared with the lesbian. This is as we would expect, and there are many contributory causes. There is a greater delicacy in speaking of women's intimate life; there is a stubborn reluctance to credit the plain fact of nature that women are capable of physical desire. More oddly, the prevailing ignorance about the nature of the urges homosexuals, male and female, wished to gratify, and the practices in which some of them engaged, worked in opposite directions. There was a general delusion among the respectable that male homosexuals invariably practised anal intercourse;* and in people whose respectable sentiments are more highly developed than their moral apprehensions, this makes a world of difference. There was no corresponding view of what lesbians might achieve in their intimate embraces; a sexually aggressive woman is not altogether easy for a man or for most women to imagine. The resourcefulness of lust in the lesbian was

---

* Barrack-room obscenities in the British Army, spoken mainly by normal and innocent boys who wish to appear knowing, turn – or used to turn – mainly on ingenious variants of this rather uncommon practice.

perhaps as much underrated as, in the case of the male, it was exaggerated.

These purely physical points are comparatively trivial no doubt. But when we are dealing with that very curious, uncritical, shockable and morally naïve thing, the corporate sexual imagination of the race, it would be a false idealism to ignore them altogether. More serious are the social differences. The male homosexual, whether chaste and celibate or sexually active, is often a bachelor, who proclaims himself, deliberately or not, by style, clothes and manner. The lesbian, in the years before 1930, which are our main concern, was often the mother of a family, appearing to the world much like other wives and mothers. It is even possible that, in some cases, husbands, trained to the doctrine that sexual enjoyment was a male prerogative – or male infirmity, according as it was viewed – were unaware.*

Alternatively, the lesbian might be a spinster; but in this case the strength of the assumption that all women wished to marry, and that all men could, if they chose,† would cause her to be viewed differently from the homosexual bachelor, with less suspicion, though perhaps with more pity or contempt.

The effect of all these differences is seen in school stories, and it is paradoxical. The girls' school stories are more, not less, outspoken. In the late Victorian stories of L. T. Meade, girls go to bed with each other, in an affectionate or emotional spirit without any great sense of daring, and still less of sin. The following passage is much later, and strange as it may seem, the context indicates an entire unconsciousness on the author's part of lesbian indications:

> Norah and Connie . . . were a recognized couple. Con, who sold gloves in a big West End establishment, was the wife and home-maker; Norah, the typist, was the husband, who planned little pleasure trips and kept the accounts and took Con to the pictures.[1]

One might compare *David Blaize* (1915), written by one of the sons of Mrs Benson, mentioned above. From the first the question of the moral and physical purity of the friendship between an

---

* For a particularly interesting case see Betty Askwith's account of Mrs Benson, wife of the Archbishop of Canterbury and mother of A. C., E. F., and R. H. Benson, in *Two Victorian Families*.

† This assumption dies hard; I remember in 1969 a very distinguished Oxford bachelor, now dead, speaking in most contemptuous tones of an equally distinguished lady, and asking 'Why did she never marry, do you think?'

older and younger boy is crucial. Both are aware of the possibility
of a lapse, and just what it would entail. This is paradoxical, but
not in the end surprising. Authors and readers were less on their
guard about lesbians; therefore they could on occasion be more
outspoken.

In one simple and important way, the lesbian novel is richer
and more various than the male homosexual novel. The latter was
written almost exclusively by male homosexuals; and widely
as these may vary in art, in intelligence, in morals, this leads to a
certain sameness. The lesbian theme is treated by heterosexual
men like Dickens, by a chaste male homosexual, Henry James,
by a purveyor of heterosexual 'dark gods' (Lawrence), by a
mannish lesbian (Radclyffe Hall), and by Djuna Barnes, a lady
with as strong a literary interest in perversion as in inversion.
And all this is additional to Swinburne, an aggressively effeminate
masochist. If we fail to find the right moral bearings, it will not
be for any lack of variety in the witnesses.

Just as an inferior writer like Elsie Oxenham might in her
innocent unawareness use language seeming to imply a lesbian
relationship, while meaning no such thing, so might a major
author, like Conrad, seem to refuse or deny the topic after setting
a scene that might appear to require it. In *Chance*, the knowing
reader is given a series of hints about Mrs Fyne; she 'had a ruddy
out-of-doors complexion and wore blouses with a starched front
like a man's shirt, a stand-up collar and a long necktie'.[2] She is
escaping from an over-possessive father when she marries. She
has a series of obsessive affections for 'girl-friends'. She is a
feminist of a crude kind, who believes that woman:

> by the mere fact of her sex was the predestined victim of
> conditions created by men's selfish passions, their vices and
> their abominable tyranny . . .[3]

When the last and current favourite, Flora de Barral, is sought
in marriage by Mrs Fyne's brother, and Mrs Fyne tries her hardest
to prevent the match, we seem to have an almost over-neat
lesbian scenario. Mrs Fyne's jealousy, Flora's search for the nearest
male likeness, in the form of a brother, to the woman to whom she
is unconsciously attracted – it all seems to fit. All the more so
when we are told that Mrs Fyne's opposition to the marriage rests
upon the fact that she:

> did not want women to be women. Her theory was that they
> should turn themselves into unscrupulous sexual nuisances.[4]

And, to crown it all, when the marriage does take place, it is, apparently, for a long time unconsummated.

And yet, all this time the knowing reader has been misled. It is not a lesbian story at all, though it is, secondarily, about feminism, and rather more insistently, about the unpredictable effect upon both women, Mrs Fyne and Flora, of being the daughters of fathers they cannot truly love and respect. The proof of this lies not only in the later development of the story, which becomes a tale of romantic seeking within marriage of two loving but estranged hearts (Captain Anthony and Flora); a more cogent indication – since it is possible at least in theory for the centre of gravity of a novel to change completely halfway – is the essential soundness of the Fyne marriage. Mrs Fyne is a militant feminist, and she has the normal quick-witted woman's exasperation at male stupidity, insensitivity and idealism. None of this makes her, even in the most rarefied sense, a lesbian.

Various views of all this are possible. The hypothesis that Conrad knew how suggestive of lesbianism some of the early passages might be, and was deliberately teasing us, cannot be disproved. But it is surely, given his known character as man and author, most improbable. More improbable still, on the same grounds, is the idea that he half-intended to treat a fully lesbian situation, and then funked it. *Chance* was Conrad's first best-seller. For all its convoluted Marlovian intricacies, it fitted, well enough, the requirements of a novel-reading public of 1912, whose general character we know. It liked romance, sentiment and propriety. There can be no doubt that *Chance* appealed to the mass of its early readers as thoroughly healthy. And, granted its view of what health was, the general reading public was surely right, and some later over-ingenious critics surely wrong. Two points need stressing. First, the extraordinarily unsuspicious character of public feeling on this question, attested alike by the calm acceptance of Elsie Oxenham's puerilities and of Conrad's misleading subtleties. This contrasts strongly with public watchfulness on other tender sexual questions, including that of male homosexuality. Lesbianism simply did not enter into most people's calculations. The young person did not notice it, and Mr Podsnap's Edwardian or Georgian successor, for once, took no alarm. This idyllic state, of course, like all idyllic states was transitory; and in 1928, with the publication of *The Well of Loneliness*, one of the most tempestuous in the fine tradition of English literary rows occurred. It had all the character of a bursting dam. A dam of ignorance, of complete unsuspiciousness was breached only by a book that no one could fail to read as lesbian. When a dam bursts the whole countryside is flooded; and it requires an effort of imagination to remember that men once stood, secure and un-suspecting, on dry ground immediately below it. The critics who have detected a real lesbian theme in *Chance* are those who have not made this effort of imagination.

But there is another, more general point, and a particularly salutary one for the writer and the readers of a book about sexual morals composed in an age which has been taught by some of its prophets, and by more of its low publicists, to exaggerate the overriding importance of sexual motives. Feminism and lesbianism are entirely separable entities. They may often go together, but so do butter and jam without ceasing to have the inherent differences of animal and vegetable.

All this is the more odd, since the lesbian theme is not, as might perhaps be expected, a complete absentee from Victorian fiction. We have seen what Swinburne made of it, but his work was not published at the time. But it is strange to find it in Dickens.

The story of Miss Wade and Tattycoram in *Little Dorrit* (1855–7) is quite as direct and outspoken in treatment as any story of love in Dickens or in any respectable novelist of the same era. Indeed, it is rather more direct and less embarrassed than the 'normal' purity of David Copperfield and Agnes, and the 'normal' sinfulness of Carker in *Dombey & Son*. In each case, but more clearly and accurately in the lesbian case, the characters and impulses are there, and acts are left to the imagination.

We may wonder why more disturbance and shock was not caused to the public. It is not difficult, on reflection, to see why. Dickens was already famous, popular, trusted. From the point of view of the reading public he was in one sense predictable, and in another, unpredictable. He was predictable because his general social and moral attitudes were known. He was healthy, a devotee of hearth and home, virtuously indignant on all proper English and Protestant themes. (The actual cynicism of certain of his opinions on sexual questions was never hinted in his published works, and known only to a few intimates.) He was unpredictable in the glorious sense that the immense inventive complexity of his creative genius left one breathless. A single novel of Dickens's

has more characters, all different and memorable, than the whole
life work of another novelist. Miss Wade is an extended, detailed
and mainly accurate study. But she is only one among fifty,
equally memorable, or more memorable characters. There was no
need to be particularly curious about her.

The situation is clear, simple and convincing. Harriet, an
illegitimate child, is taken into his home by the warm-hearted
and unimaginative English liberal businessman, Mr Meagles, as
a substitute for his dead, and companion for his surviving,
daughter. She is given the name Tattycoram, which she resents,
and required to do little services for Pet, the daughter of the house.
She comes under the influence of Miss Wade, who is also illegitimate.

Miss Wade has been driven to despair, vengefulness and lesbian
passion by her thwarted love for Henry Gowan, who later marries
Pet. This makes a convenient neatness in the plot; but it is also
broadly typical of a standard view, agreeable alike to male vanity
and to ordinary feminine feeling. It was a view that Henry James
would later challenge – the view that the lesbian is usually the
disappointed or neglected lover of men.

Yet Dickens does not allow this standard view to be unchallenged. In the notable 'History of a Self Tormentor' (Part II, chap.
XXI) we find that Miss Wade, from the age of twelve, long before
she knew Gowan, had been capable of passionate devotion to
a girl, and of terrible fits of temper and jealousy on account of
her.

Her influence over Tattycoram has a suggestion of the demonic.
Mr Meagles accuses her of having 'a perverted delight in making a
sister-woman as wretched as she is'.[5] The Meagles' home represents peace and comparative contentment. The Wade temptation
is like a temptation to self-destruction. It is true that Mr Meagles
is represented as occasionally tactless in his kindness, and Miss
Wade inveighs heavily against Harriet's subordinate position,
calling it slavery. But we are not allowed to doubt that all this is
really slander. The impeccably impartial Clennam endorses the
sound moderation of the Meagles' requirements from Harriet;
and, in any case, Miss Wade defeats her own argument by claiming
a much more absolute and exclusive authority over the girl than
the Meagles do.

Tattycoram's repentant speech cannot possibly be taken as
mistaken or ironical:

Oh! I have been so wretched . . . always so unhappy and so repentant! I was afraid of her, from the first time I ever saw her. I knew she had got a power over me, through understanding what was bad in me so well. It was a madness in me, and she could raise it in me whenever she liked. I used to think, when I got into that state, that people were all against me because of my first beginning; and the kinder they were to me, the worse fault I found in them . . . And my beautiful young mistress not so happy as she ought to have been, and I gone away from her! Such a brute and wretch as she must think me! But you'll say a word to her for me, and ask her to be as forgiving as you two are? For, I am not so bad as I was, I am bad enough, but not so bad as I was.[6]

There are several reasons why this lurid episode may be called, from a literary point of view, an auspicious start for the lesbian theme in the English novel. The great difficulty about sexual topics, in all periods perhaps, and in that period certainly, is that people cannot or will not say what they really mean. Here Dickens, obviously without any profound knowledge of the subject, but with the artist's intuition and perceptiveness, is saying what he means. He sees lesbian passion as a diabolic threat to domestic life. It is a destructive force – not merely as evil destructive of good, but as tormented and *willed* misery destructive of beauty and joy. And that threatened domestic life naturally includes not only father, mother and children but all who partake in it, servants, spinster aunts and strangers like Tattycoram. There is not even a false appearance of joy in the lesbian life; there is not even a tawdry thrill, as in the allurements of the streets. Lesbians here are like those characters in Dante 'who walked wilfully in sorrow', and the motive, too, is the same – pride. A very one-sided view, of course, but one entirely consistent with the deepest ideals of apprehensions of the age. And our enquiry will not fail to provide us with other views.

II

We now come to the only novel written in English by a major author which has the lesbian relation as its central subject. Fortunately, *The Bostonians* (1885–6) is one of James's finest works, and removes altgoether the need (which there might be otherwise) to say that the subject has only been a footnote in the work of great writers, and an obsessive concern of very inferior ones. More profound, more subtle and more detailed than what *Little Dorrit* gives us, *The Bostonians* yet has important features in common. Once again, the control of Verena Tarrant by Olive Chancellor is seen as a kind of imprisonment. In the very first chapter, Olive's smile is compared to a 'thin ray of moonlight resting upon the wall of a prison'. And once again the distinctively lesbian passion is all on one side. Verena is impressed by Olive, feels an intellectual reverence, and even a moral reverence, but she is at all times a potential wife for a man; and she is aware, without analysing it, of the wholly different nature of Olive's feeling for her. And the book ends, as the Tattycoram episode does, with a release into 'normality'. Indeed James stresses this even more than Dickens does, marrying Verena to an extremely masculine, dominant man with old-fashioned views about woman's needs and functions.

But it is only the bare scheme that is similar to that of Dickens. The milieu is utterly different. In the New England of good causes, and transcendentalism dissolving into secular concerns, the spinster has a place of influence and public respect unknown to England. There is a sense throughout the book that women are dominant, and men, most men, are feeble. Ransom's sturdy strength and uncomfortable assertiveness are seen more as a splendid resistance by a threatened race of sexual inferiors than as the tyranny of a stronger power. It is in keeping with the book's whole drift that he should be poor, and Olive rich. And he has other things beside poverty to contend with in maintaining his position as the book's only man of determination. All the other men, including Verena's father, are dragged round like slaves to meetings which with unconscious irony denounce the violent tyrannies of their race.

At the same time James has been careful to avoid presenting his Boston ladies as Amazons, intent only on dragooning the male. By way of contrast to Olive he gives us the genial sexless lady Doctor Prance, who says 'Men and women are all the same to me . . . There is room for improvement in both sexes . . .'[7]

Much more important, he gives us the excellent Miss Birdseye, the truly feminine spinster, and the truly selfless and guileless devotee of feminist causes. She is something like a norm from which Olive has deviated, and her death[8] is both a moving episode and a moral touchstone. The dying Miss Birdseye dimly foresees the marriage of Ransom and Verena, and gives it an implied blessing. Ransom is touched by her 'essentially feminine' nature; despite Miss Birdseye's unrepentant attachment to the feminist cause, it is Ransom who is soberly and tenderly in key with the feeling aroused by her death, and Olive, the militant feminist, who is dismayed and confused by the scene, and who responds to Miss Birdseye's dignified farewell, in her last recorded words, with a shriek, 'I shall see nothing but shame and ruin'.

James has chosen to make his hero a bitter opponent of feminism even in its mildest forms. By Miss Birdseye's death he ensures that we do not therefore suppose that he is making an equation between the feminism of the 'great irregular army of nostrum-mongers' and the unnatural in human and sexual terms. Miss Birdseye, the feminist spinster, and Ransom, the man with strongly masculine sexual drives, and equally strong masculine prejudices, are at one, when the feminist lesbian is cast out, or rejects herself. It is the 'natural' union of Ransom and Verena that the dying feminist approves, and the 'unnatural' one of Verena and Olive that she implicitly rejects.

At the same time James reasserts through her the dignity and charm of celibacy. After that, only the incurious or prejudiced could read the ending to mean 'As long as a girl gets a man, she won't bother her head any more about public causes.'

Like all closely-knit groups of rebels and non-conformists, the Boston ladies create their own alternative orthodoxy; and, as usual, it is a synthesis of ideas dictated by assumptions of surrounding society and conscious deviations from these. Thus 'though she [Verena] was not inclined to accept without question the social arrangements of her time, it never would have occurred to her to criticize the railways of her native land.'[9]

Naturally, Olive Chancellor, the impeccably respectable leader of Boston good causes, who wishes to persuade Verena to commit herself to a lifelong and exclusive union with herself, is particularly troubled by the dilemma of 'orthodox unorthodoxy'. From this, taken with Verena's eager naïvety, James extracts a tender and pathetic comedy.

When it comes to a question like marriage – not as fundamental, of course, as the question of railways, but still hardly to be dismissed as trivial – we find a neat reversal of attitudes. Verena, essentially ordinary, human and feminine, simply absorbs her opinions from the atmosphere. She is the sort of a girl who would have been a supporter of slavery in South Carolina, a militarist in Prussia, and an advocate of the two-nation naval standard in England. Olive is, on the contrary, timid and *deliberately* conventional because she is aware of being inherently *different*. She is as much different at heart from Miss Birdseye and the other Boston ladies as she is from the great surrounding Philistine America, which is both so like and so unlike Boston – so like it in self-righteousness and inexperience, so unlike it in rough masculinity and contempt for the intelligence. So we get this:

> She [Verena] had sat on the knees of somnambulists, and had been passed from hand to hand by trance-speakers; she was familiar with every kind of 'cure', and had grown up among lady-editors of newspapers advocating new religions, and people who disapproved of the marriage-tie. Verena talked of the marriage-tie as she would have talked of the last novel – as if she had heard it as frequently discussed; and at certain times, listening to the answers she made to her questions, Olive Chancellor closed her eyes in the manner of a person waiting till giddiness passed. Her young friend's revelations actually gave her a vertigo; they made her perceive everything from which she should have rescued her. Verena was perfectly uncontaminated, and she would never be touched by evil; but though Olive had no views about the marriage-tie except that she should hate it for herself – that particular reform she did not propose to consider – she didn't like the 'atmosphere' of circles in which such institutions were called into question . . .
>
> 'Well, I must say,' said Miss Tarrant, 'I prefer free unions.' Olive held her breath an instant; such an idea was so disagreeable to her.[10]

Olive, like Miss Wade, is felt to be inherently unhappy and destructive. But, unlike Miss Wade, and even more unlike Lawrence's Winifred Inger, she has pathos; and it springs, in part, from the pressure of ironies conveyed in passages like the one just quoted. Verena is questioning marriage simply because she has heard it questioned. She is really incapable of having anything so distinctive as an opinion. She is completely and absolutely the sort of girl that Ransom believes all good women to be – wax to receive impressions. Yet *this* is the girl upon whom Olive's restless passion has fixed. The more she talks about

women's freedom the more Olive obscurely knows that women
like Verena cannot be free. The only question is, who will
dominate them? Olive passionately desires to be that dominating
person. But being in her way sincere, believing in the cause of
free women that they are all engaged in preaching, she also wants
Verena to be what her nature will always prevent her from being
– mistress of her own destiny.

The ironies and contradictions are most intensely felt when
Olive is trying to decide whether her own and Verena's 'marriage'
should be a 'free union'. She wants to bind Verena to her for
ever; and she wants to have her freely-given devotion constantly
renewed. And she wants the solemnity of a lesbian 'marriage',
but she doesn't want to admit that it is anything (in her own eyes,
as in society's) so unnatural.

So, Olive wishes more and more to extract some definite pledge
from her:

> . . . it must be something that would have an absolute
> sanctity for Verena and would bind them together for life.[11]

At first she tries to compromise between the two incompatibles,
extracting a promise of lifelong union from Verena, and not
doing so, by simply making her promise not to marry a man.
Verena is troubled by this, feeling it 'rather awful, even if it
represented the fate one would like.'

But such a compromise will not satisfy Olive for long. Her
dilemma is terrible, when she tries to retract this last peremptory
request: 'I see it was my jealousy that spoke – my restless, hungry
jealousy.'[12]

In her desperation she reverts to the 'cause' which has been
the ostensible reason for their coming together. She invokes
the idea of priestly celibacy for the sake of this feminist cause.
Olive is especially touching at this point, where at the deepest
level of personality sincerity and hypocrisy meet. She believes in
the cause. It is not a mere excuse. She believes it to be worthy of
great sacrifices. But she knows too that what she is asking from
Verena is celibacy only in name. She is asking her not to marry a
man so that she can stay married to her, Olive.

It is a terrible thing to have to say, believe and feel two
opposite things, when one's heart is crying out for truth and purity
as well. Beautifully dramatic and clear is James's representation
of this when he makes her ask for the promise at the same time as
she refuses to have it: 'Don't promise, don't promise . . . I would

far rather you didn't. But don't fail me – don't fail me, or I shall
die!'

And Olive has moments of solitary pathos also. One is when
she is listening to music,[13] and one when she wanders in the park
and idly confronts the ordinary world of babies with their 'crude,
tender quality'.[14] This is particularly poignant for the reader,
who knows how James, unlike Olive, was able to have it both
ways. As remote as Olive herself could be from the world of
lusty infants and domestic ordinariness, he was yet a man of the
world who knew the world, and, as artist if not as man, could
rise to the apprehension of the splendour of the commonplaces,
work, fidelity, marriage, babies. He could have it both ways,
partly perhaps because he was male, but much more because the
artist can comprehend what he cannot experience. He seems to
see Olive, fastidious like himself, and sexual invert like himself, as a
poor lost sister. And in the end, when she loses Verena, the pathos
yields to tragedy. Ransom perceives her as 'some feminine firebrand of Paris revolutions, erect on a barricade, or even the
sacrificial figure of Hypatia, whirled through the furious mob
of Alexandria.'[15] *

How much of all this does Verena understand? There are many
reasons why understanding should come rather slowly. Verena
is devoted to the cause of feminism, and Olive is an effective
patron; she is vain of her gift for public speaking, and Olive is
her most effective flatterer. She is eager for intellectual culture, and Olive appears as a providential guide to it. Her sweet,
feminine egoism is soothed by the admiration of a woman older,
richer and more cultivated than her own family. She understands
from the first that Olive would prefer her not to marry, but is
startled by the passionate insistence on the promise discussed
above. She has a way of half-seeing and half-expressing the real
state of affairs, as when she tells Ransom 'Miss Chancellor has
absorbed me,'[16] without herself perceiving the full bearing of
her own words. Perhaps the most accurate summary James gives
us of her whole complex attitude is in the phrase 'tacit, tender
assent to passionate insistence'.[17]

Verena's conscience, like her thoughts and feelings, is wax
waiting to be formed. In the circumstances, it is inevitable that

---

* Hypatia was lynched – a fact known to many Victorians not well versed in
ancient history through Kingsley's novel.

Olive will be the formative power. So, when she has begun to waver in her allegiance, and to feel the pull of Ransom's passion, Verena says:

> I like him, but I want to hate my liking. I want you to keep before me all the reasons why I should . . .[18]

The false conscience is a greater threat than false passion. It is not exactly here a lesbian conscience, but a conscience shaped by the public cause, though illicitly manipulated, of course, by Olive for lesbian ends. It is touching, paradoxical, and yet wholly convincing that the innocent Verena should be influenced by an idea inherently Machiavellian. It is the idea that moral principles must give way to party spirit. James treats this idea with calm dignity, but leaves us in no doubt that it is an aberration.

As the contest intensifies, and Verena comes nearer to her eventual desertion of Olive, she comes more and more to be aware of Olive's suffering:

> She had no right to blast the poor creature's whole future. She had a vision of those dreadful years; she knew that Olive would never get over the disappointment . . . she would be incurably lonely and eternally humiliated. It was a very peculiar thing, their friendship; it had elements which made it probably as complete as any (between women) that had ever existed. Of course it had been more on Olive's side than on hers, she had always known that . . .[19]

It is one of the great merits of James's intensely intellectual comprehension of his characters that it allows him to show just how confused and partial is the understanding of the participants. The above account beautifully combines a very incomplete grasp of the facts with exact indications of what they really are. That parenthesis 'between women' tells us what we need to know. She is obscurely aware of Olive's passion, but unshaken in her adherence to the ordinary conviction of the race that the love between man and woman is far stronger than any other. 'Between women' has an air of deprecation, suggesting both the weakness of women compared with men, and the weakness of the homosexual attachment compared with the heterosexual. James has sometimes been accused, and with reason, of making all his characters too clever. Verena is a blessed exception. In passages like this, and indeed in his treatment of her throughout the book, James shows, perhaps as well as any novelist has ever done, the working of what Newman called the illative sense.

He shows how people who are incapable of reasoning as such can yet take into rational account complex impressions. He shows us what a very subtle thing is the faculty we call common sense.

There is nothing subversive of moral orthodoxies in *The Bostonians*. Verena's only true destiny is to marry a man stronger than herself and submit to his will; in this James does not differ from the wisdom of Mrs Gaskell or Trollope. All the same there is something new. Olive's temperament does not make her a freak or a fool or a criminal. It creates for her the opportunity to achieve tragic dignity. Others had achieved it before in the novel through their sexual aberrations – Richardson's Lovelace, for instance. But Olive is the first of either sex who achieves it through inversion. And as we would expect from an artist of James's calibre, she is both very near to the author's self and very far from him.

Olive receives a blow that drains her of inner life; but it was left for Lawrence to show us the actual killing of the lesbian obstacle to a man's desire for a woman. *The Fox* is typically Laurentian both in its merits and defects. The impression of the two women together and their depressed, courageous, busy life and of the farm setting is beautifully done. The symbolism of the fox, associated in the dreams of Nellie March with the young soldier who suddenly intrudes and gradually destroys the settled feminine life is finely handled, psychologically. The girl's vague disturbance at her dream association of Henry with the fox is entirely credible; and so is the suppressed link between the two that eludes her conscious mind, that both are predators who cannot be evaded. Henry is credible too for a time, with his calm, slow assumption of masculine authority, and his easy-going soldier's acceptance of the unexpected. He is entirely credible in his words. But his thoughts are altogether too Laurentian for what he is. He goes out in the December dark with a gun, and:

> suddenly, it seemed to him England was little and tight, he felt the landscape was constricted even in the dark, and that there were too many dogs in the night, making a noise like a fence of sound, like the network of English hedges netting the view. He felt the fox didn't have a chance . . . He knew the fox would be coming. It seemed to him it would be the last of the foxes in this loudly barking, thick-voiced England, tight with innumerable little houses.[20]

That is essentially the thought of a literary man at his desk, not of a soldier longing for domestic comforts after the ardours and rigours of war.

But the literary point, of course, is the mirror image of Forster's point about the forests and the night being on the side of the homosexual lovers in *Maurice*.* Here lesbian love is associated with stuffy, domestic interiors. The night, the open air and freedom are associated with Henry and his quest for normal love and marriage with Nellie March. Since the time of Wordsworth the English landscape has been extraordinarily tractable and uncomplaining, constantly invoked to prove the rightness of one morality and the wrongness of the others.

Yet even though we refrain from disputing an author's right to co-opt nature as a member of his moral committee, we may ask ourselves why it is that novelists, a civilized and sedentary tribe, should so often take it for granted that having a roof over one's head is a sign of moral decadence.†

Then comes the killing. It would not be quite right to call it murder in law, though murder seems to be its essential moral nature. Henry calls out to Jill Banford to get out of the way of the tree he is about to fell; but as he does so 'his heart held perfectly still, in the terrible pure will that she should not move.'[21] When the tree falls on her, he 'watched with intense bright eyes, as he would watch a wild goose he had shot. Was it winged, or dead? Dead!'[22]‡

Before the killing occurs, everything in the story is credible. After it, we move into a different fictional world, where the most obvious and insistent questions cannot be answered. What did local society think about the killing? Were the police called

---

* Those who do not agree may be glad to be fortified by the authority of Jane Austen. Compare the following exchange between Mrs Elton and Mr Knightley:
   'We are to walk about your gardens, and gather the strawberries ourselves, and sit under trees; and whatever else you may like to provide, it is to be all out of doors – a table spread in the shade, you know. Everything as natural and simple as possible. Is not that your idea?'
   'Not quite. My idea of the simple and natural will be to have the table spread in the dining-room.' (*Emma*, chap. XLII)
It is not easy to imagine what Forster and Lawrence would have said if their agreement with Mrs Elton had been pointed out.
† see above Chapter VIII.
‡ If it seems odd that a moralist should approve of murder, it seems even stranger that he should approve of the imagery of blood-sports applied to human prey. Yet the young man is high in the graces of Dr Leavis, who speaks of his 'profound seriousness' and his 'natural wisdom'. This is a remarkable instance of Lawrence's power of bemusing his admirers, so that they approve of what, in any other author, they would detest.

in? Was a death certificate issued, or, if not, who disposed of the
body and how? Above all, and most important for the story's
psychological truth, what was the effect on Henry of having won
his bride by killing a woman, and what was the effect on Nellie
of being won in this fashion? I would not myself admit that the
practical questions just asked can be shuffled off as irrelevant to
the story's 'poetry'. But even those who may say they can be,
must admit that the last question is crucial. 'Macbeth hath murdered sleep'; but here all we have is the inane promise 'You'll
feel better once we get over to Canada . . .'[23]

The delusion that moral consequences can be cancelled by
clearing out is shared by too many of Lawrence's heroes to let us
suppose he himself totally rejected it.

I have said, and I repeat, that in some ways this is one of the
finest stories of a great writer. But it is flawed in two very serious
ways. It is fine in its atmospheric quality, and in the extraordinary
power, in which Lawrence is here the peer of Jane Austen and
Dickens, to give the speech of simple people in such a way as to
convey a unique individuality in each. It is flawed, first, because
it does not do what it is the special province and distinction of
prose fiction to do – it does not go on to the end. It does not let
us see the ultimate consequences of the state of affairs it posits.
By the feeble device of sending the protagonists to Canada it
tramples upon the ancient and unalterable truth: *Caelum non
animum mutant qui trans mare currunt.*

Second and worse, it deliberately introduces a moral confusion.
Henry appears to triumph because he is on the side of life. The
lesbian relation is seen as sterile and deathly; the marriage of
Henry and Nellie as life-giving and liberating. But what kind of
moral system is it that castigates unchastity by condoning
murder? The answer is, of course, that it is only a pretence or an
appearance of a moral system. The moral rhetoric is only decora-
tive; it can be stripped away. When it is stripped away, we are
left with a conflict of will. Henry succeeds because he has the
stronger will. Perhaps, though the matter is not very clear, this
implies some more general statement, that a man will always have
a stronger will than a woman, if he allows it untrammelled
exercise, or that a 'natural' relationship, when fully willed, will
always be stronger than an 'unnatural' one. At all events, Henry's
will is the stronger. And so, he must conquer. Lawrence has
skilfully created his characters so that we are convinced of this.

Psychologically the story is true. But the deception comes when a moral falsehood is shuffled on to the psychological truth. Lawrence is really asking us to equate strength of will with purity of intention. He knows and we know, and the world that has endured Hitler knows, and Dr Leavis would know at any time when he was not reading Lawrence, that they are not the same thing. A great artist is misusing his powers when he tries to persuade us of the contrary.

Lawrence made one other, more peripheral, study of the lesbian topic, in chapter XII of *The Rainbow*. The episode of Ursula and Winifred Inger is carefully placed so that it shall be seen as an essentially 'normal' girl's unsteady reaction to an unsatisfactory first love for a man. And the previous chapter, entitled *First Love*, contains also the scene where Ursula sees the rough couple in the barge. The man on the barge, who is socially remote from her, had 'made her feel the richness of her own life', while the young man with whom she supposes herself to be in love, 'had created a deadness round her'. In this bewilderment she swings towards Winifred Inger, and her bewilderment is increased by her Uncle Tom's deadly account of the married life of the colliers. Winifred's critique of the male is telling:

> They make everything fit into an old, inert idea. Love is a dead idea to them. They don't come to one and love one, they come to an idea, and they say 'you are my idea', so they embrace themselves. As if I were any man's idea! As if I exist because a man has an idea of me! As if I will be betrayed by him, lend him my body as an instrument for his idea, to be a mere apparatus of his dead theory.[24]

The sexual excitement generated between the two girls is keen but superficial. In neither is there any strongly developed lesbian nature:

> A heavy, clogged sense of deadness began to gather upon her, from the other woman's contact. And sometimes she thought Winifred was ugly, clayey. Her female hips seemed big and earthy, her ankles and her arms were too thick. She wanted some fine intensity . . .

Yet on their visit to Ursula's uncle, Winifred still appears to stand for some kind of independence of spirit against a mechanical world.

Potentially, there is a deep dramatic conflict here. On the one side, the truly natural, cheapened and perverted by the mechanical, the respectable, the money-grubbing, and the kind of fake romanticism (so well criticized in Winifred's words quoted above) which is only a mask of egoism. On the other side, the 'unnatural' love of woman for woman, dignified by its contempt for hypocritical evasions, and its quest for freedom. But once again, Lawrence doesn't go on to the end. Admittedly, this is much more excusable than it is in *The Fox*, since there it was the substance of the whole story whose consequences were evaded, while here the lesbian theme is only an eddy in the story's main current. We suddenly find, for no clear reason, that Winifred is becoming associated with the mechanical world she has been criticizing. Motivated partly by fear of losing Ursula, whose affection seems to be cooling, she marries Tom Brangwen. 'His real mistress was the machine, and the real mistress of Winifred was the machine.' It is easier to understand such a sudden reversal in terms of Lawrence's own personal motives than it is in terms of the requirements of art. If Winifred's passion had been genuine and lasting, it might have seemed too uncomfortably like Rupert Birkin's feeling for Gerald Crich, which has also in the wrestling scene[25] its physical consequence, corresponding to the lesbian bathing scene. And Lawrence is concerned to show that the relation between Rupert and Gerald is different in kind from that between the two girls. Indeed, it sometimes seems as if he wishes to say that it is (or could be, if Gerald was worthy of it, as Rupert is) higher than any possible feminine relationship. So it is that *Women in Love* ends with the marriage of Ursula and Rupert seen as good but incomplete – or rather complete on her side and incomplete on his:

'Did you need Gerald?' she asked one evening.

'Yes,' he said.

'Aren't I enough for you?' she asked.

'No,' he said. 'You are enough for me, as far as a woman is concerned. You are all women to me. But I wanted a man friend, as eternal as you and I are eternal.'

'Why aren't I enough?' she said. 'You are enough for me.'

Lawrence entitled his lesbian chapter *Shame*, and so clearly signalled his intention of making a complete contrast between Ursula's friendship with Winifred and Rupert's with Gerald. Yet the contrast is only felt and willed by the author, not effectively shown to the reader. Once again it seems to be a matter of the prejudices of the man interfering with the true aims of the artist.

Different as they are, Dickens, James and Lawrence all seem to share certain assumptions imposed by the fact that they are men. All conceive the lesbian relation as a retreat from reality. Tattycoram, Verena and Ursula are all *accidental* victims; none is destined by her nature to a revulsion from what is conceived as truly natural. In each case a weakness in the self, Tattycoram's proud rebellion, Verena's political ambition, Ursula's contemptuous dissatisfaction with the male, is met by an external temptation. Each yields temporarily, with varying degrees of innocence and self-knowledge. In each case, (and this is very important) the temptation is not to wild adventure or romantic nihilism, but to a rejection of the rich possibilities of life. Each emerges at the end, as if from a prison, or at best a nursery, into the freedom of the 'normal'.

With *The Well of Loneliness* (1928), we enter for the first time a world directly corresponding to that created by the male homosexual writers discussed in the last chapter, the lesbian world seen from within. It is not surprising that the book has something of the air of a propaganda piece. Radclyffe Hall had already published several books, in which no direct lesbian hint had been given. Her friend Lady Troubridge describes the decision to write openly on this subject thus:

she had long wanted to write a book on sexual inversion, a novel that would be accessible to the general public who did not have access to technical treatises . . . It was her absolute conviction that such a book could only be written by a sexual invert, who alone could be qualified by personal knowledge and experience to speak on behalf of a misunderstood and misjudged minority.[26]

The plot is well-drawn to give the main lines of the problem. We have the incurably masculine heroine, Stephen; the old woman, acting as nurse, who has a chaste devotion to her, and sad memories of her youth and the world's condemnation; the beloved, who is married and not really lesbian in temperament, but in search of glamour and excitement; and finally there is the young girl of unformed and indeterminate sexual temperament, attracted by the masculine style of heroine, now in uniform and doing war-work. In the background there is a mother who fiercely rejects her, and a father who tenderly fears that his wish for a son has been ironically answered, since he guesses his daughter's nature and probable destiny.

The first love, the married Angela, soon takes fright and retreats to her husband, blaming all her own vagaries on Stephen. When Stephen suggests that they run away together, Angela replies:

'Are you mad?'

'No, I'm sane. It's the only decent thing, it's the only clean thing; . . . I can't go on lying about you to Ralph, [Angela's husband] I want him to know how much I adore you – I want the whole world to know how I adore you . . . I've done with these lies – I shall tell him the truth and so will you, Angela; and after we've told him we'll go away and we'll live quite openly together, you and I, which is what we owe to ourselves and our love.'

Angela stared at her white and aghast: 'You *are* mad,' she said slowly, 'you're raving mad. Tell him what? Have I let you become my lover? You know that I've always been faithful to Ralph; you know perfectly well there's nothing to tell him, beyond a few rather school-girlish kisses. Can I help it if you're – what you obviously are?'[27]

Tattycoram, Verena and Ursula were all unmarried at the time of their lesbian episodes. And, as we have seen, in each case their return to the heterosexual world was hailed as a release. Here the married Angela is treated as a coward, a slave of convention, a rejector of life and freedom for returning to her husband.

Yet it is doubtful whether, after all, that is quite what the book as a whole is saying. The masculine idea of the lesbian prison is not exclusive to the male writers; it is found in a different form here. In fact, there are two lesbian prisons in Radclyffe Hall's world; there is the prison of the tortured lesbian's own heart and the prison of the world's misunderstanding and contempt. The book's ambiguity, its failure, despite all its rhetoric and emotion, to make a clear impression on us, is due to a failure to be sure where one prison ends and the other begins. At times the author writes as if the lesbian problem was created entirely by an un-comprehending world. The condition and the life to which it leads are natural, if only people could see and admit this. But at other times, the condition appears as a curse that cannot be understood. There is a religious current in the book (Catholic in its tendency) and here too we meet the same ambiguity. Can the condition be somehow reconciled with God's laws, so that lesbians can live innocently before God? Or is some great renunciation more painful and more complete than any achieved by hetero-sexuals, positively demanded of them?

All these painful ambiguities are seen in the second lesbian encounter. Stephen is now thirty-two, and has still not experienced lesbian passion in full physical form. Mary, her girlish young friend, is willing to give herself completely:

'Have you understood? Do you realize now what it's going to mean if you give yourself to me?' Then she stopped abruptly . . . Mary was crying.

Stephen said, and her voice had grown quite toneless:

'It's too much to ask – you're right, it's too much. I had to tell you – forgive me, Mary.'

But Mary turned on her with very bright eyes: 'You can say that – you who talk about loving! What do I care for all you've told me? What do I care for the world's opinion? What do I care for anything but you, and just as you are – as you are, I love you! . . .'

Stephen bent down and kissed Mary's hands very humbly, for now she could find no words any more . . . and that night they were not divided.[28]

The last four words are perhaps the most significant and the most enigmatic in the whole book. The phrasing is biblical,* and there is a reminiscence of David's lament over Saul and Jonathan. It is perhaps unlikely that Radclyffe Hall (in no way a subtle artist), considered deeply the precise nature of the allusion made. A passage which refers to death, and to dying together as a kind of fulfilment, is transposed into a sexual union. Was there a deliberate or an unconscious reference to the powerful old pun, which treats sexual union as the 'little death'? Or is the connection merely accidental? Since the biblical passage alluded to is a lament over the dead, does the use of it here carry menace of death, or of separation and disaster which will be the death of love? It is hard, perhaps impossible to say. But one thing is clear. The biblical phrase spreads a veil of traditional dignity; it saves the necessity either for a detailed physical description or for an embarrassing vulgar euphemism. The act which was immoral according to traditional moral principles, and obscene, unnatural and disgusting in the eyes of the workaday world, has been endowed with another traditional sanctity. It is a sanctity of literary style as well as of religion.

* II Samuel, I, v 23.

The opening words of the next chapter tell us that to both the act seemed 'natural' and 'fine'. But again, this reads more as defiant assertion under the influence of the senses than as something which can really be believed and lived out by the protagonists. And if the protagonists have doubts, inevitably author and reader will have stronger ones.

The book ends with a renunciation. The man who loves and wishes to marry Mary comes to Stephen and confesses that she has defeated him. Mary is hers, and he will go away. Stephen then invents a lying tale of her own infidelity in order to force Mary to leave her, and go off with the man for ever, which she does. What does this mean? Does it mean that Stephen at last, fortified by prayer, perceives the sinfulness of the life they are leading, and renounces it, and thus leads Mary to renounce it too? Or does it mean that she senses that Mary is not strong enough to go on for ever outfacing public opinion? Or that she realizes that Mary is really heterosexual in temperament? Or is it rather an act asserting a strong moral claim? Is the author showing a woman of unalterably lesbian temperament making the greatest sacrifice of all; and proving thus that lesbians also are capable of the highest moral attainments which the world reveres, and of which only a few, of whatever sex or temperament, are ever capable?

Again it is hard to say, but the last alternative seems nearest the mark. If we select it, we read the ending as a brave statement that no inborn abnormality can take away from a human being the possibility of moral greatness. Its importance as a statement, almost a manifesto, possesses moral importance far in excess of its rather dubious literary merits. Radclyffe Hall, in her own overlush and perhaps embarrassing way, is reasserting an ancient doctrine that the respectable English world had forgotten, denied or despised. It is the doctrine stated in the words of her contemporary Von Hügel thus:

It is simply of faith that every human being is provided by God with graces sufficient for salvation.

From this point of view the storm of protest and controversy that the book raised has a line of symbolic value. The England of 1928 believed, on the whole, in the words of T. S. Eliot that I have quoted on p. 168 'that if one was thrifty, enterprising, intelligent and prudent in not violating social conventions, one ought to have a happy and successful life'. This belief is, of course, a manifest delusion, and it is a delusion which people will fight with all

their strength to retain. Seen in this light, the controversy over
The Well of Loneliness has an interest much wider and more lasting
than at first sight appears. If it is seen as a mere argument over
'decency', it is quickly dated. Standards of decency are always
changing, and cannot be convincingly linked with any fundamental moral principle. If it is seen as an episode in the decline
of the facile humanistic optimism of a nation favoured by sea
power, coal, iron and empire to believe that everyone could be
good without really trying, and everything inevitably improved
all the time, it has much more than a period interest.

Eliot's words, just quoted, were part of an introduction to
Djuna Barnes's *Nightwood* (1936). *Nightwood* is a much more
sophisticated work than *The Well of Loneliness*; and the question
that is left open in the latter receives here a clear answer. There is
no question here that lesbianism may really be natural. It is a book
about the abnormal and the unnatural in many different forms.
Lesbianism is simply one of these forms, though, as it happens,
the dominant one in the book. In *The Well of Loneliness*, there is a
clear distinction between the 'masculine' and 'feminine' members
of any lesbian pair. Here there is rather a perverse search for a total
identity with the self in the other woman's body and personality. 'A
man is another person – a woman is yourself, caught as you turn in
panic; on her mouth you kiss your own.'²⁹ The respectable world
that stands over against the troubled lesbian consciousness in Radclyffe Hall has here disappeared. The whole world is an inferno, and
those who have a specific abnormality to cling to and assert may
almost be seen as the lucky ones. If the worst temptation of all is
to forget about original sin, they are less likely than most to
succumb to it. In place of the ethereal physicality of Radclyffe
Hall's accounts of passion, we get for the first time a real vein of
lesbian coarseness. 'Arse' and 'rosebush' take the place of 'they
were not divided'. Perhaps lesbian passion was the last area left
for the venerable tradition of English literary bawdy to invade.
Paradoxically, though, this strange, overwritten, unsatisfactory
book (which it seems to me that Eliot overpraised) ends on the
side of purity. 'If only we could be chaste and disinterested' all
the characters seem to be saying in chorus, 'perhaps we could be
happy'. Certainly no reader of *Nightwood* is ever tempted to equate
lawless passion with happiness.

CONCLUSION

I end as I began with an example notable for outspokenness and for questioning received assumptions. Richardson and Miss Barnes are different in many ways, but alike in wishing to explore extreme cases. Each is very far from the standards and the experience of most people. In between we have those who used accepted moral truths to attack inconsistent social assumptions, like Jane Austen and Thackeray, eccentric individualists, like Sterne and Gissing, propounders of new doctrine, like Forster and Lawrence. Is there a common thread?

If the reader will glance back at the quotations from Newman and Tolstoy on my title page, he will be able to guess where I find it. Every writer on the relation of the sexes who is worth serious discussion at all knows that he is not dealing with an isolated part of life. One cannot just have 'views' and 'tastes' about it. As with religious questions, the response, whatever it is, is that of the whole personality, not just of the thinking mind, or the passionate heart, or the importunate body. If this is true, it follows that we are dealing with a subject where fashion is of little significance, where talk of progress or decline is out of place, where the jargon of the sociologists won't wash. Why then, it might be asked, go to the novelist rather than the theologian or the moral philosopher for instruction? Not because novelists are wiser and better than others, but because they are most skilled in revealing the obscure windings of the human heart.

References

CHAPTER I

1. *The Girl of the Period*, Saturday Review, 14 March 1868.
2. Havelock Ellis: *My Life*, p. 525.
3. Walter Bagehot: *Estimations in Criticism*. Ed. Cuthbert Lennox 1909. Vol. II, p. 258.
4. Lerner and Holmstrom: *Thomas Hardy and his Readers*, p. 44.
5. G. H. Lewes: *The Life and Works of Goethe*, Bk VII, chapter IV.
6. Geoffrey Tillotson & Donald Hawes: *Thackeray and his Readers*, p. 64.
7. *Letters of Robert Browning and Elizabeth Barrett*. Edited by Robert Browning junior. Murray 1930. Vol. I, p. 406.
8. See Gordon S. Haight: *George Eliot*, 1968, p. 238.
9. George Eliot: *Daniel Deronda*, chap. XIV.
10. ibid., chap. XXVII.
11. Coventry Patmore: *Principles of Art*. New Ed. 1898, p. 16. This book contained reprints of articles that appeared in the *St James's Gazette* in the late 1880s.
12. Howard Sturgis: *Belchamber*, chap. XIV.
13. Thackeray: *Pendennis*, chap. XVIII.
14. Trollope: *Can You Forgive Her?*, 1864, chapters XXIX and LXVI. It is worth noting that the title does not refer to the prostitute but to the life of a respectable, though wilful heroine.
15. Dickens: *Oliver Twist*, chap. XL.
16. ibid., chap. XLVII.
17. George du Maurier: *Trilby* Part VIII.
18. Richardson: *Pamela* vol. III, Letter XXII (Saturday).
19. George Eliot: *Middlemarch*, chap. LXIV.
20. Trollope: *The Small House at Allington*, 1862, chap. LV.

CHAPTER II

1. Fielding: *Joseph Andrews*, Bk I, chap. VIII.
2. ibid., Bk IV, chap. VIII.
3. Fielding: *Tom Jones*, Bk V, chap. V.
4. ibid., chap. VI.
5. ibid., Bk XV, chap. IX.
6. ibid.
7. Richardson, *Clarissa Harlowe*, Letter XXII.
7a. Letter XVI.
8. Letter XXXII.
9. Letter XCIX.
10. Letter CX.
11. Letter CXL.
12. Fielding: *Amelia*, Bk IX, chap. V.
13. ibid., Bk II, chap. VI.
14. ibid., Bk XI, chap. VI.
15. ibid., Bk XI, chap. IX.

CHAPTER III

1. Scott: *Lives of the Novelists*. Everyman, 1910, p. 182.
2. Coleridge: *Literary Remains*, pp. 141–2.
3. Thackeray: *The English Humourists*.
4. Stephen: *Hours in a Library*, New Ed. 1892. Vol. III, p. 152
5. ibid., p. 150.
6. Sterne: Edited by Douglas Grant. Rupert Hart-Davis 1950, p. 544 (All quotations from this edition).
7. ibid., p. 556.
8. ibid., p. 603.
9. ibid., p. 557.
10. ibid., p. 595.
11. ibid., p. 736.
12. ibid., p. 576.

CHAPTER IV

1. Jane Austen: *Mansfield Park*, chap. XIV.
2. ibid., chap. XVI.
3. ibid., chap. XXVII.
4. ibid., chap. XIX.
5. Jane Austen: *Emma*, chap. LI.
6. ibid., chap. XLVIII.
7. Jane Austen: *Mansfield Park*, chap. XXI.
8. ibid., chap. XXXII.
9. Jane Austen: *Emma*, chap. VIII.
10. ibid., chap. VII.
11. ibid., chap. IX.
12. ibid., chap. XIII.
13. ibid., chap. XXXII.
14. Marilyn Butler: *Jane Austen and the War of Ideas*, 1975, p. 146*n*.
15. Jane Austen: *Persuasion*, chap. VII.
16. Jane Austen: *Sense and Sensibility*, chap. V.
17. Jane Austen: *Persuasion*, chap. XIII.
18. ibid., chap. XX.

CHAPTER V

1. *Vanity Fair*, chap. XXIV.
2. ibid., chap. XXV.
3. ibid., chap. XXXV.
4. ibid., chap. XIV, end.
5. *Pendennis*, chap. LIII.
6. ibid., chap. LVI.
7. Thackeray: *The Critical Heritage*, Ed. by Geoffrey Tillotson and Donald Hawes, p. 142.
8. ibid., p. 150.
9. ibid., p. 15.
10. *Esmond*, chap. XIII of Bk II.
11. ibid., chap. XIII of Bk I.
11a. ibid., chap. X of Bk III.
12. ibid., chap. X of Bk III.
13. *Ruth*, chap. XXIII.

14. ibid., chap. XI.
15. ibid., chap. III.
16. ibid., chap. IV.
17. ibid., chap. V.
18. *Sylvia's Lovers*, chap. XV.
19. *Wives and Daughters*, chap. V.
20. ibid., chap. XXIX.
21. ibid., chap. V.
22. ibid., chap. X.
23. ibid., chap. XXXII.
24. ibid., chap. LI.

CHAPTER VI

1. Zeta: *Shadow of the Clouds*, 1847, pp. 81–2.
2. ibid., p. 68.
3. ibid. – end.
4. ibid., p. 260.
5. ibid., p. 262.
6. *Wuthering Heights*, chap. IX.
7. ibid., chap. X.
8. ibid., chap. XXIII.
9. ibid., chap. XXIX.
10. *Love's Cross-Currents*, Letter IX.
11. *Lesbia Brandon*, Ed. R. Hughes, pp. 80–1.
12. ibid., p. 132.
13. ibid., p. 67.
14. ibid., p. 115.
15. ibid., p. 165.
16. ibid., p. 100.
17. *Far From the Madding Crowd*, chap. VIII.
18. ibid., chap. XXIV.
19. ibid., chap. XXVI.
20. ibid., chap. XXVIII.
21. ibid., chap. XLIII.
22. ibid., chap. XLVIII.
23. *The Woodlanders*, chap. XV.
24. ibid., chap. XLVIII.
25. *Jude the Obscure*, Part I, chap. II.
26. ibid., Part VI, chap. VI.

27. Grant Allen: *The Woman Who Did.*
28. *Jude the Obscure*, Pt III, chap. VII.
29. ibid., Part III, chap. III.
30. ibid., Part IV, chap. VI.
31. ibid., Part II, chap. II.
32. Gissing: *The Nether World*, chap. XII.
33. ibid., chap. XXXVI.
34. Gissing: *The Crown of Life*, chap. XXX.
35. ibid., chap. XVIII.
36. ibid., chap. XIV.
37. *The Nether World*, chap. XXXIX.

CHAPTER VII

1. Leslie Stephen: *Hours in a Library*, New Ed. 1892. Vol. III, p. 11.
2. Havelock Ellis: *Studies in the Psychology of Sex*, 1897–1928.
3. Havelock Ellis: *My Life*, 1940, p. 325. Ellis lived 1859–1939, and his autobiography is posthumous.
4. W. B. Yeats: *Autobiographies*, 1956, p. 291.
5. *My Life*, p. 291.
6. ibid., p. 363.
7. Olive Schreiner: *Woman and Labour*, 1911, pp. 148–50. Five impressions of this book were called for within twelve months, and translations were made into many languages.
8. Olive Schreiner: *The Story of an African Farm*, Part II, chap. IX.
9. ibid.
10. ibid.
11. Trollope: *The Last Chronicle of Barset*, chap. XVIII.
12. *The Story of an African Farm*, Part II, chap. IV.
13. H. G. Wells: *Ann Veronica*, chap. VII.
14. *Women in Love*, chap. XIV.
15. *The Rainbow*, chap. I ('How Brangwen Married a Polish Lady')
16. ibid., chap. II.
17. ibid., chap. VI ('Anna Victrix').
18. ibid., chap. IX ('The Marsh and the Flood').
19. *Women in Love*, chap. XV.
20. ibid., chap. XI.
21. *The Rainbow*, chap. VI ('Anna Victrix').

22. ibid., chap. VIII.
23. *Women in Love*, chap. XXIII ('Excurse').

CHAPTER VIII

1. Ernest Raymond: *The Story of My Days*.
2. Dickens: *David Copperfield*, chap. VI.
3. Walter Pater: *Marius the Epicurean*, chap. IV.
4. *The Bookman*, November 1891.
5. Rolfe: *The Desire and Pursuit of the Whole*, 1934, p. 178.
6. ibid., p. 13.
7. E. M. Forster: *Where Angels Fear to Tread*, chap. X.
8. E. M. Forster: *A Room with a View*, chap. VI.
9. ibid., chap. XII.
10. E. M. Forster: *Maurice*, chap. XXX.
11. ibid., chap. I.
12. ibid., chap. XLIII.
13. ibid., chap. XLII.
14. ibid., chap. XXXVII.
15. ibid. chap. XLV.
16. ibid., chap. IX.
17. ibid., chap. XXXI.
18. L. H. Myers: *The Near and the Far*, Collected Volume 1943, p. 212.
19. ibid., p. 149.
20. ibid., p. 165.
21. ibid., p. 359.
22. ibid., p. 339.
23. ibid., p. 316.
24. ibid., p. 373.

CHAPTER IX

1. Elsie J. Oxenham: *The Abbey Girls Win Through*, 1928. The example is more striking since, though written much in the style of a school story, this is not actually a school story.
2. Conrad: *Chance*, Part I, chap. II.
3. ibid.
4. ibid., Part I, chap. VI.

5. *Little Dorrit*, Part I, chap. XXVII.
6. ibid., Part II, chap. XXXIII.
7. Henry James: *The Bostonians*, chap. VI.
8. ibid., chap. XXXVIII.
9. ibid., chap. X.
10. ibid., chap. XI.
11. ibid., chap. XIV.
12. ibid., chap. XVII.
13. ibid., chap. XVIII.
14. ibid., chap. XXXII.
15. ibid., chap. XLII.
16. ibid., chap. XXIV.
17. ibid., chap. XXXIII.
18. ibid., chap. XXXVII.
19. ibid., chap. XXXVIII.
20. *The Tales of D. H. Lawrence*, Heinemann, 1934. p. 448.
21. ibid., p. 473.
22. ibid., p. 474.
23. ibid., p. 479.
24. D. H. Lawrence: *The Rainbow*, chap. XII.
25. D. H. Lawrence: *Women in Love*, chap. XX. *The Rainbow* and *Women in Love* form, in certain respects, a continuous whole.
26. Una, Lady Troubridge: *The Life and Death of Radclyffe Hall*, Hammond, 1961, p. 81.
27. Radclyffe Hall: *The Well of Loneliness*, chap. XIX.
28. ibid., chap. XXXVIII.
29. Djuna Barnes: *Nightwood*, 1936, p. 202.

Index